HIGH
AND

C000050310

Chambers Scottish Guides

HIGHLANDS
AND ISLANDS

Roger Smith

Series editor
Kristina Woolnough

Chambers

Published 1992 by W & R Chambers Ltd
43–45 Annandale Street, Edinburgh EH7 4AZ

British Library Cataloguing in Publication Data

A catalogue record for this book is available from the British
Library

ISBN 0–550–22100–6

Acknowledgements
National and Regional Fact Files compiled by Donald Greig
Maps and town plans by Baynefield Carto-Graphics Ltd

Cover design by Creative Link, Edinburgh
Typeset by Hewer Text Composition Services, Edinburgh
Printed in England by Clays Ltd, St Ives, plc

CONTENTS

Maps and town plans

Chambers Scottish Guides

Scotland has traditionally been celebrated for two outstanding features: its history and its scenery. Romantic, compelling figures such as Robert the Bruce, Mary Queen of Scots and Bonnie Prince Charlie move across an historical landscape which is spiced with power-broking, love, political and religious intrigue, lust, murder and treachery.

Their names are known all over the world and the enduring appeal of their stories is given additional impetus by the tangible, remaining historical sites. Scattered throughout Scotland, from the Borders northwards, are battlefields where lands and crowns were won and lost and where uprisings succeeded and failed. There are caves, churches and castles where secular and religious courts were held and where refuge was sought. And there are palaces where kings and queens were born and died. As well as the buildings and ruins that document the fortunes of nobles and Scottish royalty, humbler stone monuments, settlements, houses and cottages can also be seen. These, from the prehistoric stone circles and standing stones to the 'black houses' of the Western Isles, represent largely unknown, unrecorded people who were either too ancient or too ordinary to capture the world's imagination.

Scotland's historical heritage is complemented by the country's natural heritage. The stock images of Scotland are invariably the photogenic Highland ones: jagged mountains, clear-eyed lochs and shaggy heath. Often overlooked are the more subtle charms of the Borders hills, or the hidden south-western corner of Scotland which lies around the Solway Firth. Mistakenly by-passed too is the sometimes dramatic, often picturesque east coast of the country, which stretches with indents of sandy crescents and fishing harbours from the Borders to Duncansby Head.

History, natural setting and human achievement marry in Scotland's towns and cities. Each place's architectural diversity, whether it involves loved and cherished buildings from the 17th, 18th and 19th centuries or the frequently controversial and sometimes hated efforts of the 20th century, fuses the past and the present.

For Scotland is not a museum, nor is it a national park, nor just a monument to past human endeavour. The fact of contemporary Scotland is a vital, intriguing one. New industries are slowly replacing old ones. A thriving contemporary urban culture – theatre, fiction, popular music – is successfully blending with the traditional, predominantly Highland, culture of dancing, tartan, bagpipes, accordion bands and Gaelic ceilidhs. This blending exists at the large cultural annual fixtures like the Edinburgh Festival and Glasgow's Mayfest and it exists across Scotland at the plethora of smaller-scale, local celebrations which include music festivals, family fun-days and Highland shows.

The historical and the scenic, the traditional and the contemporary – *Chambers Scottish Guides* confirm all that is known and celebrated about Scotland and they also uncover the unknown, the less familiar and the forgotten corners. The guides will be an invaluable source of reference for visitors and for residents alike. Both can take advantage of the comprehensive Gazetteer of places and attractions, both can make use of the listings of theatres, cinemas, festivals, local media, nightlife, transport and galleries. Whether employed for suggestions for family outings, Sunday jaunts or for all-season holidays, *Chambers Scottish Guides* will inform, inspire and enlighten.

As well as providing the invaluable Gazetteer and listings, *Chambers Scottish Guides* offer a broad, sometime idiosyncratic, view of Scotland in the subject panels which are interspersed throughout the Gazetteer. These panels look at aspects of Scottish history, Scottish culture and contemporary Scottish life from football to conservation. From these panels, an impression emerges of a diverse, challenging, fascinating country, one that is inspired by its past and is also tripped up by it, and one that is struggling consciously and successfully for its future. If you think you know Scotland well, there is yet more to discover. If you are travelling in Scotland for the first time, these books will guide your journey.

How to use this book

Each *Chambers Scottish Guide* consists of three sections:

The **National Fact File**, which includes information on national Scottish organizations, sports associations, airports, mainline train stations, media, Scottish currency and accommodation.

The **Regional Fact File**, which contains listings of cinemas, theatres, media, festivals, public transport facilities, tourist information offices, airports, galleries and museums specifically for the area covered by each book.

The **Gazetteer**, which provides comprehensive A–Z information about cities, towns, villages, historical sites and visitor attractions within the regions covered by each book.

The **National Fact File** is arranged alphabetically by subject and then alphabetically by entry.

The **Regional Fact File** is ordered alphabetically by subject, then by town, city or village and then alphabetically by entry.

The **Gazetteer** is alphabetical and contains entries on cities, towns and villages, and visitor attractions within each guide's area. The Gazetteer also contains several special-feature panels, which look more closely at subjects, phenomena, people and historical events associated with the area. In addition, there are a number of maps and town plans. Gazetteer entries begin with the entry heading and then give an indication of location. Mileages given are for guidance only and are not strict road mileages. Addresses, opening hours, telephone numbers and an indication of disabled access follow where appropriate. 'Free' denotes no admission charge; an entrance fee should otherwise be assumed. The letters HS or NTS before the telephone number show that the property or land is owned or managed by Historic Scotland or the National Trust for Scotland. We have adopted the Scottish Tourist Board's definitions of disabled access, and it should be noted that in many cases the visitor attractions have defined their own accessibility. It is advisable for disabled visitors to check in advance. The symbols used are:

D – unassisted disabled access

D (P) – partial access

D (A) – access with assistance

Where no letter is given, it should be assumed that access has not been assessed in the STB's scheme or that access is difficult or impossible.

Comprehensive cross-references to other Gazetteer entries and to panels have been included for ease of use. For example: **Highland games**, see panel p138. Other cross references from within one gazetteer or panel entry to another are highlighted by the use of **bold type**.

In the case of the major cities and towns – Aberdeen, Dundee, Edinburgh, Glasgow, Inverness, Perth and St Andrews, visitor attractions have been alphabetically entered as sub-headings under the main city or town heading. This procedure has also been adopted for islands and island groups.

It should be noted that three-figure telephone numbers are in the process of being phased out in Scotland. At the time of going to press, number changes had not all been implemented.

INTRODUCTION TO
THE HIGHLANDS AND ISLANDS

For the purposes of this book, 'Highlands and Islands' has been taken
to include the whole of Highland and Grampian Regions. All the
island groups from the Small Isles northwards are also included, as
are Orkney and Shetland.

Northern Scotland encompasses an extraordinary variety of scenery.
From the dramatic trench of the Great Glen to the rock stacks of St
Kilda; from the flat, water-dappled Flows of Caithness to the sub-
arctic tops of the Cairngorms; from the rich machair of the Western
Isles to the equally rich sands of Banff, Buchan and Aberdeenshire.

The area contains one large city, Aberdeen, the 'oil capital' that is
the onshore centre of the North Sea oil industry, the development of
which has provided substantial benefits to Scotland in recent years.
The next largest settlement is Inverness, often called the 'capital of
the Highlands'; other sizeable towns include Fort William, Elgin,
Thurso and on the islands, Stornoway, Kirkwall and Lerwick.

The area exhibits vast differences not just in landscape, flora and
fauna, but in its human history. Man has been settling, and thus
influencing the appearance of, this land for at least 5000 years, and
we are very fortunate that so many remains from every period of that
long human story can be seen today.

Orkney is particularly rich in prehistoric monuments, including
the Neolithic village at Skara Brae, preserved under the sand for
centuries before being uncovered 100 years ago. And yet Orkney,
even with so many reminders of its distant past, is very much a place
of the present and future, with a major oil terminal on Flotta and its
unique inter-island air service.

In many parts of the Highlands and Islands mysterious brochs
can be found, defensive masterpieces in stone dating from around
2000 years ago. Of their builders we know little: all we have is these
reminders of their skill in construction. The same applies to the Picts,
whose carved stones, dating back perhaps 1000 years, still puzzle
archaeologists.

That Scottish history went through turbulent periods is evident
throughout the area. There are over 1000 castles in Scotland as a
whole, and hundreds in the Highlands and Islands. Not all are open
to the public, but many can be seen, and each has its own story to
tell. The stark power of Corgarff in upper Strathdon or of Ardvreck
on Loch Assynt seem to fit in perfectly with their wild surroundings,
in contrast to the fantasy palace of Dunrobin on the Caithness coast,

home of the Dukes of Sutherland; and indeed to Balmoral, the royal family's Scottish country home on Deeside. In Grampian the superb Castles of Mar form a group without parallel in Britain. Many are in the care of the National Trust for Scotland.

The natural attractions of the Highlands and Islands are legion. For the walker or field naturalist, the area is a paradise. There are many magnificent nature reserves to be visited, from St Cyrus in the far south-east of the area up to Hermaness in Shetland. Major sites for birds include Sands of Forvie on the Aberdeenshire coast, Handa Island off Sutherland, the cliffs of the Bullers of Buchan, Loch of Strathbeg and a whole series along the north coast of Caithness and Sutherland. Loch Garten with its ospreys is well known, but there are also many smaller sites to be discovered by the enquiring visitor.

Mountains are on offer in every shape and size. In Sutherland the individual peaks such as Suilven and Canisp, Foinaven and Arkle rise abruptly from a flat, wet plain. In contrast, the Cairngorms present a plateau – the largest area of really high ground in Britain – split by superbly sculptured corries and cut through by dramatic hill passes. In the west near Fort William is Ben Nevis, Britain's highest mountain, climbed by perhaps 100 000 people each year; in the east are smaller hills climbed, it sometimes seems, by hardly anybody, but all have their own charm.

The coastline of the Highlands and Islands offers further riches. Magnificent sands on the east and north coasts alternate with wonderful cliffs, reaching an apogee near Cape Wrath, where the cliff at Clo Mor is the highest on mainland Britain. Even it is exceeded on the Orkney island of Hoy, where St John's Head looks down over 1100 feet to the sea below: that too is trumped at Conachair on St Kilda, that remote grouping 110 miles out in the wild Atlantic.

Recreation includes not just walking and mountaineering, but also fishing for salmon and trout, the former on glorious rivers such as the Spey, Dee and Findhorn, the latter often on remote hill lochs only reached by a hard walk. Many estates offer shooting for grouse and deer in season. Winter sport has seen great development, and there are now five ski centres, at Cairngorm, Glenshee and the Lecht in the east and at Glencoe and Aonach Mor in the west. Given sufficient snow cover, cross-country skiing is available in several areas.

Tourism and recreation is of great importance economically to the Highlands and Islands. Tourism is now worth more than farming, fishing and fish farming added together, and from being a somewhat haphazard business without central guidance and control, it is shaping itself into a major industry geared to the needs of the modern traveller. Many visitor attractions are staying open longer, at both ends of the season.

Indeed, the range of attractions is very diverse. There are well-run, and in many cases imaginative, castles, gardens, heritage centres, craft centres, farm centres, falconries, wineries and distilleries. In one day visitors can learn about the Clearances at Bettyhill, nuclear power at Dounreay, archaeology at Auckengill and glass-making in Wick. On the other hand, you could simply stay in one place, enjoying the scenery and perhaps watching the birdlife.

History and legend are natural ingredients of the tourism scene. There is still no evidence to suggest that the Loch Ness monster exists, but it attracts thousands of people to the Loch Ness area each year in the hope of a sighting. In human terms, the now rather romanticized story of Bonnie Prince Charlie and the Jacobite Risings is retold at several locations including Glenfinnan and Culloden.

Tourism apart, the Highlands and Islands economy still features agriculture and fisheries as important elements. Fish farming has been a notable success, and whisky is a major exporting industry. There are over 100 distilleries in Scotland, and the majority of them are covered by this book. The Malt Whisky Trail in Strathspey takes visitors to a number of distilleries where the process of whisky-making is explained and the result can be tasted.

For those seeking a rather different type of holiday, there is island-hopping in the Hebrides, or in Orkney and Shetland, where the midsummer light has a matchless quality and for several weeks there is almost no real darkness. These islands have a distinctive character which owes much to the strong Norse thread running through their history.

The topographical and historical richness of the area is matched by the richness of language. The meanings of many place names are given in this book. They derive in some cases from Norse but much more often from Gaelic, a language which survives and is enjoying something of a revival.

There is a vast amount to be discovered within this wonderful area, and the process of discovery, like the evolution of the topography and history of the Highlands and Islands, never ends.

National Fact File

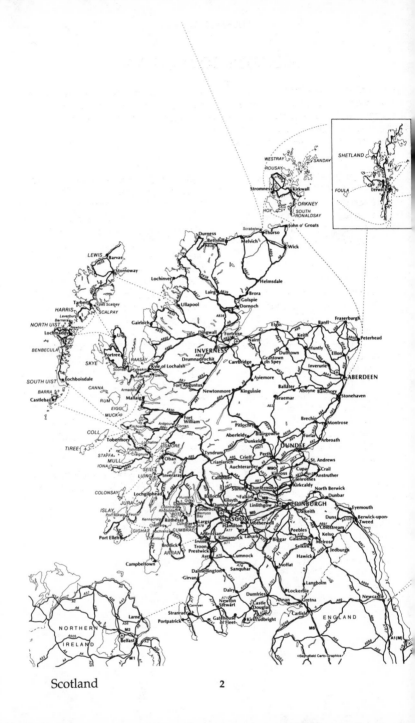

Scotland

2

ACCOMMODATION

The Scottish Tourist Board (STB: see under **Information – Associations and Organizations**) publishes a number of annual guides containing details of accommodation and grading systems throughout the country. A comprehensive booking service is offered by **Hi-Line**, run as part of the **Highland Direct Reservation System**.

CARAVANS AND CAMPING

A voluntary classification and grading scheme exists, run by the National Federation of Site Operators and the National Caravan Council, with the support of the Scottish Tourist Board (STB). Range of facilities is indicated on a descending scale from A to D, and quality of facilities by the number of ticks, varying 4–1. Other symbols are used to denote facilities, size and location of park, nature of park (static or touring), and standard of static caravans available for hire (also graded A–D). All parks in the scheme comply with the basic requirements of their site licence and, in general, with STB standards, and all have water and fire points and, where necessary, toilet blocks etc. In addition, a Thistle Commendation Scheme also indicates Holiday Static Caravan Parks, which let first-class caravans, combined with good facilities and an attractive environment. All commended parks which meet the requirements will display a Thistle plaque. Full details of sites involved in the scheme are available in STB's *Scotland: Camping and Caravan Parks*.

HOTELS, GUEST HOUSES AND SELF-CATERING

A voluntary classification and grading scheme is run by the STB, which sends inspectors to all hotels, guest houses, self-catering and bed and breakfast establishments wishing to be included. Gradings are awarded for quality, and classification indicates the range of services and facilities. Gradings are categorized as Approved (acceptable quality); Commended (good); Highly Commended (high), and Deluxe (excellent). Classification is signified by the number of crowns, varying 1–5 (minimum–comprehensive). Highly Commended Two Crown therefore indicates higher quality than Commended Four Crown, but offering fewer services and facilities. Full details of listed establishments are available in STB's *Scotland: Hotels and Guest Houses, Scotland: Bed and Breakfast* and *Scotland: Self-Catering Accommodation*.

YOUTH HOSTELS

There are 80 youth hostels in Scotland, categorized A–C in descending order, indicating facilities available. All offer dormitory accommodation and self-catering facilities. Full details are available from the Scottish Youth Hostels Association (see **Information – Associations and Organizations**), which publishes a handbook for youth hostellers in Scotland.

HIGHLAND DIRECT RESERVATION SYSTEM (HI-LINE)

Run by Highlands and Islands Enterprise, Highland Direct is an accommodation reservation service specifically for the Highlands and Islands. A brochure of all participating establishments is available by calling 0349 63434, while reservations (as well as travel information) can be made on 0349 65000 (see Highland Direct under **Information – Associations and Organizations**).

ACTIVITIES AND PASTIMES

The organizations listed here cover a range of sports and pastimes which may be of interest to the visitor. Anyone wishing to become involved with a certain activity during their stay in Scotland should contact the relevant organization. A complete list is available from the Scottish Sports Council (see **Information – Associations and Organizations**).

ARCHERY

Scottish Archery Association: Coaching Organizer, 4 Glowrorum Drive, Denny (0324 814380). Central body for archery in Scotland. Visitors may be invited to shoot with local clubs, 'as long as they hold FITA membership' (the international body for archery).

Scottish Field Archery Association: Don S. Smith, Secretary, 83 Woodend Road, Rutherglen, Glasgow (041–634 3108). Outdoor archery on a permanent woodland course of 28 targets.

ATHLETICS

Scottish Amateur Athletic Association/Scottish Women's Amateur Athletic Association: Secretary, Caledonia House, South Gyle, Edinburgh (031–317 7320/1).

BADMINTON

Scottish Badminton Union: Secretary, Cockburn Centre, 40 Bogmoor Place, Glasgow (041–445 1218).

BASKETBALL

Scottish Basketball Association: Secretary, Caledonia House, South Gyle, Edinburgh (031–317 7260).

BOWLING

Scottish Bowling Association: Secretary, 50 Wellington Street, Glasgow (041–221 8999).

Scottish Indoor Bowling Association: Secretary, 41 Montfode Court, Ardrossan, Ayrshire (0294 68372).

Scottish Women's Bowling Association: Secretary, 55A Esplanade, Greenock (0475 24140).

Scottish Women's Indoor Bowling Association: Secretary, 1 Underwood Road, Rutherglen, Glasgow (041–647 5810).

CAMPING

The Camping and Caravanning Club (Scottish Region): Ally Park, 56 Polwarth Avenue, Brightons, Falkirk (0324 715264). Scottish branch of the international affiliated organization for campers and caravanners.

CANOEING

Scottish Canoe Association: Secretary, Caledonia House, South Canoeing *cont* Gyle, Edinburgh (031–317 7314). Produces a number of videos and supplies, as well as a booklet listing names and addresses of clubs and coaching organizations throughout Scotland. Also produces a guide to

Scottish rivers, available from the above address.

CAVING

Grampian Speleological Group: 8 Scone Gardens, Edinburgh (031–661 1123).

CRICKET

Scottish Cricket Union: Secretary, Caledonia House, South Gyle, Edinburgh (031–317 7247. Produces a *Guide to Scottish Cricket* giving details of fixtures and results and including a Scottish directory of clubs, associations, universities and schools.

CURLING

Royal Caledonian Curling Club: Secretary, 2 Coates Crescent, Edinburgh (031–225 7083). A popular game among the Scots, curling is played on ice and involves sliding heavy stones with handles (curling stones) down a rink towards a target (tee).

CYCLING

CTC Scottish Cycling Council: Secretary, 11 Torridon Place, Kirkcaldy, Fife (0592 262944).

DANCE

Royal Scottish Country Dance Society: Secretary, 12 Coates Crescent, Edinburgh (031–225 3854). Worldwide society promoting Scottish Country Dance, organizing dances and events and offering instruction from beginner level to teaching standard.

Scottish Official Board of Highland Dancing: Secretary, Heritage House, 32 Grange Loan, Edinburgh (031–668 3965 a.m. only). World governing body for Highland Dancing offering information to visiting Highland dancers about championships, competitions and Highland Games they may wish to attend, and procedure for entering events.

DISABLED

Scottish Sports Association for the Disabled: Administrator, Fife Sports Institute, Viewfield Road, Glenrothes (0592 771700).

FISHING

Scottish Anglers National Association: Secretary, 5 Cramond Glebe Road, Edinburgh (031–312 7618). Governing body for the sport of game fishing in Scotland. The association does not provide an advice service to visitors, but does produce an annual report, available for a fee, which includes a useful 'Guide to SANA Club Waters', detailing clubs, waters, species, seasons and permit addresses.

Scottish Salmon Angling Federation: Secretary, 18 Abercromby Place, Edinburgh (031–556 4466).

FOOTBALL

Scottish Amateur Football Association: Secretary, Beechwood, Gateside Road, Barrhead, Glasgow (041–881 4025).

Scottish Football Association: 6 Park Gardens, Glasgow (041–332 6372). The sport's main governing body.

Scottish Football League: Secretary, 188 West Regent Street, Glasgow

(041–248 3844). Publishes the *Scottish Football League Review* giving details of all clubs, and contact names and addresses.

Scottish Women's Football Association: Administrator, Kelvin Hall, Argyle Street, Glasgow (041–337 1455).

GAMES (HIGHLAND AND BORDER)

Scottish Games Association: Secretary, 24 Florence Place, Perth (0738 27782). Central organization for Highland and Border Games throughout Scotland.

GENEALOGY

Scottish Genealogy Society: 15 Victoria Terrace, Edinburgh (031–220 3677). Nominal membership fee. Does not carry out professional record searching, but can supply members with a list of professional researchers.

GLIDING

Scottish Gliding Association: Secretary, Glenfinart Park, Ardentinny, near Dunoon, Argyll (0369 81256).

GOLF

Scottish Golf Union: Secretary, The Cottage, 181A Whitehouse Road, Edinburgh (031–339 7546).

Scottish Ladies Golfing Association: Secretary, Chacewood, 49 Fullarton Drive, Troon (0292 313047).

HANG GLIDING

Scottish Hang Gliding Federation: Peter Shields, Secretary, 1 Lochbrae Drive, High Burnside, Glasgow (041–634 6688). Scotland has only one hang gliding school, Cairnwell Hang Gliding School, Cairnwell Mountain, by Braemar, Aberdeenshire (03397 41331). Visitors already qualified should contact the above address in Glasgow for information on the nearest club.

HOCKEY

Scottish Hockey Union: Executive Administrator, Caledonia House, South Gyle, Edinburgh (031–317 7254). Contact point for non-national clubs and associations interested in participating in Scotland.

ICE HOCKEY

Scottish Ice Hockey Association: President, 16 Glencairn Road, Ayr (0292 266203).

LACROSSE

Scottish Lacrosse Association: Secretary, Geddes House, Parleyhill, Culross, Dunfermline (0383 880602).

LAWN TENNIS

Scottish Lawn Tennis Association: Secretary/National Coach, 12 Melville Crescent, Edinburgh (031–225 1284).

LITERATURE

Association for Scottish Literary Studies: c/o Department of English Literature, University of Glasgow, Glasgow (041–339 8855 ext 5549). National association promoting the study, teaching and writing of

Scottish literature and the study and teaching of Scottish languages.

Poetry Association of Scotland: Secretary, 38 Dovecot Road, Edinburgh (031–334 5241). Originally established in 1924, the association is today a registered charity promoting poetry through readings and related activities.

MOUNTAINEERING

The Mountaineering Council of Scotland: Kevin Howett, National Officer, Flat 1R, 71 King Street, Crieff (0764 4962). Representative body for Scottish hill-walkers, rock and ice climbers, ski mountaineers and cross-country skiers of all standards. It directly funds winter and summer training courses for members at Glenmore Lodge in the Cairngorms (the national Scottish Outdoor Centre).

ORIENTEERING

Scottish Orienteering Association (SOA): Secretary, 7 Lawson Avenue, Banchory (033 02 3145). Formed in 1961, the association is now a subsidiary branch of the British Orienteering Federation (BOF), the governing body of the sport in the UK, which is affiliated to the International Orienteering Federation.

PARACHUTING

Scottish Sport Parachute Association: Secretary, 47 Great Southern Road, Aberdeen (0224 586510).

PARAGLIDING

Cloudbusters Paragliding School: Peter Shields, Chief Inspector,

9 Lynedoch Place, Glasgow (041–634 6688). Courses available for novices to advanced pilots. Information about nearest clubs available from the above address.

PÉTANQUE

Scottish Pétanque Association: Bob Boyle, National Secretary, 1 Arbroath Crescent, Stirling (0786 70619). The National Secretary of the association defined pétanque (peyt-onk) as being the 'proper name for the French game of boules'. With the exception of a few events which are only open to licensed players, all games are open to the public. Lists of affiliated clubs and contacts and a fixtures list are available from the above address.

RAMBLING AND RIGHTS OF WAY

The Ramblers' Association (Scotland): Scottish Officer, Kelinbank, Church Place, Freuchie, Fife (0337 58065).

Scottish Rights of Way Society: Secretary, Mrs Judith Lewis, John Cotton Business Centre, 10/2 Sunnyside, Edinburgh (031–652 2937).

RIDING

Scottish Trekking and Riding Association: Secretary, Tomnagairn Farm, Trochry, by Dunkeld (035 03 220).

ROWING

Scottish Amateur Rowing Association: Secretary,

11 Spottiswoode Street, Edinburgh (031–229 2366).

RUGBY

Scottish Rugby Union: Secretary, Murrayfield, Roseburn Street, Edinburgh (031–337 9551).

SHINTY

The Camanachd Association: Secretary, Algarve, Badabrie, Banavie, Fort William (0397 772461). A game like hockey, shinty is played mainly in the Highlands and Islands with a curved stick called a caman.

SHOOTING

British Association for Shooting and Conservation: Director of Development – Scotland, Scottish Centre, Trochry, by Dunkeld (035 03 226).

Scottish Clay Target Association: Secretary, 10 Balgibbon Drive, Callander (0877 31323).

SKIING

Scottish National Ski Council: Administrator, Caledonia House, South Gyle, Edinburgh (031–317 7280). Governing body representing and regulating skiing in Scotland. Produces a number of leaflets about its activities and skiing in Scotland.

SUB AQUA

Scottish Sub Aqua Club: Secretary, Cockburn Centre, 40 Bogmoor Place, Glasgow (041–425 1021). Central organization for sub aqua and diving clubs throughout Scotland.

SURFING

Scottish Surfing Federation: Secretary, South Pitblae House, Fraserburgh (0346 23600).

TUG-OF-WAR

Scottish Tug-of-War Association: Fiona Watson, Secretary, Laurelbank, 3 Riverside Villas, Catrine, Mauchline (0290 51502).

WATER SKIING

Scottish Water Ski Association: Secretary, Caledonia House, South Gyle, Edinburgh (031–317 7217).

WINDSURFING

Scottish Windsurfing Association: Secretary, c/o RYA Scotland, Caledonia House, South Gyle, Edinburgh (031–317 7217). The association publishes a guide to recognized windsurfing centres throughout the UK and abroad.

YACHTING

Royal Yachting Association Scotland: Secretary, Caledonia House, South Gyle, Edinburgh (031–317 7388). Videos, handbooks and log books for all RYA training and examination schemes are available from the above address. The *RYA Yearbook and Race Programme* is a useful guide to sailing in Scotland, giving comprehensive details of affiliated clubs and organizations, events and topics of general interest to all in the sailing community.

FESTIVALS (NATIONAL) AND PUBLIC HOLIDAYS

FESTIVALS

Burns Night: 25 January.
Celebrations marking the birthday of Scotland's national poet Robert Burns in 1759 have no effect on public facilities and services. Burns Night Suppers are held either on the evening of the 25th or on nearby dates at hotels, local halls, and in private houses.

St Andrew's Day: 30 November.
Celebrations for Scotland's patron saint do not constitute a statutory public holiday, and few amenities are affected. In the evening, St Andrew's Night dances and ceilidhs are held in hotels and local halls.

PUBLIC HOLIDAYS

English public holidays do not apply in Scotland, although some English-associated companies do recognize them. Bank holidays affect banks only. The following list gives the main bank holidays each year: 1 January*, 2 January, Friday before Easter, first and last Monday in May, first Monday in August, 30 November, 25 December*, 26 December. Spring and autumn holidays are taken instead of public holidays. Dates vary from year to year, but are usually on a Monday. Local holidays marking particular dates or occasions relevant to specific areas vary considerably between towns and regions. Full details of public holidays are available in *Public Holidays in Scotland*, published and updated annually by the Glasgow Chamber of Commerce (30 George Square, Glasgow (041–204 2121). The booklet costs £1.00. The STB publishes a free booklet, *Events in Scotland*, which lists events and festivals for the year throughout the country.

* New Year's Day and Christmas Day are taken by shops, offices, factories etc, although many hotels may remain open.

FOOD AND DRINK

DRINKING

Licensed hotels can serve drinks to residents at any time. Although licensing laws allow bars to open for 12 hours a day, public houses are usually open 1100–1430, and 1700–2300, Monday–Sunday, although not all choose to open on Sunday, and many, especially in cities, stay open later (some until 0130–0200). The same restrictions apply to licensed restaurants.

The legal age for drinking in Scotland is 18. Some landlords and publicans reserve the right to refuse admittance to minors, so it is always advisable to ask permission to bring children in.

Off-licences (liquor stores) selling beers, wines and spirits for private consumption are generally open 1100–2200 (Monday–Saturday, closed Sunday). It is illegal for anyone under the age of 18 to attempt to buy alcohol from an off-licence.

Scottish beer comes in a variety of forms. The standard request is for a pint of 'heavy' or 'special' but what exactly this means depends on what part of the country you're in. Generally, heavy is the equivalent of the Englishman's 'bitter', but is sweeter and fuller bodied. If you ask for a pint of heavy in Edinburgh, you're likely to be served '80 shilling' or, if you specifically request it, '70 shilling'. A few pubs also serve '90 shilling'. All three are cask-conditioned beers which have carbon dioxide pumped through them, making them creamy rather than fizzy. Their names – 70, 80 and 90 shilling – refer to the original price of a keg of beer in days gone by. Ninety shilling has the greatest proof (alcoholic content) and 70 the least. Elsewhere, the same request for a pint of heavy is likely to secure a pint of Special. These are pressurized beers which are fizzy rather than creamy. Lager is another option, originally imported from Germany and Denmark, but now produced in Scotland. A pressurized beer, it is roughly equal in strength to 70 shilling, although some stronger lagers are available.

Chasers are a small measure of spirit (usually whisky), drunk simultaneously with a pint of beer. Whisky remains one of Scotland's favourite drinks and best-known exports. A nip and a dram are both equal to roughly one measure. Visitors should note, however, that measures in Scotland tend to be larger than those in England.

PUBLIC HOUSES

The Scottish pub is something of an institution. Although in larger towns restaurants are now widely available, in more rural areas they can be few and far between, in which case it is the pub which provides a focal point for eating. Pubs provide an excellent alternative for a cheap and filling lunch or dinner. Some pubs offer a 'Family Room', usually to one side of the main bar, where minors can eat either on their own or with their parents.

RESTAURANTS

A voluntary listing scheme for restaurants was introduced by the STB in 1973. Called 'The Taste of Scotland', it is now independently run, and covers restaurants, inns and coffee shops throughout Scotland which have applied for membership and paid the required fee. All applicants are visited by inspectors and, if up to standard, subsequently included in *The Taste of Scotland Guide*. Participants display the Taste of Scotland logo, a soup tureen encircled by the words 'The Taste of Scotland'. A list of all participating establishments is available from the Taste of Scotland office (see **Information – Associations and Organizations**). Restaurant guides, such as *Michelin* and the *Good Food Guide*, generally contain a Scottish section, albeit somewhat limited, and there are one or two specifically Scottish food guides.

LANGUAGE

ENGLISH

Spoken throughout Scotland, although variations in accent can often be difficult to understand.

SCOTS

Dialects vary from region to region. Visitors are most likely to hear 'broad' Scots around Glasgow and the Central Region. Geographically, in the Borders and from Dundee northwards, dialects change frequently.

GAELIC

Gaelic is still a living language in the Outer Hebrides (road signs on the Isle of Lewis are exclusively in Gaelic and bilingual in the rest of the region) and in pockets elsewhere, such as the Isle of Skye. Roughly 87 000 people in Scotland (about 2 per cent of the population) either speak, read or write Gaelic. The language is undergoing something of a renaissance at present, and it is estimated that over 3000 Scots are now learning Gaelic. Forecasts are that by 1993 broadcasting time for Gaelic television programmes will have trebled to 300 hours (see **Sabhal Mor Ostaig**, and **An Comunn Gaidhealach** under **Information – Associations and Organizations**).

MEDIA

The magazines and newspapers listed below are published in Scotland for a specifically Scottish market. British national papers often have Scottish sections or correspondents. Freesheets are free local newspapers distributed to each home in a particular area, often aimed at a certain district of a city or rural community. Some, along with regional newspapers, are listed in the Regional Fact File.

MAGAZINES

The List: 14 High Street, Edinburgh (031–558 1191). Contemporary magazine covering art, books, clubs, film, music, sport, television, theatre and travel, particularly in the Central Belt, covering Glasgow and Edinburgh. Published fortnightly (Thursday) and available from bookshops and newsagents.

Scots Magazine: Bank Street, Dundee (0382 23131). Scotland's oldest magazine was first published in 1739 in Edinburgh. In addition to articles of general Scottish interest, it has regular features on areas of Scotland and aspects of Scottish culture, and a classified section covering holidays, accommodation, books, shooting, fishing, livestock, and public notices. On sale on the last Friday of every month, it is available either by subscription or from newsagents and some bookshops.

Scottish Field: The Plaza Tower, The Plaza, East Kilbride (03552 46444). Up-market, glossy magazine offering the best of Scottish contemporary life. Articles cover people, lifestyles, fashion, culture, landscape, natural history and attractions, as well as history and heritage. Published monthly and available from newsagents.

Scottish Historical Review: Company of Scottish History Ltd, Aberdeen University Press, Farmers Hall, Aberdeen (0224 630724). Intellectual/academic magazine of essays on Scottish history, book reviews and lists of articles written about Scotland. Available by subscription only from the above address.

Scottish Home and Country: 42 Heriot Row, Edinburgh (031–225 1934). 'The Magazine of the Scottish Women's Rural Institutes' was founded in 1924. Published monthly, it offers features on crafts, fashion, gardening, books and cookery, all with a strong Scottish emphasis. Available on subscription in Scotland and abroad.

Scottish World: PO Box 1, Oban, Argyll (0631 62079). Covers all aspects of life in Scotland, such as clans, history and art; published quarterly and available on subscription or from newsagents.

What's On: 9a St Bernard's Crescent, Edinburgh (031–332 0471). Describing itself as 'the magazine for the Scottish leisure and tourism industry', *What's On* rivals *The List* as Scotland's equivalent of *Time Out*, providing details of events around Scotland. Covers exhibitions, theatre, film, music, food and drink; published monthly and available from newsagents.

DAILY NEWSPAPERS

Daily Record: Anderston Quay, Glasgow (041–248 7000).

Dundee Courier and Advertiser: 7 Bank St, Dundee (0382 23131).

The Herald: 195 Albion Street, Glasgow (041–552 6255). Formerly called the *Glasgow Herald*.

Press and Journal: PO Box 43, Lang Stracht, Mastrick, Aberdeen (0224 690222).

The Scotsman: 20 North Bridge, Edinburgh (031–225 2468).

SUNDAY NEWSPAPERS

Scotland on Sunday: 20 North Bridge, Edinburgh (031–225 2468).

Scottish Sunday Express: Park House, Park Circus Place, Glasgow (041–332 9600).

Sunday Mail: Anderston Quay, Glasgow (041–242 3403).

Sunday Post: Courier Place, Dundee (0382 22214); 144 Port Dundas Road, Glasgow (041–332 9933).

NATIONAL RADIO

(Regional channels listed under Regional Fact File)

BBC Radio Scotland: Broadcasting House, Queen Margaret Drive, Glasgow (041–330 2345); Broadcasting House, Queen Street, Edinburgh (031–225 3131). MW: 810 kHz/370m, VHF: 92.95 MHz.

BBC1–5: can be received throughout the country on the following frequencies, although quality of reception varies:
Radio 1 – MW: 1053 kHz/285m, 1089 kHz/275m
VHF: 97.7–99.6 MHz.

Radio 2 – VHF: 88–90.2 MHz.
Radio 3 – MW: 1215 kHz/247m.
VHF: 90–92.5 MHz.
Radio 4 – LW: 198 kHz/1515m.
VHF: 95.8, 94.9 MHz.
Radio 5 – MW: 693 kHz, 909 kHz.
In addition, BBC Radio Scotland is broadcast on MW: 810 kHz/370m, VHF: 92.95 MHz.

There is no national independent radio channel (in 1992); some independent regional channels (listed separately) are available.

TELEVISION

BBC Scotland: Broadcasting House, Queen Margaret Drive, Glasgow (041–330 2345); Broadcasting House, Queen Street, Edinburgh (031–225 3131). BBC1 and BBC2 are both received throughout the country, with some programme variations from England, including Scottish news bulletins.

British Sky Broadcasting: 6 Centaurs Business Park, Grant Way, Isleworth, Middx (071–782 3000). Broadcasts five channels to special receivers.

Channel 4 Television Company Ltd: 60 Charlotte Street, London (071-631 4444). Programmes received nationally throughout Britain.

Independent Television Association: Knighton House, 56 Mortimer Street, London (071–636 6866). Central organization for independent television stations. ITV programmes vary between regions: Scottish Television (STV), Borders Television and Grampian Television are listed in Regional Fact Files.

MONEY AND BANKS

BANKING

Scotland has four national banks.

Bank of Scotland plc: Head Office, The Mound, Edinburgh (031–442 7777). Fully independent.

The Royal Bank of Scotland plc: Head Office, 42 St Andrew Square, Edinburgh (031–556 8555). Fully independent.

Clydesdale Bank plc: Head Office, 30 St Vincent Place, Glasgow (041–223 2000). Part of National Australia Bank group.

TSB Scotland plc: Head Office, 120 George Street, Edinburgh (031–225 4555). Part of the TSB Group (head office in London).

All four banks have branches in the major Scottish cities, while both the Royal Bank of Scotland and the Bank of Scotland provide a comprehensive network of branches and autotellers throughout the country, which can be used by cardholders from other banks. Signs showing which cards can be used are displayed at autotellers.

CURRENCY

Scottish currency is the same value as English currency, although there are variations in the design of banknotes depending on the bank of issue. One pound notes are still legal tender in Scotland, along with the new one pound coins.

TRAVEL AND TRANSPORT

AIRPORTS

Scotland's main airports are at Glasgow and Edinburgh. Regional airports are located at Aberdeen and Prestwick, and there are a number of smaller airfields throughout the country (Dundee, Inverness and around the Highlands and Islands). Regional airports are listed in Regional Fact Files. Central address: **Scottish Airports Ltd**: St Andrews Drive, Glasgow Airport, Paisley, Renfrewshire (041–887 1111).

BUSES/COACHES

Scottish Citylink: St Andrew Square Bus Station, Edinburgh (031–557 5717); Victoria Coach Station, 164 Buckingham Palace Road, London (071–730 0202).

Caledonian Express/Stagecoach: Walnut Grove, Kinfauns, Perth (0738 33481).
Both run services from London and cities throughout England to Aberdeen, Dumfries, Dundee, Edinburgh, Fort William, Glasgow, Inverness, Lochalsh, Oban, Perth and Stirling. Stagecoach also run to Thurso.
Details of coach times and routes are available from the **Travel Centre**, Buchanan Street Bus Station, Glasgow (041–332 7133).

Scottish Postal Board: Royal Mail Public Relations Unit, West Port House, 102 West Port, Edinburgh EH3 9HS. Post enquiries only. Produces an annual *Scottish Postbus Guide*, giving full details of postbus services throughout Scotland.

DRIVING

Driving in Scotland is on the left-hand side. The road network throughout the country is generally good, with either motorway or dual carriageway links between Glasgow, Edinburgh and the north, including Stirling, Perth and Dundee.
  Visitors should take extra care when driving on small country roads – many of which are single-track – particularly in the north of the country. In addition, during wintertime it is advisable to check on relief maps whether routes go over high roads, as snow can soon block them.

FERRIES

Comprehensive ferry services are run, particularly around the north of the country and to outlying islands.

Caledonian MacBrayne Ltd (popularly known as Cal Mac): The Ferry Terminal, Gourock (0475 33755).

Orkney Islands Shipping Company Ltd: 4 Ayre Road, Kirkwall, Orkney (0856 2044).

P&O European Ferries: Enterprise House, Channel View Road, Dover (0304 203388).

P&O Ferries Orkney and Shetland Services: P&O Ferries Terminal, Jamieson's Quay, Aberdeen (0224 589111).

Sealink British Ferries: Sea Terminal, Stranraer (0776 2262).

Shetland Islands Council: Grantfield, Lerwick, Shetland (0595 2024).

Western Ferries (Argyll) Ltd/Western

Ferries Clyde Ltd: 16 Woodside Crescent, Glasgow (041–332 9766).

TRAINS

InterCity trains connect Scotland with the rest of the UK. If taking a bicycle on trains, check in advance about availability of space, as reservations are compulsory on some services. Full details are available in the leaflet *ScotRail Welcomes Cyclists*.

Edinburgh Waverley Station: Waverley Bridge (031–556 2451).

Glasgow Central Station: Gordon Street (041–204 2844).

Glasgow Queen Street Station: (041–204 2844).

TRAVEL TICKETS

Reduced Price Tickets: Issued by British Rail, these can save money on most routes around the country. Ask for details of Standard, Cheap Day and Saver tickets, as well as Weekly, Monthly and 3-Monthly season tickets if your stay in Scotland is longer.

Travelpass: Issued by Highlands and Islands Enterprise, Travelpass allows 8 or 13 days' unlimited travel around the Highlands and Islands, including the Outer Hebrides, by bus, train and ferry. Passes also cover travel by train or bus (Scottish Citylink) from Glasgow, Edinburgh or Aberdeen to the Highlands and back again. Further details, and passes, are available from British Rail in Edinburgh, Glasgow, Paisley, Aberdeen, Stirling and Inverness; from St Andrew Bus Station (Edinburgh), Buchanan Street Bus Station (Glasgow); and from Caledonian MacBrayne (address under Ferries above).

Festival Cities Rover: Issued by British Rail, this allows unlimited travel for any three or seven consecutive days between Edinburgh, Kirkcaldy, North Berwick, Stirling, Glasgow and intermediate stations.

Freedom of Scotland Rover Ticket: Issued by British Rail, this allows unlimited train travel (also covering Caledonian MacBrayne ferries and Firth of Clyde steamers) from Wick and Thurso in the north to Carlisle and Berwick in the south, for 4, 7, 10 or 15 days.

Highland Rover Airpass: British Airways offers a 'Highland Rover Airpass', which allows travel on up to eight Highlands and Islands flights over a minimum of eight days.

WEATHER

Misconceptions about Scottish weather are common: that the whole of Scotland is covered by snow in winter for example, and that it rains a lot in summer.

In fact the eastern part of Scotland is rather dry; the annual average rainfall for Edinburgh is similar to that for London. The higher areas are wet, but even there the rainfall is seasonal. In the west of Scotland the driest months are April, May and June and the wettest are September to January.

As for sunshine, the chart shows the extreme east of Scotland (Dunbar) to have an excellent sunshine record (although the absolute record for hours of sunshine in a day is held by Tiree with 329 hours in a month in May 1946 and May 1975).

Full details of Scotland's climate are available in *The Climate of Scotland – Some Facts and Figures*, on sale at HMSO Bookshops or from the Meteorological Office, Saughton House, Broomhouse Drive, Edinburgh (031–244 8362/3).

Average number of days with snow on ground at 9am (1951–80)

Location	Jan	Feb	Mar	Apr	May	Jun	Jul	Aug	Sep	Oct	Nov	Dec	Year
Shetland													
Lerwick	7.5	7.8	3.8	1.4	0.1	0.0	0.0	0.0	0.0	0.2	2.4	4.9	23.1
Western Isles													
Stornoway	3.5	2.8	1.4	0.2	0.0	0.0	0.0	0.0	0.0	0.0	1.0	1.5	10.4
Highland													
Wick	5.4	5.6	2.2	0.5	0.0	0.0	0.0	0.0	0.0	0.0	1.5	3.0	18.2
Nairn	5.5	5.6	1.7	0.2	0.0	0.0	0.0	0.0	0.0	0.0	0.8	2.7	16.5
Grampian													
Braemar	15.6	15.9	9.7	2.4	0.1	0.0	0.0	0.0	0.0	0.3	4.6	10.4	59.0
Craibstone (nr Aberdeen)	9.6	9.6	4.9	0.9	0.1	0.0	0.0	0.0	0.0	0.2	2.6	4.7	32.6
Tayside													
Perth	5.7	5.2	1.2	0.1	0.0	0.0	0.0	0.0	0.0	0.0	0.5	2.4	15.1
Lothian													
Edinburgh													
Royal Botanic Gdn.	5.0	5.3	1.1	0.2	0.0	0.0	0.0	0.0	0.0	0.0	0.5	1.9	14.0
Royal Observatory	5.5	6.1	1.8	0.3	0.0	0.0	0.0	0.0	0.0	0.0	1.0	2.0	16.7
Penicuik	9.6	9.3	3.8	0.9	0.1	0.0	0.0	0.0	0.0	0.0*	1.9	4.7	30.3
Dunbar	1.7	2.6	0.4	0.1	0.0	0.0	0.0	0.0	0.0	0.0	0.2	0.6	5.6
Strathclyde													
Tiree	1.4	1.2	0.4	0.1	0.0	0.0	0.0	0.0	0.0	0.0	0.1	0.4	3.6
Glasgow Airport	3.5	1.8	0.7	0.1	0.0	0.0	0.0	0.0	0.0	0.0	0.6	1.3	8.0
Auchincruive (nr Ayr)	2.3	1.7	0.7	0.1	0.0	0.0	0.0	0.0	0.0	0.0	0.5	0.6	5.9
Dumfries & Galloway													
Eskdalemuir	10.1	9.6	4.7	0.7	0.0*	0.0	0.0	0.0	0.0	0.0*	1.9	5.0	32.0

Note: 0.0* in the 30-year period indicates there was only one day with snow lying at 0900 hours in this month.

Average rainfall in mm (1951–80)

Location	Jan	Feb	Mar	Apr	May	Jun	Jul	Aug	Sep	Oct	Nov	Dec	Year
Shetland													
Lerwick	127	93	93	72	64	64	67	78	113	119	140	147	1177
Orkney													
Kirkwall	105	71	72	54	53	57	55	77	88	110	120	121	983
Western Isles													
Benbecula	129	86	89	62	65	76	83	83	119	139	140	132	1203
Stornoway	115	77	80	66	62	67	72	74	103	126	129	125	1096
Highland													
Ullapool	119	84	93	76	73	83	80	92	115	155	159	161	1290
Achmore (nr Plockton)	104	68	70	56	56	63	78	82	107	112	124	112	1032
Portree (Skye)	182	116	129	93	91	104	113	118	170	204	203	210	1732
Onich (nr Fort William)	200	132	152	111	103	124	137	150	199	215	220	238	1981
Wick	81	58	55	45	47	49	61	74	68	73	90	82	783
Fort Augustus	112	72	83	58	72	61	65	82	103	124	126	140	1098
Nairn	48	34	33	36	43	46	62	75	50	54	60	52	593
Glenmore Lodge	96	64	71	68	76	73	87	107	80	96	100	106	1024
Grampian													
Gordon Castle	55	44	42	42	51	55	77	89	57	66	75	67	720
Braemar	93	59	59	51	65	55	58	76	73	87	87	96	859
Craibstone (nr Aberdeen)	77	57	54	51	62	54	79	83	68	78	80	80	821
Tayside													
Pitlochry	94	59	52	47	64	62	65	72	70	76	69	94	824
Arbroath	50	40	40	38	48	44	62	67	50	52	54	54	599
Perth	70	52	47	43	57	51	67	72	63	65	69	82	738
Fife													
St. Andrews	62	48	44	39	50	44	61	68	55	55	63	64	653
Lothian													
Edinburgh (Royal Botanic Garden)	47	39	39	38	49	45	69	73	57	56	58	56	626
Dunbar	46	33	33	33	47	41	55	68	47	48	55	49	555
Borders													
Floors Castle (Kelso)	55	43	38	40	55	51	63	75	57	59	63	57	656
Central													
Callander	164	113	115	81	97	86	97	113	141	147	175	193	1522
Strathclyde													
Tiree	120	71	77	60	56	66	79	83	123	125	123	123	1106
Inveraray Castle	210	132	150	115	106	124	137	148	209	225	228	252	2036
Eallabus (Islay)	139	85	92	70	67	74	93	93	128	139	149	149	1278
Glasgow Airport	96	63	65	50	62	58	68	83	95	98	105	108	951
Auchincruive (nr Ayr)	82	50	53	47	51	58	80	91	100	97	99	93	901
Aros (Mull)	210	116	142	97	96	109	120	133	199	208	203	220	1853
Dumfries & Galloway													
West Freugh (nr Stranraer)	100	65	67	53	55	57	70	82	98	100	105	103	955
Loch Dee	236	154	168	130	121	122	142	184	214	222	241	263	2197
Dumfries	103	72	68	55	71	63	77	93	104	106	109	104	1023
Eskdalemuir	150	99	108	86	94	95	107	122	142	140	153	160	1456

1″ = 25.4mm

Average bright sunshine in hours (1951–80)

Location	Jan	Feb	Mar	Apr	May	Jun	Jul	Aug	Sep	Oct	Nov	Dec	Annual	Annual total
Shetland														
Lerwick	0.7	1.9	2.7	4.5	4.9	5.3	4.0	3.8	3.2	2.0	1.1	0.5	2.9	1056
Orkney														
Kirkwall	1.0	2.3	3.1	4.9	5.2	5.4	4.3	4.1	3.4	2.4	1.3	0.7	3.2	1160
Western Isles														
Stornoway	1.2	2.5	3.6	5.2	6.0	5.9	4.2	4.4	3.6	2.5	1.5	0.8	3.4	1256
Benbecula	1.3	2.5	3.7	5.8	6.5	6.5	4.6	4.9	3.8	2.5	1.6	0.9	3.7	1361
Highland														
Prabost (Skye)	1.3	2.7	3.5	5.2	6.0	5.8	4.1	4.3	3.3	2.3	1.5	1.0	3.4	1243
Onich (nr Fort William)	0.9	2.2	2.9	4.4	5.3	5.0	3.7	3.8	2.9	2.1	1.1	0.6	2.9	1059
Wick	1.3	2.6	3.4	5.0	5.2	5.4	4.4	4.3	3.7	2.8	1.6	1.0	3.4	1240
Nairn	1.4	2.8	3.6	4.9	5.3	5.6	4.7	4.3	3.9	2.9	1.8	1.2	3.5	1290
Fort Augustus	0.8	2.1	2.9	4.2	5.0	5.0	3.8	3.8	2.9	2.0	1.0	0.6	2.9	1044
Glenmore Lodge (nr Aviemore)	0.8	2.4	3.4	4.4	5.1	5.2	4.2	4.1	3.5	2.6	1.1	0.5	3.1	1137
Grampian														
Braemar	0.8	2.0	2.9	4.5	5.2	5.5	4.9	4.2	3.4	2.1	1.1	0.6	3.1	1137
Craibstone (nr Aberdeen)	1.7	2.7	3.4	5.0	5.6	6.0	5.2	4.7	3.9	3.1	2.1	1.5	3.7	1367
Tayside														
Perth	1.4	2.3	3.2	5.1	5.7	6.0	5.5	4.5	3.7	2.7	1.8	1.1	3.6	1309
Arbroath	1.8	2.9	3.6	5.6	6.1	6.4	5.9	5.2	4.4	3.2	2.4	1.6	4.1	1499
Fife														
St. Andrews	1.8	2.6	3.4	5.1	5.8	6.2	5.6	4.9	4.2	3.1	2.2	1.5	3.9	1415
Lothian														
Edinburgh														
(Royal Botanic Garden)	1.5	2.4	3.2	4.9	5.7	6.1	5.5	4.8	4.0	3.0	2.0	1.3	3.7	1400
Dunbar	1.8	2.8	3.7	5.4	6.1	6.7	6.1	5.4	4.4	3.4	2.4	1.7	4.2	1523
Strathclyde														
Tiree	1.4	2.4	3.7	5.8	6.9	6.6	5.1	5.2	3.9	2.5	1.5	0.9	3.8	1400
Glasgow Airport	1.3	2.2	3.1	5.1	6.0	6.2	5.3	4.7	3.7	2.6	1.6	1.0	3.6	1303
Prestwick Airport	1.6	2.8	3.5	5.6	6.8	6.7	5.7	5.2	4.0	2.9	1.9	1.3	4.0	1465
Dumfries & Galloway														
Dumfries	1.5	2.5	3.2	4.9	5.8	6.1	5.1	4.9	3.7	2.9	2.0	1.3	3.7	1338
Eskdalemuir	1.3	2.2	2.9	4.5	5.3	5.4	4.6	4.3	3.3	2.5	1.8	1.2	3.3	1198

MISCELLANEOUS

EMERGENCY PHONE NUMBERS

Directory Enquiries: 192. Free from phone-boxes; 42 pence per call otherwise.

Operator: 100. Free.

Police/Fire/Ambulance/Mountain Rescue/Coastguard: 999. Free.

LAW

The Scottish legal system differs from that in England. Unlike most legal systems, it is based neither solely on Roman Law (as in France and Germany), nor is it derived completely from English law (as in America). Instead, it is a mixture of composite sources, having evolved its principles over the centuries on the basis of past cases.

The most senior lawyer in Scotland is the Lord Advocate, who is responsible for all criminal prosecutions, discharging his functions through the Crown Office. He is also a member of the government, although his role as a lawyer takes precedence over that as a politician.

The legal profession in Scotland has two branches: advocates and solicitors. Further information is available from the **Law Society of Scotland** (see under **Information – Associations and Organizations**).

LOCAL GOVERNMENT

Scottish local government as it is recognized today came into existence on 16 May 1975. It is on a two-tier basis, with nine regional councils (such as Strathclyde, Tayside and the Borders) and 53 district councils (such as Glasgow City, Angus and Berwickshire). In addition there are three island councils for Orkney, Shetland and the Western Isles which perform the tasks of both regional and district councils. In general, regional councils provide large-scale services such as transport and education within their area, while district councils are responsible for local planning, housing, environmental affairs, tourism and amenity services.

POPULATION

Britain: 55 780 000 (1981).

Scotland: 5 130 735 (1981).

At the time of going to press, preliminary figures of the 1991 census put Scotland's population at 4 957 289. Also apparent is the first evidence of the 'urban clearances' which have pushed up house prices in many rural areas of the country, with increasing numbers of people leaving their homes in the city for a peaceful retreat in the country. It is estimated that over the past two years (1989–91), almost 14 000 people have migrated to Scotland, many from England. Islands such as Skye, Mull and Arran now have sizeable English populations.

RELIGION*

Of Scotland's various Christian denominations, the largest is the Church of Scotland, with an official membership of 822 985 (1988), although it is likely that considerably more people identify themselves as belonging to the Church of Scotland without formally being members of it. Its structure is presbyterian, with regions split into parishes, and its doctrine evangelical. It is governed by the General Assembly of the Church of Scotland, which meets once a year in Edinburgh in May to review policies and discuss reports. The Roman Catholic Church is Scotland's second largest, with 793 620 members (1988), while Scottish Episcopal Church membership stands at 59 940 (1987).

Also functioning along the lines of the presbyterian tradition is a conservative presbyterian group, with a membership of around 12 250 (1988). This includes the Reformed Presbyterian Church, found mostly in the Lowlands, and the Free Church of Scotland and Free Presbyterian Church, which are found mostly in the western Highlands and Islands.

Other religious groups present in Scotland include the Religious Society of Friends (Quakers), whose membership is around 550 (1988), and a number of Christian organizations, including Independent Evangelical Churches, various house Churches and the Christian Brethren, which have a combined total membership of over 17 800 (1984). Judaism is represented, with Hebrew congregations in each of Scotland's four major cities accounting for 4200 people, while the Muslim population, mostly Asian, is estimated to be between 15 000 and 20 000 (1988). Hindus and Sikhs are also present (although no figures are available), and for several years now there has been a Buddhist community at Langholm in the Borders.

TELEPHONES

British Telecom pay-phones can be found throughout the country. Although the Mercury network is increasing, Mercury telephones are still found mostly in larger cities. British Telecom telephones accept either coins (all except one penny and the new five pence coins) or phone-cards; the latter are available from post offices and some newsagents. British Telecom has replaced the traditional red call-box (telephone booth) with modern glass booths, although a handful of old ones have been allowed to remain in locations where they have been thought more appropriate. New booths marked with a green stripe or sign accept phone-cards or those with a pink stripe or sign, coins. International Direct Dialling is possible to most countries.

TOURISM IN SCOTLAND

Tourism in Scotland has traditionally consisted of a three-month summer influx of visitors from June to August, followed by increased activity (both domestic and international) at the end and beginning of the year for the skiing season. Attributes constantly

* Statistics throughout are based on the Fact Sheet *Religion in Scotland*, issued by the Scottish Office (see Information – Associations and Organizations), in conjunction with HMSO. At the time of going to press a new Fact Sheet is being prepared, updated to provide comprehensive information on religion in Scotland, and available from the Scottish Office.

highlighted have been beautiful scenery, wild open spaces, the Edinburgh Festival in August, and the opportunity to indulge in some healthy country living.

This situation is changing, however, and the emphasis is no longer on making the most of a few months of the year, but on how to sustain tourism in Scotland right through from January to December, and in a way that brings maximum benefits to visitors and locals alike. As in so many countries around the world, Scotland is now trying to make the most of her resources without allowing them to become worn, run-down and over-exploited. To this end, moves are afoot throughout the country to implement new policies aimed at opening up less visited areas, raising standards of accommodation, and, generally, spreading the load more evenly in terms of both geographical location of attractions and seasonal accessibility. In addition, conservation bodies are continually working with all aspects of Scottish wildlife, fauna and flora (see **Information – Associations and Organizations** for a number of the main ones). For the visitor this will ensure a better quality of stay at any time of the year, while for the Scots it means the continued preservation of their land, and the ensuing economic benefits.

INFORMATION – ASSOCIATIONS AND ORGANIZATIONS

An Comunn Gaidhealach: 109 Church Street, Inverness (0463 231226). One of several Gaelic organizations based at the Church Street office, dealing with the Gaelic language and culture past and present.

Forestry Commission:
231 Corstorphine Road, Edinburgh (031–334 0303). A government department, the Forestry Commission manages over one million hectares of forest (60 per cent in Scotland), provides a source of employment and revenue in more rural areas, is responsible for training and research, and provides many recreational facilities.

Friends of the Earth Scotland:
Bonnington Mill,
70–2 Newhaven Road, Edinburgh (031–554 9977). Scottish headquarters of environmental group.

Highlands and Islands Enterprise:
Bridge House, 20 Bridge Street, Inverness (0463 234171). Development agency for the Highlands and Islands, investing roughly 25 per cent of its budget in tourism.

Highland Direct: Hi-Line House, Station Road, Dingwall, Ross-shire (0349 65000). A comprehensive holiday booking service run by Highlands and Islands Enterprise.

Historic Scotland: 20 Brandon Street, Edinburgh (opening times and admission charges, 031–244 3101; Friends of Historic Scotland, 031–244 3099; all other enquiries, 031–244 3144). Government body working to protect Scotland's

built heritage, caring for over 330 properties throughout Scotland, including Edinburgh and Stirling Castles, Dryburgh Abbey, the Meigle Sculptured Stones, Dallas Dhu Distillery and St Andrews Cathedral. Membership of 'Friends of Historic Scotland' is open to anyone and benefits include 'unlimited free entry (and directory) to all properties; concessions at English and Welsh monuments, and a quarterly newsletter'. For non-members Scottish Explorer Tickets are available for 7 or 14 days (family tickets also), offering reduced entrance fees to over 70 sites.

Law Society of Scotland:
26 Drumsheugh Gardens, Edinburgh (031–226 7411). The governing body of the solicitor branch of the Scottish legal profession.

National Trust for Scotland:
5 Charlotte Square, Edinburgh (031–226 5922). There are over 100 historic castles, houses, gardens and areas of open countryside in the Trust's care in Scotland. A registered charity, the National Trust for Scotland was formed in 1931 and now welcomes in excess of one and a half million people per year to properties in its care. Members are admitted free to all properties, while non-members are charged an entrance fee at most sites.

Royal Highland and Agricultural Society of Scotland: Edinburgh Exhibition and Trade Centre, Ingliston, Edinburgh (031–333 2444).

Royal Society for the Protection of Birds (Scotland): Scottish

Headquarters, 17 Regent Terrace, Edinburgh (031–557 3136). Scottish branch of the national organization, working to protect birds throughout Scotland. Produces a series of useful leaflets, as well as an excellent map, *Where to Watch Birds in Scotland*, matching areas of the country with species of birds.

Sabhal Mor Ostaig Gaelic School: An Teanga, Isle of Skye (04714 373). Started in 1973 as a summer school, Sabhal Mor Ostaig (The Big Barn) has grown to become a popular centre for innovative further education, as well as one of the world's leading authorities on Gaelic language and culture. Courses and information are offered on every aspect of Gaelic culture, from song and clarsach to language and writing skills.

Saltire Society: 9 Fountain Close, 22 High St, Edinburgh (031–556 1836). Promotes culture and heritage of Scotland through lectures, publications etc.

Scotland's Gardens Scheme: 31 Castle Terrace, Edinburgh (031–229 1870). Works with and publishes details of several hundred private gardens around Scotland which are periodically opened to the public. Directory available from the above address, or from outlets such as National Trust shops and Tourist Information Offices.

Scottish Arts Council: 12 Manor Place, Edinburgh (031–226 6051). Part of the Arts Council of Great Britain, promoting the arts in Scotland. Information on theatres throughout the country.

Scottish Conservation Projects: Balallan House, 24 Allan Park, Stirling (0786 79697). Conservation charity founded in 1984, inviting people of all ages to become involved in preserving the Scottish countryside. Working 'holidays' learning skills such as dry-stone dyking and wildlife management.

Scottish Enterprise: 120 Bothwell Street, Glasgow (041–248 2700). A Government-funded body which oversees and monitors development throughout the country. Grants aid towards development and administers the Enterprise Trust scheme.

Scottish Field Studies Association: Kindrogan Field Centre, Enochdhu, Blairgowrie, Perthshire (0250 81286). Offers courses at its Perthshire field centre aimed at increasing understanding of the Scottish countryside.

Scottish Natural Heritage: Battleby, Redgorton, Perth (0738 27921) and 12 Hope Terrace, Edinburgh (031–447 4784). In existence from 1 April 1992, created by the merger of the Countryside Commission for Scotland and the Nature Conservancy Council in Scotland. Functions include giving planning advice to authorities, providing financial assistance for tree-planting, landscape enhancement and recreation provisions establishing nature reserves, researching species and sites and granting aid to conservation bodies.

Scottish Office: Information Department, New St Andrew's House, Edinburgh (031–244 5199). The publicity office of Scotland's administrative headquarters produces a number of useful fact sheets about issues relevant to Scottish life today. These cover a wide range of topics, including religion, education and social work and are available by post or phone-call from the above address. No personal callers.

Scottish Sports Council: Caledonia House, South Gyle, Edinburgh (031–317 7200). Umbrella organization for sports in Scotland, information on main sporting bodies throughout the country.

Scottish Tartans Society: Scottish Tartan Museum, Drummond Street, Comrie, Perthshire (0764 70779). International headquarters maintaining the Register of all Publicly Known Tartans. Research department will answer questions 'on the origin of Scottish names, their connections with clans and families, and their associated tartans'. Fees are charged for time spent searching records and compiling reports. The society does not deal with enquiries concerning heraldry or genealogy. Individual and associate membership available.

Scottish Tourist Board: 23 Ravelston Terrace, Edinburgh (031–332 2433); 19 Cockspur Street, London (071–930 8661).

Scottish Wildlife Trust: 25 Johnston Terrace, Edinburgh (031–226 4602). Voluntary body conserving Scottish wildlife, with over 60 reserves throughout the country.

Scottish Youth Hostels Association: 7 Glebe Crescent, Stirling (0786 51191). Central office and information point for Scotland's 81 youth hostels.

Taste of Scotland: 33 Melville Street, Edinburgh (031–220 1900). (See listings under **Food and drink – Restaurants**.)

Regional Fact File

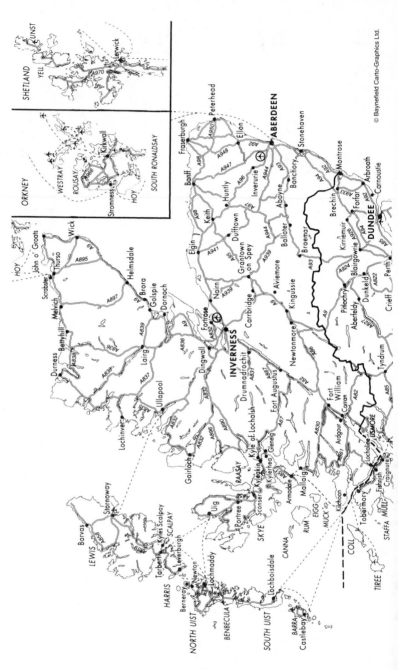

© Baynefield Carto-Graphics Ltd.

30

CINEMAS

Aberdeen

Cannon: Union Street (0224 591477).

Capitol Theatre and Cinema: Union Street (0224 583141).

Odeon: Justice Mill Lane (0224 587160).

Aviemore

Speyside Cinema: Aviemore Centre (0479 810624).

Benbecula, Isle of

Sgoil Lionacleit Community School: Liniclate (0870 2211). Regular film screenings (mainstream).

Elgin

Playhouse: High Street (0343 542680).

Fort William

Studio Cinemas: Cameron Square (0397 705095).

Inverness

Riverside Screen: Eden Court (0463 221718).

Scala 1 and 2: Twin Cinemas, Strothers Lane (0463 233302).

Inverurie

Victoria Cinema: West High Street (0467 21436).

Lewis, Isle of

Seaforth Hotel: James Street, Stornoway (0851 2740). Mainstream films throughout the week (except Sundays).

Orkney

Phoenix Cinema: Junction Road, Kirkwall (0856 874407).

Peterhead

Playhouse: Queen Street (0779 73494).

FESTIVALS/EVENTS

The festivals listed below are those which are likely to be of most interest to visitors. Dates are based on those of 1991 and should be checked with Tourist Information Offices.

Aberdeen
End March–April: Scottish Connection Festival.
End May: City of Aberdeen Milk Race (cycling).
End May–June: Festival for the Environment.
June, third week: Bon Accord Festival.
Highland Games.
June, fourth week: Bon Accord Steam Engine Rally.
July–August: Aberdeen Arts Carnival.
July, third week: International Football Festival. City of Aberdeen Bowling Tournament.
August, second–fourth week: International Youth Festival.
August, second week: Quaich Golf Tournament.
Rose Day.
August, fourth week: Clydesdale Horse Show.
Flower Show.
September–October: Arts Centre Drama Season.
October, second–third week: Aberdeen Alternative Festival.
November, third week–December, third week: Christmas Shopping Festival.

Aberlour
March, first week: Spring Flower Show.
August, first week: Highland Games.

August, third week: Summer Flower Show.

Aboyne
August, first week: Highland Games. Kincardine and Deeside Pipe Band Championships.

Aden
September, first week: North of Scotland Horse and Pony Driving Show.

Alford
July, third week: Alford Cavalcade.

Arisaig
August, second week: Highland Games.

Aviemore
End January: Annual Show Rally of the Siberian Husky Club of Great Britain (Glenmore).
February, first week: Nordic Ski Festival.
March, second week: Badenoch and Strathspey Music Festival.
March, fourth week: 'Euro-Curl' International Curling Competition.
June, third week: Midsummer Music Festival. Stakis Cycle Tour (starts and finishes in Aviemore). Midsummer Firework Display.
End June: Highland Balloon Festival.
End October: Glenfiddich indoor shinty tournament.
December, third week: Torchlight Procession.

Ballater
May, first–second week: Royal Deeside Golf Week.
August, first–second week: Victoria Week.
August, second week: Highland Games.

Banchory

May, second week: Festival of Scottish Music.

End July: Deeside Agricultural Show.

August, fourth week: Deeside Steam and Vintage Rally.

Banff

May, first week: Banffshire Horticultural Association Daffodil Show.

July, first week: Mobil North Sea Yacht Race.

Barra, Isle of

July, first–second week: Feis (Festival) Bharraigh.

July, first week: Highland Games.

July, first/second week: Heaval Hill Race.

Boat of Garten

July, first week: Gala Day.

Bonar Bridge

September, fourth week: Invercharron Highland Games.

Braemar

September, first or second week: Highland Gathering.

Brora

September, second or third week: Sutherland Biathlon.

Buckie

July, third week: Peter Fair.

End July–August: Four Day Open Golf Tournament.

August, second week: 'Keswick in Buckie'.

End August: Flower Show.

Burghead

January, second week: Burning of the Clavie.

End June: North of Scotland Pipe Band and Drum Corps Championships.

Carrbridge

September, third week: Ceilidh Week.

Cullen

July, second week: Gala.

August, first week: Arts, Crafts and Hobbies Festival.

August, second week: Open Golf Tournament.

August, third week: Flower Show (Deskford).

Dingwall

July, second week: Highland Games.

Dornoch

July, third week: Sutherland County Show.

August: Festival Week. Carnegie Shield Golf Tournament.

August, second week: Highland Gathering.

September: Royal Dornoch Golf Week.

Drumtochty

End June: Highland Games.

Dufftown

1 January: Boys' Walk.

July, fourth week: Gala Week.

End July: Highland Games.

September, third week: Autumn Festival.

Duffus

August, third week: Horticultural Show.

Dunbeath

July, third week: Highland Games.

Durness

July, fourth week: Highland Gathering.

Elgin
End March/April: Easter Bonnet
Parade, Millbuies.
June: Fiddle Festival.
July: Highland Games.
September: Fiddler's Rally.
Bothy Ballads Competition.

Findhorn
July, third week: Regatta.
July, fourth week: Findhorn Week.

Fochabers
End August: Flower and Honey
Show.

Forres
June, first week: Scottish Week.
July, first week: Highland Games.
End July–August: Grant Cup Open
Amateur Golf Tournament.
September, first week: Flower
Show.
October, first week: Macallan Horse
Trials (Burgie).

Fort William
May, first or second week: Scottish
Six-Day International Motorcycle
Trials.
June, first week: Three Peaks Yacht
Race (finishing point).
July, first week: Great Glen Sheep
Dog Trial.
July, fourth week: Lochaber
Highland Games.
Fort William Cow Hill Race.
September, first week: Ben
Nevis Race.

Fraserburgh
End July: Fish Festival.

Glenfinnan
August, third week: Glenfinnan
Gathering and Highland
Games.

Golspie
May, third week: Sutherland
Triathlon.
June, first week: Ben Bhraggie
Mountain Bike Race.
Sutherland/Caithness Provincial
Mod.
End July–August: Gala Week.
August: Golspie Open Golf.
Vintage Car Rally.
Sutherland Sheepdog Trials.

Grantown-on-Spey
June, fourth week: Highland
Games.
End July–August: Festival
Fortnight.
August, second week: Agricultural
Show.
August, third week: Horticultural
Show.

Halkirk
July, fourth week: Highland
Games.

Helmsdale
August, third week: Helmsdale and
District Highland Games.
August, fourth week: Loth and
Helmsdale Flower Show.

Invergarry
July second/third week: Highland
Games.

Invergordon
August, fourth week: Highland
Games.

Inverness
End March: Folk Festival.
July, third–fourth week: Country
and Western Festival.
August, second week: Marymas
Fair.
Annual Three-Day Antique Fair.
End August: Northern Meeting
Piping Competition.

Keith

April, third week: Spring Flower Show.

May, fourth week: Budgerigar Show.

June, second–third week: Festival of Traditional Music and Song.

June, third/fourth week: Highland Games.

August, second week: Agricultural Show.

August, third week: Budgerigar Show.

End August: Summer Flower Show.

Kemnay

May, first week: River Don Raft Race.

Kilmore

June, second week: Highland Games.

Kingussie

July, fourth week: Gala Week.

Lairg

August, third week: Crofter's Show.

Latheron

July: Latheron Agricultural Society Show.

Lewis, Isle of

March, first–second week: Lewis and Harris Sports Festival.

End June: Lewis/Harris Mods.

July, third week–August: Harris Gala Fortnight.

July, second–fourth week: Lewis Carnival (Stornoway).

West Side Agricultural Show (Barvas). Highland Games (Tong).

Lochinver

August, second week: Assynt Highland Games.

Lossiemouth

March, third week: Spring Flower Show.

July, third week: Moray Open Amateur Golf Tournament.

September, third week: Summer Flower Show.

Mey

August, second week: Mey and District Highland Games.

Morvern

July, first/second week: Gala Week and Highland Games.

Nairn

June, third week: Street Party.

June, fourth week: Arts, Crafts and Music Festival.

End June: Craft and Country Fair.

July, first week: Children's Week.

July, second/third week: Vintage Vehicle and Steam Rally.

July, fourth week: Gala Week. Sheepdog Trials.

August, first–third week: Fairground Fortnight.

August, first week: Agricultural Show.

August, second week: Activities Week.

August, third week: Highland Games.

Nethybridge

August, second week: Highland Games.

New Byth

End June: New Byth and District Steam and Vintage Rally.

New Deer

July, third/fourth week: New Deer Show.

New Pitsligo

May, second week: Festival of Doric Plays and Sketches.

Festivals/Events (cont.)

End September: Annual Exhibition of New Pitsligo Visual Arts.

Newtonmore
August, first week: Highland Games and Clan MacPherson Rally with Craig Dhu Hill Race.

Orkney
1 January: New Year's Day Ba' (Kirkwall).
February: Drama Festival (Kirkwall).
February, fourth week: Opening of Sea Trout Season (Stromness).
May, fourth week: Orkney Traditional Folk Festival (Stromness).
June, third week: High Island Half Marathon (Hoy).
June, third–fourth week: St Magnus Festival (Kirkwall and Stromness). Finstown Regatta. Midnight Foursomes Golf Competition (Kirkwall).
End September: Sea Angling Festival (Stromness).
End October: Close of Sea Trout Season.
November, fourth week: Orkney Cage Bird Society Annual Show.
25 December: Christmas Day Ba'.

Peterhead
July, fourth week: Scottish Week.

Plockton
End July–August: Plockton Regatta.

Rothiemurchus
End July: Highland Games.
August, first week: Craft Fair.

Scrabster
July, fourth week: Caithness Agricultural Society Show.

Shetland
End January: Up Helly Aa (Fire Festival). As well as Lerwick's Up Helly Aa (both of which mark the winter solstice), many others take place in the first few weeks of the year.
March, second week: Young Fiddler of the Year Competition (Lerwick).
March, third week: Drama Festival (Lerwick).
May, first week: Shetland Folk Festival.
May, third week: Bergen to Shetland International Yacht Race. Norwegian National Day Parade.
May, fourth week: Haggis Hurling (Lerwick).
June, fourth week: Simmer Dim Motorcycle Rally. Mid Summer Carnival.
June: Round Bressay Yacht Race. Round Foula Yacht Race.
July: Fetlar and Yell Sheepdog Trials.
August, second week: Round Skerries Yacht Race. Cunningsburgh Agricultural Show.
August, third week: Lerwick Regatta.
September: Viking International Sea Angling Festival.
October, third week: Shetland Accordion and Fiddle Festival.

Skye, Isle of
June, third week: Skye Week
June, fourth week: Donald MacDonald Quaich (Piping Competition, Armadale).
End July–August: Skye Folk Festival.
August, first week: Highland Games (Portree).

Stonehaven
June, third or fourth week: R.W. Thomson Memorial Vintage Vehicle Rally.

July, second week: Highland
   Games.

Strathdon
August, fourth week: Lonach
   Gathering.

Strichen
May, second week: Buchan
   Heritage Festival.
May, third week: Old Tyme Dance.

Strontian
June, third week: Sheep Shearing
   Competition.

Thurso
June, first week: Caithness Music
   Festival.
July, first week: Caithness
   Highland Gathering.
July, second week: Gala week.

Tomintoul
July, third/fourth week: Highland
   Games.

Turriff
June, first week: Pipe Band
   Contest.
August, first week: Turriff Show.

Uist, Isles of
June, first or second week: Uist
   Mod.
July: North Uist Games,
   South Uist Games.
July, third week: Feis Tir an Eorna
   (North Uist Festival).
July, third or fourth week: North
   Uist Agricultural Show.
   South Uist Agricultural Show.
End July/August: Uist Sea Angling
   Competition.
August, second or third week: Feis
   Tir a'Mhurain (South Uist
   Festival).

Wick
June, first week: Caithness Music
   Festival.
July, fourth week: Gala Week.

GALLERIES

Galleries listed below are intended as a quick reference guide only and cover those of most interest in each area. Galleries which are included as part of a museum are listed under Museums, unless they merit particular mention, in which case there is an entry for both the gallery and the museum.

Aberchirder

North-East Falcony Centre: Bruntbrae Farm, north of Aberchirder (02616 602). Arts and crafts gallery at the only falconry centre in the north of Scotland. Also, daily displays and commentary involving falcons, owls and buzzards.

Aberdeen

Arts Centre Gallery: King Street (0224 635208). Changing exhibitions of photography and work from community projects.

Art Gallery: Schoolhill (0224 646333). Permanent collection of contemporary artists and changing exhibitions by local and foreign artists.

James Dun's House: Schoolhill (0224 646333). Changing arts and crafts exhibitions (see Museums also).

Peacock Artspace: 21 Castle Street (0224 639539). Exhibitions by local, national and international artists.

Aviemore

Clan Art Gallery: Aviemore Centre (0479 811100). Original oil paintings and watercolours.

Ballater

McEwan Gallery: Glen Gairn (on A939, 03397 55429). Eighteenth–20th-century oil paintings, watercolours, prints and rare Scottish and golf books.

Buckie

Peter Anson Gallery: Town House West, Cluny Place (0542 32121). Watercolours of the east-coast fishing communities. Also here, **Maritime Museum** (see Museums).

Drumnadrochit

Art Gallery: The Green (04562 695). Paintings by Highland artists and prints, cards, books, brass and ceramics.

Durness

Balnakiel Craft Village: west of Durness. Mainland Britain's most north-westerly community, located in a previous Ministry of Defence Early Warning Station. Buildings have been converted to create a village largely dedicated to arts and crafts: pottery, printmaking, painting, patchwork, leather and horncraft are a few of the skills put to use.

Evanton

Fyrish Gallery: 17 Balconie Street (0349 830851). Local artists and touring exhibitions.

Grantown-on-Spey

Strathspey Gallery: 40 High Street (0479 3290). Original wildlife and local paintings.

Inverness

Highland Printmakers Workshop and Gallery: 20 Bank Street (0463 712240). Wide range of original contemporary art, workshop

acilities for etching, relief,
ithography, screenprinting and
process photography.

Greenfield Gallery: Bow Court,
54 Church Street (0463 224781).
Original oil paintings, watercolours,
prints and engravings of Scottish
porting and natural history
ubjects.

Lewis, Isle of

An Lanntair: Town Hall, Stornoway
(0851 3307). Gallery of changing
exhibitions, usually of local artists'
work, and a programme of music,
readings and drama.

Muirneag Galleries: Brue, Barvas
(085184 240). Original oil
paintings of the Western Isles and
hand-painted prints of traditional
Hebridean scenes and customs.

Lyth

Lyth Arts Centre: (095584 270).
Summer displays of contemporary
art.

Mey

Royal Gallery: Castle Arms Hotel
(084785 244). Unique collection of
photographs of Her Majesty Queen
Elizabeth the Queen Mother and
the royal family in Caithness.

Orkney

Black Pig Gallery: Victoria Street,
Kirkwall (0856 874328). Temporary
exhibitions of arts and crafts.

Pier Arts Centre: Victoria Street,
Stromness (0856 850209). Permanent
and changing exhibitions of arts
and crafts.

Soli Deo Gallery: Anchor Buildings,
Bridge Street, Kirkwall (0856 3356).
Small exhibition area and shop with
locally made figurines. Also here

is the **Orkney Gallery** (0856 5345),
exhibiting works by local artists.

Scourie

Dorothy Dick Gallery: 47 The Village,
by Lairg (0971 2013). Wood carvings
and cast sculptures, paintings and
prints.

Shetland

Old Haa: Burravoe, Yell (095782
339). Changing exhibitions of arts
and crafts, often related to local
history, as well as videos and
photographs.

Skye, Isle of

Gallery/Art Centre: An Tuireann,
Struan Road, Portree (0478 3306).
New gallery opened in 1991 hosting
art exhibitions, workshops and art
and craft classes.

Orbost Art Gallery: Orbost House,
Dunvegan (047022 207). Original
paintings by a resident couple.

Skye Original Prints: 1 Wentworth
Street, Portree (0478 2388).

Croft Studio: Dunvegan (047022 383).
Paintings, arts and crafts, and Celtic
designs.

Little Gallery: Portnalong (047842
254). Paintings of Skye.

Strathdon

Candacraig Gallery: (09756 51226).
Changing exhibitions of fine art,
sculpture and craft throughout
the year.

Tarves

Tolquhon Gallery: Tolquhon (06513
2343). Changing exhibitions of
local work.

GOLF CLUBS/ASSOCIATIONS

Visitors are welcome at the courses listed below, but are advised to telephone ahead to check times. Note that many clubs require written applications, particuarly for groups, and often with at least 21 days' notice. Full details of golf clubs are usually available from Tourist Information Offices in the relevant areas. Ask for the leaflet *Golf in the Scottish Highlands and Islands* which provides a comprehensive list and descriptions of the courses in the north of Scotland. Also available is a *Highland Golf Trail* leaflet showing course locations in relation to each other around the Highlands. Moray District produces a useful publication, *Moray for Golf*, which provides a selection of hotels and bed and breakfast establishments which offer weekly packages, including a visitor's five-day golf ticket. Details and leaflets can be obtained from Tourist Information in Elgin (address at end).

Aboyne

Aboyne Golf Course (03398 86328). 18 hole.

Alford

Alford Golf Club: (09755 62178). 9 hole.

Alness

Alness Golf Club: (0349 883877). 9 hole.

Ballater

Ballater Golf Club: Victoria Road (03397 55567). 18 hole.

Banchory

Banchory Golf Course: (03302 2365). 9 hole.

Banff

Duff House Royal Golf Club: Barnyards (02612 2062). 18 hole.

Braemar

Braemar Golf Club: Cluniebank Road (03397 41618). The highest 18 hole course in Britain.

Brora

Brora Golf Club: Golf Road (0408 21417). 18 hole.

Buckie

Buckpool Golf Club: Barhill Road (0542 32236). 18 hole.

Strathlene Golf Club: Portessie (0542 31798). 18 hole.

Carrbridge

Carrbridge Golf Club: Inverness Road (047984 674). 9 hole.

Cruden Bay

Cruden Bay Golf Club: Aulton Road (0779 812285). 18 hole championship links and 9 hole course (telephone in advance).

Cullen

Cullen Golf Club: The Links (0542 40685). 18 hole.

Dornoch

Royal Dornoch Golf Club: Golf Road (0862 810219). 18 hole.

Struie Golf Club: Golf Road (0862 810219). 18 hole.

Dufftown

Dufftown Golf Club: Glenrinnes (0340 20325). 18 hole.

Durness

Durness Golf Club: (097181 364). 8 hole.

Elgin

Elgin Golf Club: Hardhillock, Birnie Road (0343 542338). 18 hole.

Ellon

McDonald Golf Club: Hospital Road (0358 20576). 18 hole.

Forres

Forres Golf Club: Edgehill Road (0309 72261). 18 hole (telephone in advance).

Muiryshade Golf Club: (0309 72949). 8 hole.

Fort Augustus

Fort Augustus Golf Club: (0320 6460). hole.

Fortrose

Fortrose and Rosemarkie Golf Club: (0381 20529). 18 hole.

Fraserburgh

Fraserburgh Golf Club: Corbie Hill, Philorth (0346 28287). 18 hole.

Gairloch

Gairloch Golf Club: (0445 2407). hole.

Garmouth

Garmouth and Kingston Golf Club: (034387 388). 18 hole.

Golspie

Golspie Golf Club: Ferry Road (04083 3265). 18 hole.

Grantown-on-Spey

Grantown-on-Spey Golf Club: Golf Course Road (0479 2079). 18 hole.

Harris, Isle of

Harris Golf Club: 14 miles south of Tarbert (0859 2078). 9 hole.

Hopeman

Hopeman Golf Club: (0343 830578). 18 hole.

Huntly

Huntly Golf Club: Cooper Park (0466 2643). 18 hole.

Invergordon

Invergordon Golf Club: (0349 852715). 9 hole.

Inverness

Inverness Golf Club: (0463 239882). 18 hole.

Torvean Golf Club: (0463 237543). 18 hole.

Inverurie

Inverurie Golf Course: Davah Lands (0467 20193). 18 hole.

Keith

Keith Golf Club: Fife Keith (05422 2469). 18 hole.

Kemnay

Kemnay Golf Club: Monymusk Road (0467 42225). 9 hole.

Kingussie

Kingussie Golf Club: Gynack Road (0540 661374). 18 hole.

Golf Clubs/Associations (cont.)

Kintore

Kintore Golf Club: (0467 32631). 9 hole.

Lewis, Isle of

Stornoway Golf Club: (0851 2240). 18 hole.

Kyle of Lochalsh

Kyle Golf Club: (0599 4751). 9 hole.

Lochcarron

Lochcarron Golf Club: half a mile east of the village (05202 311). 9 hole.

Longside

Longside Golf Club: West End (077982 558). 9 hole.

Lossiemouth

Moray Golf Club: Stotfield Road (034381 2018). Two 18 hole courses, one of championship standard.

Macduff

Royal Tarlair Golf Club: Buchan Street (0261 32897). 18 hole.

Muir of Ord

Muir of Ord Golf Club: (0463 870825). 18 hole.

Nairn

Nairn Dunbar Golf Club: (0667 52787). 9 and 18 hole courses.

Nethybridge

Abernethy Golf Club: (47982 305). 9 hole.

Newtonmore

Newtonmore Golf Club: Golf Course Road (05403 328). 18 hole.

Orkney

Orkney Golf Club: one mile from Kirkwall (0856 872457). 18 hole.

Stromness Golf Club: (0856 850593). 18 hole.

Westray Golf Club: Isle of Westray (08577 28). 9 hole.

Peterhead

Peterhead Golf Club: Craigewan Links (0779 72149). 18 hole and junior 9 hole courses.

Reay

Reay Golf Club: (084781 1288). 18 hole.

Rothes

Rothes Golf Club (03403 443). 9 hole and 18 hole courses.

Shetland

Shetland Golf Club: three miles from Lerwick (059584 369). 18 hole.

Skye, Isle of

Sconser Golf Club: 12 miles south of Portree (secretary: 0478 2192). 9 hole.

South Uist

Askernish Golf Club: five miles north-west of Lochboisdale (contact South Uist Tourist Information Centre: 08784 286). 9 hole.

Spey Bay

Spey Bay Golf Club: (0343 820424). 18 hole.

Stonehaven

Stonehaven Golf Club: Cowie (0569 62124). 18 hole. Visitors welcome except Saturdays.

Strathpeffer

Strathpeffer Spa Golf Club:
(0997 21219). 18 hole.

Tain

Tain Golf Club: (0862 2314). 18 hole.

Tarland

Tarland Golf Club: (03398 81413).
9 hole course (advisable to
telephone first).

Thurso

Thurso Golf Club: (0847 63807).
18 hole.

Torphins

Torphins Golf Course: (03398 82493).
9 hole.

Turriff

Turriff Golf Club: Rosehall
(0888 62745). 18 hole.

Westhill

Westhill Golf Course: (0224 740159).
18 hole.

Wick

Wick Golf Club: (0955 2726). 18 hole.

HALF-DAY CLOSING

Wednesday
Aberlour, Alford, Buckie, Cullen,
Elgin, Ellon, Findochty, Fochabers,
Forres, Garmouth, Glenlivet,
Hopeman, Inverbervie, Inverness,
Inverurie, Keith, Kemnay
(and/or Saturday), Kintore
(and/or Saturday), Laurencekirk,
Mosstodloch, Nairn, Newburgh,
Oldmeldrum, Pitmedden,
Portgordon, Portknockie, Rathven,
Rothes, Rothiemay, Stonehaven,
Tarland, Tarves, Tomintoul.

Thursday
Aboyne, Archiestown, Ballater,
Banchory, Beauly, Braemar
(October–May; no half-day closing
June–September), Burghead,
Craigellachie (post office closes
Wednesday), Fort Augustus,
Huntly, Insch, Kincardine
O'Neil, Lhanbryde, Lossiemouth,
Lumphanan, Methlick, Rhynie,
Torphins.

LEISURE/SPORT CENTRES

These include swimming pools, ski slopes, bowling alleys, ice rinks, general athletics grounds and gymnasia.

Aberchirder

Aberchirder Bowling Club: North Street (04665 665). Visitors welcome.

Aberdeen

Aberdeen Skating Rink: Stoneywood Road (0224 724454). Skating sessions and skate hire.

Aberdeen Superbowl: 197 George Street (0224 643001). Tenpin bowling.

Beach Leisure Centre: Beach Promenade (0224 647647). Sports hall, leisure pool, health centre and climbing wall.

Bon Accord Swimming and Leisure Centre: Justice Mill Lane (0224 587920/575676). Swimming pool, Turkish baths, sauna, solarium and fitness centre.

Codona's Amusement Centre and Park: Beach Boulevard (0224 581909). Scotland's largest fun-fair.

Flagship Leisure Centre: Bridge Place (0224 572876). Swimming pool, snooker, multi-gym and health club.

Kaimhill Dry Ski Slope: Garthdee Road (0224 311781). Skiing throughout the year.

YMCA: 52 Skene Terrace (0224 643291). Badminton, snooker, table tennis, weights, gym, keep fit classes and swimming pool.

Aberlour

Community Centre: Speyside High School, Mary Avenue (0340 871641).

Badminton, table tennis, carpet bowls and other activities. Swimming pool also here.

Aboyne

Aboyne Community Centre: Bridge View Road (03398 86222). Swimming pool, squash, badminton, table tennis and games hall.

Alford

Pleasure Park: Greystone Road (09755 62380). Dry ski slope, swings and roundabouts.

Aviemore

Aviemore Centre: (0479 810624). All-weather leisure centre with swimming pool, ice rink, sauna, solarium, squash courts, snooker tables and amusements.

Aviemore Ski School: Aviemore Centre (0479 810310). Ski hire and ski school from December to April. Dry ski slope and ski lessons all year.

Banchory

Recreation Ground: Dee Street (contact District Council Office: 03302 2878). Putting, tennis, crazy golf, trampoline and outdoor table tennis.

Swimming Pool: Banchory Academy (03302 3357). Indoor pool.

Banff

Community Centre: Bridge Street (02612 2450). Indoor tennis, badminton, table tennis, snooker and darts.

Swimming Pool: Bellevue Road (02612 5754). Modern indoor pool.

Benbecula, Isle of

Sgoil Lionacleit Community School:

Leisure/Sport Centres (cont.)

Liniclate (0870 2211). Swimming pool, games hall and outdoor pitches.

Braemar

Bowling Club: Glenshee Road (03397 41666). Lawn bowls.

Buckie

Swimming Pool: South Pringle Street (0542 32841). Indoor pool.

Carrbridge

Carrbridge Ski School: (047984 246/328). Sports hire and ski school.

Slochd Nordic Ski School: Slochd (047984 666). Forest trails, ski hire and ski touring.

Dingwall

Dingwall Leisure Centre: (0349 64226). Indoor swimming pool, games hall, fitness room, table tennis and indoor bowling.

Elgin

Fitness 'N' Fun Leisure Centre: 130 High Street (0343 549307). Multi-gym, dance studio, saunas and sunbeds.

Swimming Pool: North Street (0343 542509). Pool, sauna and solarium.

Fochabers

Swimming Pool: Burnside Caravan Park, Keith Road (0343 820362).

Forres

Swimming Pool: Sanquhar Road (0309 72984).

Fort William

Lochaber Leisure Centre: Belford Road (0397 704359/703886). Swimming pool, sauna, sunbeds, squash courts, fitness room, jacuzzi and climbing wall.

Nevis Range: Torlundy (administration 0397 705825; skiing conditions 0397 705855). Skiing on Aonach Mor.

Fraserburgh

Community Centre: Alexandra Terrace (0346 28788). Snooker, table tennis and indoor bowling carpets.

Leisure Centre: Seaforth Street (0346 26663). Indoor bowling centre with facilities for a wide variety of indoor sports.

Swimming Pool: Alexandra Terrace (0346 28627). Swimming pool, sauna, Turkish baths and solarium.

Huntly

Swimming Pool: Castle Street (0466 2397).

Cooper Park: Castle Street (Gordon District Council: 0467 20981). Tennis, putting, miniature golf, trampoline and roller-skating.

Inverbervie

Sports Centre: Kirkburn (0561 61182). Keep fit, bowls, badminton, roller discos, outdoor tennis courts, putting green and crèche facilities.

Inverness

Swimming Pool: (0463 233799). Indoor pool, solarium, multi-gym, fitness room, sauna, jacuzzi and sunbeds.

Inverurie

Swimming Pool: Chelsea Road (0467 20654). Indoor pool.

Keith

Community Centre: Banff Road

(05422 2028). Table tennis, darts, snooker, badminton, archery, trampolines and other activities.

Swimming Pool: Banff Road (05422 2370).

Kincraig

Loch Insh Watersports and Skiing Centre: Insh Hall (05404 272). Downhill and cross-country skiing and watersports.

Laurencekirk

Mearns Sports Centre: (05617 519). Multi-gym, badminton, five-a-side football and a variety of other sporting activities.

Lewis, Isle of

Sports Centre: Sandwick Road, Stornoway (0851 2603). Swimming pool, sports hall, squash and badminton courts.

Lossiemouth

Swimming Pool: Community Education Centre, Coulardbank Road (034381 2047). Variety of other activities also available here.

Nairn

Nairn Sports Club: Viewfield Drive (0667 54523). Four all-weather tennis courts, squash courts, multi-gym, sauna and solarium.

Swimming Pool: near Nairn West Beach (0667 53061). Indoor pool and steam room (telephone ahead to check opening times).

Orkney

Kirkwall Swimming Pool: Kirkwall Grammar School (0856 3219). Indoor pool.

Stromness Swimming Pool: North End Road (0856 850552). Indoor pool.

Peterhead

Fishing permits for salmon, trout and sea trout fishing are available from Robertson Sports, 1–3 Kirk Street (0779 72584).

Community Centre: Queen Street (0779 77277). Theatre, disco area, sports hall, indoor climbing wall, squash courts and multi-gym.

Swimming Pool: Queen Street (0779 71757). At the same location as the Community Centre (see above), with sauna and solarium.

Shetland

Clickimin Centre: Lochside, Lerwick (0595 4555). Sports hall, badminton, short tennis, football, fitness suite, sauna and solarium.

North Mainland Pool: Brae (080622 321). Indoor swimming pool.

Unst Leisure Centre: Baltasound, Unst (095781 577). Indoor swimming pool.

Whalsay Leisure Centre: Symbister, Whalsay (08066 678). Indoor swimming pool.

Yell Leisure Centre: Mid Yell, Yell (0957 2222). Indoor swimming pool.

Skye, Isle of

Swimming Pool: Park Road, Portree (0478 2655). Indoor pool. Keys for the tennis and squash courts on Bridge Road should be picked up from here.

Wet Weather Centre: Sligachan (047 852 204). Restaurant and activities area, suitable for children.

Stonehaven

Leisure Centre: (0569 63162). Swimming, badminton, table tennis, basketball, netball,

Leisure/Sport Centres (cont.)

volleyball, five-a-side football, sunbed, fitness room and crèche facilities.

Swimming Pool: (0569 62134). Indoor pool.

Thurso

Thurso Leisure Centre: Meadow Lane (0847 64588). Sauna, gymnasium and exercise equipment.

Tomintoul

Glenmulliach Nordic Ski Centre: (08074 356). Cross-country and Nordic ski centre.

Turriff

Gateway Community Centre: Victoria Terrace (0888 62562). Pool table, table tennis and coffee bar.

Swimming Pool: Queen's Road (0888 62528). Modern, indoor pool.

Turriff Bowling Club: Bowling Green Road (0888 62676). Outside green and indoor rinks.

Ullapool

Ullapool Leisure Centre: (0854 2679). Games hall and fitness room.

LIBRARIES

Aberchirder

Aberchirder Library: Main Street (04665 607).

Aberdeen

Central Library: Rosemount Viaduct (0224 634622).

Aboyne

Aboyne Library: Community Centre (03398 86004).

Alness

Alness Library: High Street (0349 882674).

Ballater

Ballater Library: Station Square (03397 55628).

Banchory

Banchory Library: Dee Street Car Park (03302 3784).

Banff

Banff Library: High Street (02612 5052).

Barra, Isle of

Barra Library: Castlebay Community School, Castlebay (08714 4471).

Benbecula, Isle of

Benbecula Library: Sgoil Lionacleit Community School, Liniclate (0870 2211).

Buckie

Buckie Library: Town House West, Cluny Place (0542 32121).

Burghead

Burghead Library: 16 Grant Street (0343 830186).

Cruden Bay

Cruden Bay Library: Station Road (0779 812815).

Cullen

Cullen Library: Seafield Road (0542 41140).

Dingwall

Dingwall Library: Old Academy, Tulloch Street (0349 63163).

Dufftown

Dufftown Library: Balvenie Street (0340 20282).

Elgin

Elgin Library: Grant Lodge, Cooper Park (0343 542746).

Ellon

Ellon Library: Station Road (0358 20865).

Fettercairn

Fettercairn Library: Fettercairn School (05614 442).

Findochty

Findochty Library: 30 Commercial Street (0542 32184).

Fochabers

Fochabers Library: 55 High Street (0343 821434).

Forres

Forres Library: Forres House, High Street (0309 72834).

Libraries (cont.)

Fraserburgh

Fraserburgh Library: King Edward Street (0346 28197).

Grantown-on-Spey

Grantown-on-Spey Library: High Street (0479 3175).

Harris, Isle of

Tarbert Library: Barmore Road (08802 820424).

Hopeman

Hopeman Library: Forsyth Street (0343 830188).

Huntly

Huntly Library: The Square (0466 2179).

Inverbervie

Inverbervie Library: Church Street (0349 852698).

Invergordon

Invergordon Library: Main Street (0349 852698).

Inverness

Culloden Library: (0463 792531).

Harbour Road Library: 31a Harbour Road (0463 235713).

Inverness Library: Farraline Park (0463 236463).

Inverurie

Inverurie Library: Town Hall (0467 21619).

Keith

Keith Library: Union Street (05422 2223).

Kintore

Kintore Library: (0467 32949).

Laurencekirk

Laurencekirk Library: Johnston Street (05617 298).

Lewis, Isle of

Stornoway Library: Keith Street (0851 3064).

Lossiemouth

Lossiemouth Library: Town Hall Lane, High Street (034381 3334).

Macduff

Macduff Library: High Street (0261 33289).

Mintlaw

Mintlaw Library: Newlands Road (0771 23366).

Nairn

Nairn Library: High Street (0667 52367).

Oldmeldrum

Oldmeldrum Library: The Square (065 12 3008). **Local History** information is available from the Genealogy Department, Library Headquarters, Meldrum Meg Way (065 12 2707).

Orkney

Kirkwall Library: Laing Street (0856 873166).

Stromness Library: Hellihole Road (0856 850907).

Peterhead

Peterhead Libary: St Peter Street (0779 77778; located under Arbuthnot Museum).

Portgordon

Portgordon Library: 1 Gordon Square
(0542 35478).

Portknockie

Portknockie Library: 24 Park Street
(0542 41149).

Portsoy

Portsoy Library: Aird Green
(0261 43891).

Rosehearty

Rosehearty Library: Church Terrace
(03467 219).

Rothes

Rothes Library: 4 Seafield Square
(03403 281).

Shetland

Lerwick Library: Lower Hillhead
(0595 3868).

Skye, Isle of

Portree Library: Somerled Square
(0478 2697).

Stonehaven

Stonehaven Library: Evan Street
(0569 62136).

Strichen

Strichen Library: Water Street
(07715 347).

Tain

Tain Library: Stafford Street
(0862 2391).

Thurso

Thurso Library: Davidson's Lane
(0847 63237).

Tomintoul

Tomintoul Library: Tomintoul School
(08074 271).

Turriff

Turriff Library: Grange Villa, The
Square (0888 62539).

Whitehills

Whitehills Library: Loch Street
(02617 240).

Wick

Wick Library: Sinclair Terrace
(0955 2864).

LOCAL MEDIA

NEWSPAPERS

Aberdeen Press and Journal:
published by Aberdeen Journals
Ltd, Lang Stracht, Mastrick,
Aberdeen (0224 690222).

Caithness Courier: 1 Sir George's
Street, Thurso (0847 62015/62499).

East Ross Herald and Post: Castlebank
House, High Street, Dingwall (0349
61323/61360).

Highland News Group Ltd:
6 Henderson Road, Inverness (0436
239311). **Inverness and Nairnshire
Herald** also here.

Inverness Courier: 9–11 Bank Lane,
Inverness (0463 233059).

Strathspey and Badenoch Herald: (and
other local publications) published
by Moray and Nairn Newspaper
Company Ltd, 54 High Street,
Grantown-on-Spey (0479 2102).

Orcadian: 9 Victoria Street, Kirkwall
(0856 873249/872574).

Ross-shire Journal: Docharty Road,
Dingwall (0349 63436).

Shetland Times Ltd: Prince Alfred
Street, Lerwick (0595 3622).

Stornoway Gazette Ltd: 10 Francis
Street, Stornoway (0851 2687).

West Highland Free Press: Unit
1, Broadford Industrial Estate,
Broadford, Isle of Skye (04712 464).

Also at 1 Wentworth Street,
Portree, Isle of Skye (0478 2388).
Part of the West Highland
Publishing Company (same
address).

RADIO

BBC Radio Aberdeen: Beechgrove
Terrace, Aberdeen (0224 625233).
93.1 FM.

BBC Radio Highland: Culduthel
Road, Inverness (0463 221711).
92.4–94.7 FM.

BBC Radio Orkney: Castle Street,
Kirkwall (0856 873939). 93.7 FM.

BBC Radio Nan Gaidheal: Church
Street, Stornoway, Isle of Lewis
(0851 705000). 94 FM

BBC Radio Shetland: Brentham
House, Harbour Street, Lerwick
(0595 4747). 92.7 FM; VHF: 92.6/7.

Moray Firth Radio: Scorguie Place,
Inverness (0463 224433). MW: 1107
kHz/271m; 97.4 FM.

North Sound Radio: 45 Kings Gate,
Aberdeen (0224 632234). MW: 1035
kHz/290m; VHF: 96.9 MHz.

**Shetland Islands Broadcasting
Company Ltd:** Market Street, Lerwick
(0595 5299/5181). 96.2 FM.

TELEVISION

BBC Television: Beechgrove Terrace,
Aberdeen (0224 625233).

Grampian Television: Queen's Cross,
Aberdeen (0224 646464).

MUSEUMS

The list of museums below represents a cross-section of those found throughout the area but is intended as a quick reference guide only. Full details of museums in specific locations are obtainable from the relevant Tourist Information Office. Museums of special interest are included in the gazetteer.

Aberdeen

James Dun's House: Schoolhill (0224 646333). Restored 18th-century house, gallery and audio-visual presentations.

Marischal Museum: Marischal College, Broad Street (0224 273131). Changing exhibitions of arts, crafts and customs of people throughout the world, from ancient to modern times including Scottish prehistoric weapons, tools and archaeological remains.

Alford

Railway Museum: The Station (09775 62292). Exhibition and photographs on the advent of the railway in Alford.

Alness

Farm Museum: Dalmore (0349 883978). Farming history and equipment and children's farm, with some rare breeds.

Archiestown

Ladycroft Farm Museum: Elchies (03406 274). Agricultural equipment through the ages.

Ardersier

Fort George and Military Museum: by Ardersier (0667 62777). Eighteenth-century fortress, still used by the army, with a military museum.

Banchory

Banchory Museum: Burgh Buildings, High Street (0779 77778). Local history display, including silver, costume, ceramics and photographs.

Banff

Banff Museum: High Street (02612 5052). Local history, Banff silverware and award-winning natural history exhibition.

Cromarty

Cromarty Courthouse: Church Street (03817 418). Local history exhibition and audio-visual display, and a reconstructed court case in the newly converted courthouse at Cromarty.

Dingwall

The Museum: Town House, High Street (0349 62116). Military collections, maps, photographs, traditional Highland kitchen, a smithy interior, the old town clock and the history of the county town of Ross from the Bronze Age to the present.

Dufftown

Dufftown Museum: Clock Tower (0340 20501). Local history museum.

Elgin

Elgin Museum: 1 High Street (0343 543675). Palaeontology, archaeology and natural history.

Moray Motor Museum: Bridge Street, Bishopmill (0343 544933). Veteran, vintage and classic cars and motorbikes, and motorabilia.

Museums (cont.)

Ellon

'Remains to Be Seen': Quilquox Croft, Ythanbank (03587 229). Museum of period costume, lace and accessories.

Fettercairn

Mearns Heavy Horse Centre and Farm Museum: Durie Mains Farm, Luthermuir (067484 447). Clydesdale horses, mares and foals on show. Farm carts, horse harnesses and other items, harness room and blacksmith shop.

Fochabers

Folk Museum: Pringle Church, High Street (0343 820362). Museum of local interest and the largest collection of horse-drawn vehicles in north-east Scotland.

Tugnet Ice-House: Spey Bay, by Fochabers (0309 73701). History of the River Spey and salmon fishing.

Forres

Falconer Museum: Tolbooth Street (0309 73701). Local and natural history, temporary exhibitions.

Fraserburgh

Fishermen's Memorial Room: Fishermen's Mission, Shore Street (0346 28388). Tribute to local men who lost their lives at sea.

Gairloch

Gairloch Heritage Museum: (044583 243). Award-winning museum illustrating all aspects of life in a typical West Highland parish from the Stone Age to the present day.

Glenkindie

Glenkindie Museum: (09756 41286). Memorabilia and local history museum, located in Glenkindie shop.

Glenlivet

Drumin Country Museum: Drumin Farm (08073 210). Collection of household and farm equipment from ages past in an early 19th-century farmhouse. Open on request.

Huntly

Brander Museum: The Square (0466 2179). Collection of local history material.

Inverness

Inverness Museum and Art Gallery: Castle Wynd (0463 237114). History, natural history and archaeology of the Highlands.

Inverurie

Carnegie Museum: Town Hall (0467 21619). Exhibits relating to the history of Inverurie, specializing in archaeology.

Latheron

Clan Gunn Heritage Centre and Museum: Latheron (0955 4771). History of the Clan Gunn and local history exhibits in the Old Parish Church of Latheron (1735).

Lochroistean Centre: Uig Historical Society, Uig (085175 456). Crofting exhibition, including photographs and historical artefacts.

Ness Historical Society (Comunn Eachdraidh Nis): Lionel Old School and Dell Mill, Port-of-Ness (085181 576). Exhibition relating to crofting life around Ness and a restored 19th-century grain mill.

Shawbost Folk Museum: Shawbost (085171 213). Artefacts relating to all aspects of life on Lewis; collection put together by local children.

Lossiemouth

Lossiemouth Fisheries and Community Museum: Pitgaveny Street (034381 3772). Fishing industry displays and a reconstruction of Ramsay Macdonald's study, with original furnishings.

Monymusk

Monymusk Arts Centre: (04677 220). Arts and crafts and a farming museum in an 18th-century lapidary mill. Open by appointment only.

Nairn

Fishertown Museum: Laing Hall, King Street (0667 52064). Displays and photographs of old Fishertown, Nairn.

New Pitsligo

Northfield Farm Museum: Northfield (07717 504). Farm machinery, smiddy and aviary.

Orkney

Corrigal Farm Museum: Corrigall, Harray (085677 411). Restored 19th-century farm buildings with a collection of farming relics.

Kirbuster Farm Museum: Kirbuster, Birsay (085672 268). Farm machinery and implements and other intriguing artefacts.

Orkney Wireless Museum: Church Road, St Margaret's Hope (0856 83 462). Collection of equipment, including a wartime radio from Scapa Flow, maps, charts and photographs.

Stromness Museum: 52 Alfred Street, Stromness (0856 850025). Natural and maritime history museum.

Peterhead

Arbuthnot Museum: St Peter's Street (0779 77778). Peterhead's history as Britain's main whaling and fishing port, based on the collections of local trader Adam Arbuthnot.

Pitmedden

Pitmedden Garden and Museum of Farming Life: (06513 2352). Formal gardens, visitor centre and museum. Pétanque court available by appointment.

Rhynie

Anderson Bay Museum: Rhynie School, Essie Road (046 46 257). Small collection of material connected with a Seaforth Highlander who served in the Egyptian army. Visits by appointment only.

Shetland

Pier House: Symbister, Whalsay (0595 3535 ext 315). Displays illustrating Shetland's trading links with the Hanseatic ports.

Scalloway Museum: Main Street, Scalloway (059588 256). The history of Scalloway.

Shetland Croft House Museum: Voe, Dunrossness (0595 5057). Restored 19th-century croft house and furnishings.

Shetland Museum: Lower Hillhead, Lerwick (0595 5057). Displays relating to the history of Shetland life.

Tingwall Agricultural Museum: Veensgarth, Gott (059584 344). Displays relating to all aspects of a working croft.

George Waterson Memorial Centre: Fair Isle (contact Anne

Museums (cont.)

Sinclair, 03512 244). Displays relating to island living. Open by appointment only.

Skye, Isle of

Borreraig Park Exhibition Croft: by Dunvegan (047081 311). Agricultural machinery and implements and natural history exhibits.

Giant Angus MacAskill Museum: Dunvegan (047022 296). Exhibits relating to Angus MacAskill, recorded in the *Guinness Book of Records* as the tallest Scotsman and tallest 'true' giant at 7 feet 9 inches.

Luib Folk Museum: near Broadford (04712 427). Thatched-cottage museum with displays on the living conditions on Skye in the early 20th century.

Skye Museum: seven miles north of Uig (047052 279). Exhibits and buildings, including a smithy and weaver's house, relating to crofting life on Skye.

Stonehaven

Tolbooth Museum: The Harbour (0779 77778). Fishing and local history exhibits.

Tain

Tain and District Museum and Clan Ross Centre: Castle Brae (0862 2140). History of the royal burgh of Tain and Clan Ross, including Tain silver, early charters and documents and an extensive collection of unique historic photographs.

Thurso

Thurso Heritage Museum: Town Hall, High Street (0847 62459). Local history museum.

Tomintoul

Tomintoul Museum: The Square (08074 285). Exhibitions on rural life, wildlife and landscape, including a reconstructed farmhouse kitchen with original domestic equipment, and a display on peat working, with a peat cart, tools, photographs and diagrams.

Turriff

Session Cottage Museum: Castle Street (contact Turriff Heritage Society: 0888 63451). Limited opening hours: contact Tourist Information for details. Small museum with historic local artefacts in a 250-year-old cottage.

Ullapool

Lochbroom Museum: Quay Street (0463 2356). Rock collection and a variety of artefacts relating to all aspects of the area's history.

Wick

Wick Heritage Centre: Bank Row (0955 3385). Prize-winning local history museum, notable for its exhibition on the herring industry and for the 'Johnston Collection' of photographs of mid 19th–20th-century life in the north of Scotland.

NIGHTLIFE

The venues listed below are those which are known 'night-time spots'. Away from larger towns and cities it becomes more difficult to pin down regular venues but, as a guideline for entertainment-seekers, if you're in a more rural area, try the local hotels to see either if they are hosting events in their public bars or if they have a local information board. Tourist Information Centres may also have details.

Aberdeen

Caesar's Palace: 7 Crown Street (0224 210286). Often has live bands.

The Cotton Club: 491 Union Street (0224 581858). Regular karaoke nights.

Eagles Night Club: 120 Union Street (0224 640641). Popular with an 'older' crowd.

Mr G's: 70 Chapel Street (0224 642112). Over 21s disco, middle-of-the-range music.

Alford

Haughton Arms Hotel: Main Street (09755 62026). Offers music and dancing on Saturday evenings.

Banchory

Burnett Arms Hotel: 25 High Street (03302 4944). Offers the Accordion and Fiddle Club on the second and last Monday of June to August and on the last Monday of each month from September to May. On the first and third Sunday of each month there is also a jazz evening, as well as live music every Sunday.

Buckie

Ziggy's Nightclub and Disco: Commercial Road. Thursday–Saturday. Popular local disco.

Dingwall

Legends (Dingwall) Ltd: High Street (0349 65055/65057). Local disco.

Grantown-on-Spey

Ben Mhor Hotel: High Street (0479 2056). Offers live music every Saturday night during the summer season.

Craiglynne Hotel: Woodlands Terrace (0479 2597). Offers live music with local artists every Monday, Tuesday, Thursday and Friday. Wednesday is a dance night.

Grant Arms Hotel: The Square (0479 2526). Offers live entertainment every Tuesday and Thursday.

Royal British Legion: (0479 2212). Offers dancing and live music every Friday and Saturday.

Waterford Hotel: The Square (0479 2202). Offers weekly discos as well as Grantown Accordion and Fiddle Club on the second Wednesday of each month.

Invergordon

After Dark Night Club: High Street (0349 853004). Local disco and night club, occasional live bands.

Inverness

Beaufort Hotel: Culduthel Road (0463 222897). Hosts the Folk Club each Sunday.

Cummings Hotel: Church Street (0463 232531). Offers traditional music, songs, dancing and Highland humour Monday–Saturday.

Nightlife (cont.)

Dillingers Nightclub: 25 Union Street (0463 225362). Disco seven nights a week.

Inverness Ice Centre: Bught Park (0463 235711). Hosts the Inverness Country and Western Club every Tuesday.

Inverness Jazz Platform holds regular concerts throughout the year. Contact Tourist Information (0463 234353) or the secretary (0463 238113) for further details.

Market Bar: Market Lane (off Church Street) (0463 220203). Live music every night, folk on Saturday.

Mr G's: 9–21 Castle Street (0463 233322). Night club and disco, live bands occasionally during the week.

Keith

Seafield Arms Hotel: Mid Street (05422 7025). Hosts the Accordion and Fiddle Club on the first Tuesday of the month.

Lewis, Isle of

Twilights: Seaforth Hotel, James Street, Stornoway (0851 2740). Local disco, open Wednesday–Friday.

Lossiemouth

Beach Bar: Commerce Street (03481 3164). Hosts the Folk Club on Tuesdays.

Orkney

Casablanca: Junction Road, Kirkwall (0856 875038). Local disco. Some nights for under 18-year-olds.

Matchmakers: Albert Hotel, Kirkwall (0856 876000). Disco and night club.

Shetland

Posers: Grand Hotel, Commercial Street, Lerwick (0595 2826). Local disco with resident DJ.

Skye, Isle of

Evening events are usually held in hotels and community halls. During the summer season some restaurants have resident bands who normally play once a week. Try **Green House Restaurant** (047072 293) in Struan and **Cuillin Hills Hotel**, Portree (0478 2003).

Thurso

Features: Sir George's Street (0847 65800). Disco and live bands.

ORGANIZATIONS

The organizations included here have been chosen to cover those areas, places and subjects which are likely to be of most interest to the visitor. Scotland has many hundreds of local organizations which, as well as providing interesting information about their area, are also a good way of meeting local people. Tourist Information Offices usually carry some details of organizations, as do local libraries (listed above).

Aviemore

Strathspey Railway Association: enquiries to Aviemore Speyside Station, Dalfaber Road, Aviemore (0479 810725). Organization founded in 1972 to support and promote steam railways, now with a line running from Aviemore to Boat of Garten.

Braemar

Braemar Royal Highland Society: Coilacreich, Ballater (03397 55377). Organizers of the famous Braemar Gathering (see Festivals/Events).

Buckie

Buckie District Fishing Heritage Society: Seaview Place (next to the library) (0542 32093). Extensive collection of photographs and artefacts relating to the history of Buckie, particularly its fishing industry.

Grantown-on-Spey

Strathspey Angling Association: Secretary, 61 High Street (0479 2684). Offers weekly tickets for salmon fishing on the association's seven-mile stretch of the River Spey and 12-mile stretch of the River Dulnain.

Inverness

Association for Film and Television in the Celtic Countries: c/o The Library, Farraline Park (0463 226189). Details of Gaelic broadcasting.

Highland Family History Association: c/o Reference Room, The Library, Farraline Park (0463 236463). Genealogical contact point.

Inverness and District Bed and Breakfast Association: Mrs M. Mansfield, 3a Resaurie, Smithton (0463 791714). Details of bed and breakfast hosting in the area.

Macduff

Banffshire Horticultural College: c/o The Secretary, 17 Souter Street (0261 32416). Organizes a number of popular shows throughout the year.

New Deer

New Deer Agricultural Association: c/o The Secretary, Shevado, Maud (07714 675). Organizers of the annual New Deer Show.

Orkney

Orkney Arts Society: contact Mr G. Rendal, 13a Bridge Street, Kirkwall (0856 874803). Local contact point for information about the arts in Orkney.

Orkney Folk Festival Society: PO Box 4, Stromness (contact Mr Johnny Mowat: 0856 850773). Organizers of the annual Orkney Folk Festival.

Orkney Heritage Society: contact Dr Raymond Lamb, 48 Junction Road, Kirkwall (0856 872632). Information about the Orkney Archaeological Archive, and contact point for the Heritage Society, a

Organizations (cont.)

local pressure group working to conserve Orkney's archaeological and man-made heritage.

St Magnus Festival Committee: contact Mrs D. Rushbrook, Strandal, Nicolson Street, Kirkwall (0856 872669). Organizers of the St Magnus Festival (June).

Shetland

Shetland Anglers' Association: Club House, Burns Lane, Lerwick (0595 4945 Thursday–Friday evenings only). Will provide information about angling in Shetland. Information is also available from the Tourist Office, from where permits can be obtained.

Shetland Field Studies Trust: Fort Charlotte, Lerwick (0595 5321). Information relating to Shetland's natural history.

Shetland Film Archive: Shetland Library, Lower Hillhead, Lerwick (0595 3868). Collection of films and videos showing much of Shetland's past life.

Shetland Folk Festival Society: Burns Lane, Lerwick (0595 4757). Organizers of the Shetland Folk Festival.

Tingwall, Whiteness and Weisdale History Group: contact Alister Smith at R.W. Bayes, 143 Commercial Street, Lerwick (0595 3951). Details of local history, including genealogy, can be made available by arrangement.

Skye, Isle of

Sabhal Mor Ostaig Gaelic School: see INFORMATION – ASSOCIATIONS AND ORGANIZATIONS in the National Fact File.

Turriff

New Blyth and District Steam and Vintage Club: The Secretary, 4 Sunnybank Cottages, Crudie (08885 634). Organizers of the annual steam and vintage rally.

Turriff and District Agricultural Association: The Secretary, Whitefield, Forglen, Banff (04665 267). Organizers of the annual Turriff Show.

THEATRES/CONCERT HALLS

Aberdeen

Tickets for theatre events in Aberdeen are available from the **Aberdeen Box Office**, Union Street (0224 641122).

Arts Centre: King Street (0224 635208). Workshops, music and community events.

His Majesty's Theatre: Rosemount Viaduct (0224 641122). Musicals, local and touring productions, drama and dance.

Music Hall: Union Street (0224 641122). All types of music from around the world.

Aviemore

Aviemore Centre: (0479 810624). Varied programme throughout the year.

Ellon

Haddo House Hall Arts Trust: Haddo House (06515 770). Regular plays and concerts throughout the year.

Inverness

Eden Court Theatre: Bishops Road (0463 239841). Music, drama, films and light entertainment throughout the year.

Orkney

Orkney Arts Theatre: Mill Street, Kirkwall (0856 872047). Local and visiting performers.

Shetland

Isleburgh Community Centre: King Harald Street, Lerwick (0595 2114). Central information point for dramatic and musical performances at both the community centre itself and the nearby **Garrison Theatre**.

Thurso

Mill Theatre: Princes Street (0847 63572). Local and visiting productions.

TOURIST INFORMATION

Area Tourist Boards

Aberdeen Tourist Board: St Nicholas House, Aberdeen (0224 276276).

Aviemore and Spey Valley Tourist Board: Main Road, Aviemore (0479 810363).

Banff and Buchan Tourist Board: Collie Lodge, Banff (02612 2789).

Caithness Tourist Board: Information Centre, Whitechapel Road, Wick (0955 2596).

Fort William and Lochaber Tourist Board: Cameron Centre, Cameron Square, Fort William (0397 703781).

Inverness, Loch Ness and Nairn Tourist Board: 23 Church Street, Inverness (0463 234353).

Isle of Skye and South-West Ross Tourist Board: Meall House, Portree, Isle of Skye (0478 2137).

Kincardine and Deeside Tourist Board: 45 Station Road, Banchory (03302 2066).

Moray District Tourist Board: 17 High Street, Elgin (0343 542666).

Orkney Tourist Board: 6 Broad Street, Kirkwall (0856 872856).

Ross and Cromarty Tourist Board: Information Centre, North Kessock, Ross-shire (0463 73505).

Shetlands Islands Tourism: Market Cross, Lerwick, Shetland (0595 3434).

Sutherland Tourist Board: The Square, Dornoch (0862 810400).

Western Isles Tourist Board: 4 South Beach Street, Stornoway, Isle of Lewis (0851 73088).

Local Information Centres

Tourist Information Centres in main towns are usually open all year. Those in smaller towns, such as Strathpeffer and Thurso, and subsidiary offices, such as that at Broadford, on the Isle of Skye, are mostly open from April to October, although a small handful are just from May to August/September. As a general guideline, offices located in town car parks, libraries or museums are open for the summer season only.

Aberdeen: St Nicholas House, Broad Street (0224 632727).

Aboyne: Ballater Road Car Park (03398 86060).

Alford: Railway Museum (09755 62052).

Aviemore: Grampian Road (0479 810363).

Ballachulish: Car Park (08552 296).

Ballater: Station Square (03397 55306).

Banchory: Dee Street Car Park (03302 2000).

Banff: Collie Lodge, St Mary's Car Park (02612 2419).

Barra, Isle of: Main Street, Castlebay (08714 336).

Bettyhill: Clachan (06412 342).

Bonar Bridge: (08632 333).

Braemar: Balnellan Road (03397 41600).

Buckie: Cluny Square (0542 34853).

Carrbridge: Main Street (047984 630).

Crathie: Car Park (03397 42414).

Cullen: 20 Seafield Street (0542 40757).

Daviot: Daviot Wood (046385 203).

Dornoch: The Square (0862 810400).

Dufftown: The Clock Tower, The Square (0340 20501).

Durness: Sango (097181 259).

Elgin: 17 High Street (0343 543388/542666).

Ellon: Market Street Car Park (0358 20730).

Forres: Falconer Museum, Tolbooth Street (0309 72938).

Fort Augustus: Car Park (0320 6367).

Fort William: Cameron Square (0397 703781).

Fraserburgh: Saltoun Square (0346 28315).

Fyvie: Fyvie Castle Car Park (06516 597).

Gairloch: Auchtercairn (0445 2130).

Grantown-on-Spey: High Street (0479 2773).

Harris, Isle of: Pier Road, Tarbert (0859 2011).

Helmsdale: Coupar Park (04312 640).

Huntly: The Square (0466 792255).

Inverness: 23 Church Street (0463 234353).

Inverurie: Town Hall, Market Place (0467 20600).

John O'Groats: County Road (095581 373).

Keith: Church Road (05422 2634).

Kingussie: King Street (0540 661297).

Kirkwall: 6 Broad Street (0856 872856).

Kyle of Lochalsh: Car Park (0599 4276).

Lerwick: The Market Cross (0595 3434).

Lewis, Isle of: 4 South Beach Street, Stornoway (0851 703088).

Lochcarron: Main Street (05202 357).

Lochinver: Main Street (05714 330).

Mallaig: East Bay (0687 2170).

Mintlaw: Aden Heritage Centre (0771 23037).

Nairn: 62 King Street (0667 52753).

North Kessock: North of Inverness Bridge on the A9, (0463 73505).

Peterhead: 56 Broad Street (0779 71904).

Ralia: by Newtonmore on the A9 (05403 253).

Shiel Bridge: (059981 264).

Skye, Isle of: Broadford (04712 361). Meall House, Portree (0478 2137).

Spean Bridge: Car Park (0397 81 576).

Stonehaven: 66 Allardice Street (0569 62806).

Strathpeffer: The Square (099721 415).

Stromness: Pier Head Ferry Terminal (0856 850716).

Strontian: The Square (0967 2131).

Thurso: Riverside (0847 62371).

Tomintoul: The Square (08074 285).

Turriff: Swimming Pool Car Park, Queen's Road (0888 63001).

Uist, Isle of: Pier Road, Lochboisdale, South Uist (08784 286).
Pier Road, Lochmaddy, North Uist (08763 321).

Ullapool: West Shore Street (0854 2135).

Wick: Whitechapel Road (0955 2596).

TRANSPORT

AIR

There are several airstrips throughout the region, including those located at Lerwick, and on the Fair Isle and Unst in Shetland; Stornoway on the Isle of Lewis; the Isle of Benbecula and Isle of Barra. Visitors are advised to contact either Loganair (Loganair Ltd., Glasgow Airport, Abbotsinch, Paisley 041–889 3181) or British Airways (your nearest BA travel shop, or 041–332 9666/031–225 2525) for further information on air travel around Shetland and the Western Isles. British Airways offers a 'Highland Rover Airpass' which allows travel on up to eight Highlands and Islands flights over a minimum period of eight days.

Aberdeen Airport and Heliport: Dyce (0224 722331). Domestic, national and international flights.

Inverness Airport: Dalcross (0463 232471).

Kirkwall Airport: Kirkwall (0856 872421).

Wick Airport: Half a mile north of Wick off the A9 (0955 2215).

BUS

Local mail vans will carry a few passengers and are an interesting way to travel to remote places. Refer to the *Scottish Postbus Guide* (from the Royal Mail Public Relations Unit, West Port House, 102 West Port, Edinburgh) for details and times.

Aberdeen Bus Station (Northern Scottish): Guild Street (0224 212266). Terminus for long-distance, airport and local buses, around the north in particular.

Bluebird Northern: Guild Street Bus Station, Aberdeen (0224 591381). Local services throughout the area and express services throughout Scotland.

Elgin Bus Station: High Street, Elgin (0343 544222).

Fort William Bus Garage: North Road, Fort William (0397 702373).

Grampian Transport: 395 King Street, Aberdeen (0224 637047). Services in and around the Grampian area.

Highland Omnibuses: Park Road, Portree, Isle of Skye (0478 2647). Local bus service throughout Skye and Lochalsh.

Highland Scottish: Seafield Road, Inverness (0463 237575). Services around the Highlands.

Inverness Bus Station: Farraline Park, off Academy Street (0463 233371).

Nairn Bus Station: King Street, Nairn (0667 53355).

Scottish Postal Board: Royal Mail Public Relations Unit, West Port House, 102 West Port, Edinburgh EH3 9HS (postal enquiries only). Full details of post-bus services and routes throughout Scotland.

Skyeways and Clan Coaches: Kyle of Lochalsh (0599 4328). Service to and from Uig/Portree to Glasgow and Inverness.

Thurso Bus Station: Lovers' Lane, Thurso (0847 63123).

FERRIES

Caledonian MacBrayne Ltd: The Ferry Terminal, Gourock, Renfrewshire (0475 33755). Serving most of the Inner and Outer Hebrides (and Clyde Estuary).
Lochboisdale (08764 288).
Lochmaddy (08763 337)

ortree (0478 2075)
tornoway (0851 2361)
arbert (0859 2444)

&O Ferries (Orkney and hetland Services): Jamieson's Quay, Aberdeen (reservations Aberdeen/Lerwick: 0224 572615); crabster/Stromness: 0856 50655/6). Serves mainland cotland–Orkney–Shetland, and Orkney–Shetland.

Shetland Islands Council runs inter-sland ferries: information from Tourist Information in Lerwick. The **Shetland Tourist Organization** publish an *Inter-Shetland Transport Timetable*, containing details of all ail, sea and road services.

RAIL

Aberdeen (0224 594222).

Aviemore (0479 810221).

Dingwall (0349 62242).

Huntly (0466 2705).

Invergordon (0349 853710).

Inverness (0463 238924).

Inverurie (0467 21384).

Keith (05422 2517).

Nairn (0667 53196).

Thurso (0847 62058).

Wick (0955 2131).

Gazetteer

ABERCHIRDER
Grampian

On A97 12m N of Huntly.

Asking directions for Aberchirder might prove unproductive, for the village is known locally as Foggieloan (possibly meaning a grassy lane). It is a small, quiet place, but still a centre for the hamlets round about, and the Foggie Show, held every August, is one of the best in the area. Two miles south of Aberchirder is Bridge of Marnoch. In 1841 a walkout by the church congregation here – unhappy over the imposition on them of an unpopular minister – was one of the events leading to the establishment of the Free Church of Scotland in 1843. There is a standing stone in the grounds of the ruined Old Church, where St Marnoch, a reputed miracle worker, is said to be buried. Also at Bridge of Marnoch are **Cloverleaf Fibre Stud**, which breeds llamas, alpacas and other animals for their fleeces, and the **Old Manse of Marnoch Herb Garden**. A couple of miles west of Aberchirder is the ruin of Crombie Castle, a 16th-century L-plan tower.

ABERDEEN
Grampian

On A92, A93, A96 and A944, 85m NE of Perth.

The granite city facing the cold North Sea is full of great historical and cultural interest – and of colour, particularly in the spring and summer. The city is noted for its superb floral displays, especially roses, and regularly wins prizes in the Britain in Bloom competition.

Aberdeen has a long history, receiving its royal charter in 1179. The city was largely rebuilt in the 14th century and established its credentials as a seat of learning early, its university being 500 years old. Set up as two colleges, it united in 1641, divided again after the Restoration and reunited only in 1860. Aberdeen's mercat cross of 1686, in Castle Street, is one of the most notable in Scotland with heraldic panels and coats of arms. Provost Ross's House in Shiprow, which now houses the city's **Maritime Museum**, dates from 1593. In the same year Marischal College was founded. Its 1906 rebuilding is considered to be one of the finest achievements in granite anywhere in the world. Older yet is **Provost Skene's House** opposite the college. It dates from 1545 and has rooms devoted to several different periods including Georgian and Regency. The educational theme continues in Schoolhill with Robert Gordon's Institute of Technology, founded as a school in 1739 and now a centre for offshore research.

Aberdeen's harbour is always busy with oil support vessels and is the departure place for ferries to Orkney and Shetland. The fish market, opened by the Queen in 1982, is the largest in Scotland. Union Street, named for the union of the parliaments of Britain and Ireland, is the main shopping centre. A mile or so inland is Old Aberdeen, centred on the university and the largely 16th-century St Machar's Cathedral. Notable buildings include the graceful King's College Chapel with an elegant lantern tower and fine wood-carvings. Nearby are Georgian houses in the Chanonry and the Town House of 1788, now a library.

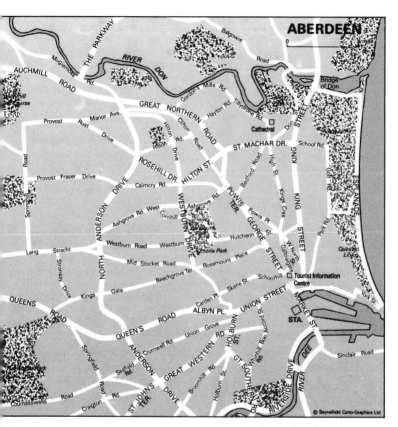

Town plan of Aberdeen

Aberdeen has many outdoor spaces, including Seaton Park beside the River Don. Here and in Duthie Park by the River Dee you can enjoy a riverside stroll, while out to the west, Hazelhead Park has a small zoo, nature trails and three golf courses. The outdoor theme continues at Beechgrove Terrace where, in the grounds of the BBC studios, the very popular *Beechgrove Garden* series is made. Aberdeen is a city which repays exploration on foot, whether through the old city, the parks, or along the long, breezy beach, now being redeveloped. Starting here, you could, if you wished, walk all the way to **Newburgh** on the sand, watching the helicopters shuttling from Dyce airport out to the rigs and back. Aberdeen is prosperous, proud and far from prim.

ABERDEEN, CROMBIE WOOLLEN MILL

Off Great Northern Road (A96) in Woodside, Aberdeen. All year except Christmas and New Year holidays. Mon–Sat 0900–1630, Sun 1200–1630. D. Free. (0224 483201).

The visitor centre and museum tell the story of the famous Crombie cloth. There is a riverside mill, shop, restaurant and coffee shop, and walks are laid out.

ABERDEEN, CRUICKSHANK BOTANIC GARDENS

The Chanonry, Old Aberdeen. May–Sept, Mon–Fri 0900–1630, Sat–Sun 1400–1700; Oct–Apr, Mon–Fri 0900–1630. D (P). Free (0224 272704).

Beautiful gardens contain shrubs, herbaceous and alpine plants, heathers, rockeries and water gardens. Plants from many different countries make this a quiet oasis in the busy city.

ABERDEEN, JONAH'S JOURNEY

120–122 Rosemount Place (0224 647614).

Runner-up in the Scottish Tourist Board Community Awards (1987), this innovative museum offers insight into life 3000 years ago, with a firm emphasis on hands-on experience and participation.

ABERDEEN, MARITIME MUSEUM

Provost Ross's House, Shiprow (0224 585788).

This is a 16th-century shipmerchant's home with models, artefacts and paintings on the fishing industry, local shipbuilding, the North Boats and North Sea Oil and gas. There is also a National Trust for Scotland shop and visitor centre.

ABERDEEN, PROVOST SKENE'S HOUSE

Guestrow, off Broad Street (0224 641086).

This is the oldest domestic dwelling house in Aberdeen. Today, it is restored and furnished in period style and incorporates a museum of civic and domestic life.

ABERDEEN, THE SATROSPHERE

ustice Mill Lane, off Union treet.

ll year. Mon, Wed–Fri 1000–1600, Sat 000–1700, Sun 1330–1700. D (0224 13232).

Children of all ages will enjoy this hands-on' science and technology how with dozens of try-it-yourself xhibits which explore the worlds f sound, light, energy and the nvironment. There is a café nd shop.

ABERDEEN, WINTER GARDENS, DUTHIE PARK

olmuir Road or Riverside Drive. ll year. Daily, 1000–30 mins efore dusk. D (P). Free 0224 583155).

Large conservatories contain 600 pecies of cactus, many tropical lants and trees, an aviary, fish anks and turtles. There is also a raditional Japanese garden, water ardens and sculpture, plant shop nd café, and band concerts in ummer. The park has a children's lay area and boating ponds.

ABERLOUR
Grampian

On A95 midway between Grantown-on-Spey nd Keith.

Aberlour – or to give its full name, Charlestown of Aberlour – is a lanned village, established in 1812 y Charles Grant of Wester Elchies.

Before Grant developed the village, it was known as Skirdustan, from the dedication of the original parish church to St Drostan, who is said to have used the waters of the Lour, which flows into the Spey here, for baptisms. This is, of course, **whisky** country, and in a neat link between holy water and the 'water of life', St Drostan's Well is found in the grounds of Aberlour Distillery, founded in 1826 on the banks of the Lour and still producing both malt and blended whisky today.

Aberlour also claims to produce 'the best shortbread in the world', using traditional ingredients and a recipe unchanged for over a century. The Speyside Way footpath, on the track of a disused railway, passes through the town. The 'village shop', in the main street, is partly preserved in early 20th-century style.

ABOYNE
Grampian

On A93 30m W of Aberdeen.

The neat Deeside village of Aboyne was described by the 19th-century writer George Walker as 'a lodging-house town full of sportsmen with gay knickerbockers of a loud pattern and Turkish caps'. The loud knickerbockers and Turkish caps have gone, but the visitors still come. The large green is the venue for the Aboyne Highland Games each summer. There is a golf course, and a gliding centre, from which these graceful craft rise above the surrounding hills. West of Aboyne, off B976, is **Glen Tanar Estate** and further away on the road to Ballater is **Muir of Dinnet** nature reserve.

ACHARACLE
Highland

On A861 15m W of Strontian.

The small village of Acharacle lies
on flat ground at the west end of
Loch Shiel, and at the east of the
long peninsula of **Ardnamurchan**. An
excellent community newspaper,
De Tha Dol (What's New) is produced
here, and the village hall gets
regular visits from musical and
theatrical companies. To the west,
a minor road leads past the glorious
sands of Kentra Bay to Ardtoe,
where the White Fish Authority set
up an experimental research station
in 1965. East along Loch Shiel
is Claish Moss National Nature
Reserve, a large raised peat bog
covering 1408 acres. On the loch
is the island of Eilean Fhianain,
where an old chapel dedicated to St
Finnan is said to be the saint's last
resting place. To the west, the River
Shiel makes its short, swift passage
into Loch Moidart. Four miles to the
north is **Castle Tioram**.

ACHILTIBUIE
Highland

*On minor road 15m from Drumrunie on
A835 (10m N of Ullapool).*

The narrow, winding road to
Achiltibuie goes through superb
scenery, passing Lochs Lurgain,
Bad a'Ghaill and Osgaig and then
running back along the coast. From
a car park by Loch Lurgain, the
superb little mountain Stac Polly
can be climbed. Achiltibuie (Gaelic
for 'field of the yellow stream') is
a crofting township, and an ideal
centre for active holidays: the
possibilities for walking, fishing or
nature study are endless. Offshore
are the **Summer Isles**, noted for their
wildlife; regular boat trips run from
Achiltibuie. Also in Achiltibuie
are the **Hydroponicum** and the
Smokehouse.

ACHNACARRY
near Gairlochy, Highland

Off B8005 12m N of Fort William.

Achnacarry (field of the fish-trap)
has been the home of the chiefs
of Clan Cameron for centuries.
The present house is 18th century.
During World War II it was used
as a base for troops engaged in
commando training; they are
commemorated by the memorial
above **Spean Bridge**. The house itself
is not open to view, but a converted
croft house in the grounds contains
the excellent **Clan Cameron Museum**.
A mile north of Achnacarry, at the
east end of Loch Arkaig, there is
a car park and a forest walk to the
Eas Cia-Aig, a series of waterfalls.

ACHNASHEEN
Highland

*At the junction of A832 and A890, 16m W
of Garve.*

The small hamlet of Achnasheen
lies at the junction of two major
roads and on the Kyle of Lochalsh
rail line. Its hotel has served
travellers, walkers and fishermen
for many years. Mail and postbus
services spread out from here
along Glen Carron and through the
dramatic defile of Glen Docherty
to Wester Ross and Torridon.
Achnasheen means 'field of

rainstorms', a name it does not wholly deserve.

ACHNASHELLACH
Highland

On A890 12m SW of Achnasheen.

While there is little reason for the motorist to stop at Achnashellach (meaning 'field of willows'), the Kyle of Lochalsh railway does stop there, and many walkers use the halt as a start point to get into the fine mountains that ring Glen Carron. From the station, walks lead north through the forest and north-east over the Coulin Pass, a very old right of way.

ADEN COUNTRY PARK
Grampian

On A950 1m W of Mintlaw.
All year. Daily. D (P) (0771 22857).

Most of Scotland's country parks are close to large centres of population; Aden sits in the rolling Buchan countryside ten miles west of **Peterhead**. Its 230 acres include picnic areas, a caravan site, adventure playground, visitor centre, café and shop. Walks go through woodland including an arboretum, loch and a stretch of the South Ugie Water. The award-winning **North-East of Scotland Agricultural Heritage Centre** is within the park.

ALFORD
Grampian

On A944. 25m W of Aberdeen.

In the 1860s, the railway from **Aberdeen** via Kintore reached Alford, and the community relocated its centre nearer the station instead of at Bridge of Alford, a mile to the west. The railway has long gone but you can still take a steam train here on the narrow-gauge Alford Valley Railway, which runs in summer from the old station through Murray Park and Haughton Country Park. The latter is based around Haughton House, formerly owned by the Farquharson family and now a caravan site run by the regional council. Alford today is a small, neat market town with many stone houses, and is a good base for exploring the delights of **Strathdon**. It is also the home of the **Grampian Transport Museum**.

ALNESS

Off A9 8m NE of Dingwall.

The town of Alness is much quieter now that it is bypassed by the A9. Alness Bay, on the north side of the Cromarty Firth, has good sand and, behind the town, the Alness Burn tumbles through forestry to the sea. There is a golf course and good **fishing**. The Dalmore Distillery, on the Invergordon road, is sometimes open to visitors. The River Averon is crossed here by two notable bridges. The road bridge is a Thomas Telford design, dating from 1810 and with more decoration than most of his bridges. It can be viewed from the adjacent footbridge. A little way downstream and rather screened by trees and bushes is a fine Joseph Mitchell railway viaduct, in castellated style.

It was built in 1862 and still carries the railway.

ALTNAHARRA
Highland

On A836 20m N of Lairg.

The hotel at Altnaharra, much used by fishermen, stands at the head of Loch Naver and in the shadow of Ben Klibreck, a fine Munro. To the east, the B873 leads through Strath Naver, where the wholesale clearance of people took place (see Bettyhill), to the west an unclassified road leads through Strath More to Dun Dornadilla or Dun Dornaigil, a fine broch, and to Ben Hope, the most northerly Munro in Scotland.

APPLECROSS
Highland

On minor roads off A896 between Kishorn and Shieldaig.

The Applecross peninsula thrusts into the Inner Sound opposite Raasay and Skye. Until recently the only road access was over the notorious Bealach na Ba (pass of the cattle), a twisting ascent to over 2000 feet often closed in winter. Car parks and viewpoints at the summit give magnificent panoramas, and also provide easy access to Beinn Bhan and other Applecross hills, whose dramatic cliffs hold many superb rock climbs. There is now a road from Shieldaig round the coast to Applecross village and beyond, a lovely drive with magnificent seaward views. St Maelrubha founded a chapel on Applecross Bay in the seventh century. The saint is said to have planted five apple trees in the shape of a cross, giving the place its name, but a more likely, if prosaic, derivation is Abercrossan, the estuary of the river which reaches the sea here. The west coast of the peninsula holds a number of small crofting communities.

ARBUTHNOTT
Grampian

On B967 3m W of Inverbervie.

The Arbuthnott family have been major landowners in the Mearns for nearly 1000 years; Arbuthnott House sits above the Bervie Water and a mile to the east, in a tranquil location, is the sandstone church dedicated to St Ternan. Parts are 13th century, and the Arbuthnott Aisle (c1500) is a good example of Scottish Gothic style. J.L. Mitchell, better known as the author Lewis Grassic Gibbon, is buried here, outside the 'Kirk of Kinraddie' as he named it in his novel *Sunset Song*.

ARCHIESTOWN
Grampian

On B9102 4m W of Aberlour.

This is another planned village, established in 1760 by Sir Archibald Grant of Monymusk and given his name. A disastrous fire destroyed much of the village in 1783, but it was rebuilt. In the centre is a large memorial to local men killed in World War I, unveiled in 1920 by the Duke of Richmond and Gordon Archiestown is a neat, quiet village today, slightly off the tourist trail through Strathspey.

ARDCLACH
Highland

Minor road off A939 9m SE of Nairn.

Ardclach, a tiny settlement on the River Findhorn, is notable for its Bell Tower. Built in 1655 on a promontory above the river, it was used both to call worshippers to the nearby church and to act as a watch-tower. It can be visited by obtaining a key from the guardian.

ARDGAY
Highland

On A836 15m W of Tain.

The small, quiet settlement of Ardgay retains a separate identity from its neighbour, **Bonar Bridge**, having its own hotels and shops. The railway still comes through on its long inland loop to **Lairg**, and ten miles west up Gleann Mor is **Croick Church**. The stone on a plinth beside the road marks the former site of Ardgay's winter market.

ARDGOUR
Highland

Access from Corran Ferry (A82, 8m S of Fort William) or via A861 from Drumfern (A830, 10m W of Fort William).

Between Loch Eil, Loch Shiel and Glen Tarbert is the land of Ardgour (possibly meaning 'height of goats'), a mountainous area cut through by superb glens ideal for the hardy walker. Garbh Bheinn (rough hill), well seen from the Glen Tarbert road, typifies the rugged nature of the area. The small settlements cling to the loch shores, with the Ardgour Hotel at the west side of the short Corran car ferry crossing. There is also a passenger-only ferry from Fort William to Camasnagaul.

ARDNAMURCHAN
Highland

B8007 from Salen leads 25m W to Ardnamurchan Point.

The peninsula of Ardnamurchan sticks out like a long foot testing the waters of the Atlantic. Geologically the area is very interesting with a number of ancient basaltic 'ring dykes', best seen from the air. The single-track B8007 winds westward from Salen along Loch Sunart to pass Glenborrodale with its luxury hotel, curves inland round Ben Hiant and reaches the sea again at Kilchoan, an attractive village with a neat church serving the scattered parish. Also here are the ruins of Mingary Castle, a 14th-century stronghold of the MacIans, a sept of Clan Donald. It was under siege several times, lastly in 1644. It can be seen by walking down a track from the village.

From Kilchoan a passenger ferry (summer only) runs across to Tobermory on Mull. The road continues past the turnoff to Sanna Bay, a glorious stretch of sand with a caravan park, to reach Ardnamurchan Point, the most westerly extremity of the British mainland. The lighthouse here, designed by Alan Stevenson, dates from 1848. It used to be possible to climb to the top (with permission) but the light is now, like many others, automatic in operation. From Ardanamurchan Point, there are views out to Coll and the **Small**

Isles, and there is usually plenty of birdlife to be seen and heard.

ARDVRECK CASTLE
near Lochinver, Highland

On N shore of Loch Assynt by A837, 10m N of Ledmore Junction, 10m E of Lochinver. All times, free.

The gaunt ruin of this 16th-century Macleod stronghold sits on a peninsula in Loch Assynt, surrounded by wild mountainous country. The Marquess of Montrose took refuge here in 1650 after his defeat at Culrain, near Bonar Bridge, but was betrayed and taken to Edinburgh for execution. The castle was largely destroyed in 1672 by a Mackenzie raiding party.

ARISAIG
Highland

On A830 35m W of Fort William.

After passing Loch nan Uamh, where a cairn marks the landing of Bonnie Prince Charlie in August 1745, and his departure a year later, the A830 winds through woods, accompanied by the railway, to meet the sea again at the village of Arisaig before continuing to Morar and Mallaig. Arisaig has its own railway station, a hotel, several guest houses and a camping and caravan site. The church tower incorporates a clock dedicated to the Gaelic poet Alasdair Macmhaigstair Alasdair, who died at the Battle of Culloden in 1746. From Arisaig you look out to the Small Isles, with the Sgurr of Eigg prominent. Boat trips can be taken in summer. The coast here is blessed with fine sandy beaches.

ARNISDALE
near Glenelg, Highland

On minor road 9m S of Glenelg.

The road south from Glenelg climbs through forestry to Upper Sandaig. From here a path leads down to Sandaig itself, the 'Camusfearna' of Gavin Maxwell's otter books. The road continues below the slopes of Beinn Sgritheall to reach the sea, makes one last climb and then swoops down to the neat village of Arnisdale, set around Camas Ban (white bay) on Loch Hourn. The road continues for a mile to Carron, from where a lovely path leads along Loch Hourn. Across the loch is Knoydart.

ASSYNT
Highland

Between A837 and A838 in Sutherland.

The area between Loch Assynt and Loch Shin is one of the wildest in Scotland. The only road is the minor one serving the scattered community in Glen Cassley: that apart, all is mountain, moor and loch, the home of eagles, deer and much other wildlife. It is a superb area for the walker and naturalist, but caution should be exercised and local advice taken in the shooting season. The twin high points are Ben More Assynt and its neighbour Conival, both Munros, reached from Inchnadamph. Up the River Traligill are limestone caves where the river 'sinks' below ground; they can safely be explored. At the northern end of the area is Britain's highest waterfall, Eas Coul Aulin, and on an island on Loch Assynt is Ardvreck Castle.

AUCHENBLAE
Grampian

*On minor roads off A94 or B966, 6m N of
Laurencekirk.*

East of the large Drumtochty
Forest, the village of Auchenblae
sits snugly on a gentle hillslope.
The 1829 church is on the site of
a much earlier chapel dedicated
to St Palladius, whose bones were
interred here. The church serves
the large parish of Fordoun. In
medieval times Auchenblae was
famous for the three-day Paddy's
Fair (originally St Palladius's Fair),
when business and pleasure became
one and many were the sore heads
afterwards.

AUCKENGILL
Highland

On A9 10m N of Wick.

There are several features of interest
in this small settlement on the
Caithness coast. As well as the **John
Nicolson Museum**, there are three
follies, one of which formerly held
weather recording instruments;
another was called Mervin's Tower
after a small boy who spent all his
spare time here with the workmen.
A lane leads down to Auckengill
harbour, with a small pier and a
shingle beach backed by fine cliffs.
A clifftop path leads south to a
ruined **broch**; birdlife is likely to
include fulmars, shags and plovers.

AULTBEA
Highland

On A832 12m N of Gairloch.

South of Aultbea, the road from
Poolewe climbs high above Loch
Ewe; viewpoint car parks give
splendid panoramas of the **Torridon**
mountains and out to the north
end of **Skye**. Nearer the village, the
beauty of the scene is marred by
an ugly naval base. Aultbea itself
has shops and a hotel, and from
it minor roads lead out either side
of the peninsula to the north. The
drive to Mellon Udrigle via Laide is
well worth taking: from the small
sandy beach a magnificent view
opens out across Loch Broom to the
hills of Sutherland, and round to
the majestic mountain An Teallach.
From Achgarve an old track can be
walked across the peninsula to the
deserted village of Slaggan, above
another fine beach.

AVIEMORE
Highland

*Off A9, 80m N of Perth, 30m S of
Inverness.*

Aviemore has been through a
number of phases in its history.
Before the railway came in the
1850s there was just an inn and
a few houses on one of General
Wade's **military roads**. Then the
trains arrived, and so did the
people. The village grew, and
became well known as a centre for
sporting holidays, especially **fishing**
on the River Spey. Mountaineers
too used it as a base for exploring
the **Cairngorms**. In this century it
declined, until far-sighted people
saw the opportunities for winter
sports in the area, and the ski area
on Cairn Gorm was opened in
the 1960s. A consortium led by Sir
Hugh Fraser (later Lord Fraser of
Allander) built the Aviemore Centre

with its hotels, shops and leisure complex. Many feel its architecture is quite alien to the Highland scene, and there are currently plans to redevelop it on more aesthetically pleasing lines; but it does attract many thousands of visitors all year round.

High season for **skiing** (given sufficient snow) is February to April but there is always much else to do – walking, mountain biking, cross-country skiing in the forest, birdwatching and so on. Behind Aviemore is the Craigellachie Nature Reserve, which has a fine birch wood with walks laid out; see also **Rothiemurchus**. For steam train enthusiasts, the **Strathspey Railway** runs to **Boat of Garten**.

The island of Eilean Munde in the loch has a Macdonald burial ground.

BADBEA
Highland

Off A9 6m N of Helmsdale.

On the A9 between **Helmsdale** and **Berriedale** is a car park from which the former crofting village of Badbea is reached. A walk of about half a mile leads to the remains of the settlement formed here when people cleared from their home glens were forced to try to scrape an existence on the coast, in inhospitable conditions, with poor land and no livestock. Interpretive panels tell the story. Nearby is Ousdale Broch, with its guard-cell and stair still intact.

BALLACHULISH
Highland

On A82 12m S of Fort William.

Ballachulish (once known as Laroch) made its living, and nearly wrecked its environment, by quarrying slate. It was the most important source of roofing material for much of Scotland. Ballachulish slate has contributed greatly to the appearance of Scottish vernacular architecture, and the distinctive dark grey slates can be seen all over the country. Extensive quarrying took place here from the late 17th century up to 1955, when the slateworks closed. A great deal of landscaping has gone on in recent years, and the scars are much ameliorated. The Tourist Information Centre off the A82 has interpretive material on the slate quarries. As well as the village here, there are settlements called South and North Ballachulish either side of the bridge that straddles the Loch Leven narrows and replaced the former ferry crossing in 1975.

BALLATER
Grampian

On A93 40m W of Aberdeen, 17m E of Braemar.

Douce, solid and sure of itself, Ballater straddles the River Dee as if guarding the wilder upper reaches from an eastern invasion. It has become Royal Deeside's principal town, offering visitors a wide range of accommodation. Shops proudly display the royal coat of arms, granted for supplying the needs of **Balmoral Castle**, a few miles to the west. Ballater has a grid street pattern which was planned when mineral-rich waters were discovered at Pannanich Wells, east of the town, in the late 18th century. The waters are still there, but Ballater's modern success comes more from its royal neighbours and from the undiminished beauty of the surrounding forests, glens and hills. Walks can be taken to the top of Craigendarroch (crag of oaks) or Craig Coillich (crag of the cockerel) or along the former railway line to Cambus o'May.

BALMACARA
Highland

On A87 3m E of Kyle of Lochalsh. NTS (059 986 207).

The estate of Balmacara extends to 5600 acres of the Kyle/Plockton peninsula. In **Lochalsh Woodland Garden**, the policies of Lochalsh House (not itself open), walks are laid out and there is a seasonal interpretive display. On the A87 there are several viewpoint car parks commanding the outlook to **Skye** across Loch Alsh and east towards **Kintail**; the minor road across to **Plockton** has further fine views. **Kyle of Lochalsh** is the main crossing-point for Skye, presently by ferry but, if current plans come to fruition, soon by a bridge: it is also a rail terminal.

BALMEDIE COUNTRY PARK
Grampian

Off A92 5m N of Aberdeen.

An area of dunes and foreshore has been laid out with walks, picnic areas and car parks. The sandy beach is excellent for children, but the area also holds a historical curiosity. South and north of Balmedie are points marked on the Ordnance Survey map as 'End of Base'. In 1817, along this straight coastline, an exact five-mile base line was measured out, to be used for the Principal Triangulation of the United Kingdom, which was not published until 1858. The measurements made then are only now being replaced by satellite surveying and mapping.

BALMORAL CASTLE AND GROUNDS
Grampian

On A93 9m E of Braemar, 50m W of Aberdeen. The castle ballroom with paintings and other exhibits is open

May–Jul, Mon–Sat 1000–1700. The grounds are also open, and there is a shop and refreshment room. D (P) (03397 42334).

The present Balmoral Castle, completed in 1855, replaced an older building which stood here when **Queen Victoria** and Prince Albert first visited the area in 1848. They fell in love with Deeside, and purchased the estate soon afterwards. It stretches from the river to the 'steep frowning glories of dark Lochnagar', as the poet Byron had it, and beyond. The royal family still visit Balmoral in late summer each year, staying in the castle and attending the Gathering at **Braemar** on the first Saturday in September. Balmoral is built of Glen Gelder granite, and was designed by William Smith of Aberdeen. Nearby is Crathie Church, where the royal family worship while staying here. The church was built in 1895, the royal family contributing to the cost.

BALVENIE CASTLE
near Dufftown, Grampian

On A941 1m W of Dufftown.
Apr–Sept, Mon–Sat 1000–1900, Sun 1400–1900.

Founded as a moated stronghold by the Comyns in the 13th century, most of what remains today is later 15th- and 16th-century work by Earls of Atholl. Balvenie was occupied by Cumberland's troops in 1746 but is now an atmospheric ruin. It stands in the grounds of the **Glenfiddich Distillery**.

BANCHORY
Grampian

On A93 18m W of Aberdeen.

Banchory (fair hollow) is full of solid, well-established houses: the church dates its foundation back to St Ternan, who is said to have established a monastery here in the fifth century. Just south of the town, the River Dee is joined by the Feugh, a rapid, tumbling burn, and at Bridge of Feugh a car park enables visitors to stop and watch for salmon leaping upstream. Banchory was the birthplace of the great fiddle player James Scott Skinner (1843–1927), known as 'the Strathspey King' after the many dance tunes he composed. He is marked by a plaque in the High Street and also by a restaurant bearing his name. The perfume and cosmetic makers, **Ingasetter**, are located in Banchory.

BANFF
Grampian

At junction of A97/A98, 35m E of Elgin, 26m W of Fraserburgh.

Situated where the River Deveron meets the sea, Banff is a handsome town with many old buildings. The burgh dates back at least to the 12th century, when it was a member of the Northern Hanseatic League, trading with European ports. The Town House of 1765 is a James Adam design, and at the Plainstones is the 16th-century mercat cross. There are several fine churches, including the episcopal St Andrews (Archibald Simpson, 1833) and the parish church of St Mary's, dating from 1790 with a high steeple. High Shore is a good group of 17th-century houses near the harbour.

In High Street is the Castle, actually an 18th-century mansion designed by William Adam and now council offices. Adam was also responsible for **Duff House**, over the building of which there was a long wrangle which led to a lawsuit between the architect and the Earl of Fife. There are good walks along the coast and up the Deveron, as far as the old Bridge of Alvah three miles to the south. Banff retains its character today and, in common with other towns on this coast, enjoys a mild, generally dry climate. Just across the Deveron is the neighbouring town of **Macduff**.

BARRA
Western Isles

Reached by regular car ferry from Oban: journey time about 5 hrs.

Barra, near the south end of the long chain of Outer Hebridean islands, is named after St Barr, whose church stood at Cille-bharra, where carved stone slabs can still be seen. Of later date, and an unmistakable Barra landmark, is Kisimul Castle, home of the MacNeils of Barra, set on a small island off Castlebay, Barra's only town. The ferry from Oban passes Kisimul to arrive at Castlebay Pier, always a busy scene. From Castlebay the A888 circles the island, a 14-mile trip of great variety and beauty. Heading north-west the road passes Loch Tangusdale, with the ruined Castle Sinclair on an islet. The 1974 Isle of Barra Hotel is passed then, as an historical contrast, opposite the turning to

Borve are two ancient standing stones which are said to mark the resting place of a Norse warrior. At Craigston there is a small cottage museum.

The road continues to North Bay, where a minor road leads north past the superb sands of Traigh Mor (big sands), used at low tide as Barra's airport, to the three small chapels at Cille Barra, one of which has been roofed to shelter the carved slab stones. The author Compton Mackenzie is buried here, in sight of the island of Eriskay, the setting for his famous novel *Whisky Galore*. From Eoligarry there is a passenger ferry to Ludag on South Uist. Returning to North Bay, the statue of St Barr with his stave raised, completed in 1975 by a Barra artist, Margaret Somerville, can be seen. At Brevig there are standing stones. Barra is a Catholic island, and high on the shoulder of Heaval is the well-known Madonna of the Sea, a marble statue erected in 1954 by the Welcome Home Fund for Seamen. Heaval is Barra's highest hill at 1255 feet, and is an easy climb rewarded with a stupendous panorama of sea and islands, including Vatersay, south of Barra, and connected by a causeway opened in 1991.

BARRA, KISIMUL CASTLE

Castle Bay. May–Sept, Wed and Sat afternoons only. Enquire locally for times (08714 336).

Kisimul probably dates back to the 13th century, though much is 16th century and later. It is the traditional home of the chiefs of the MacNeils of Barra, and has recently been restored by the 45th chief, an American architect.

BAXTERS VISITOR CENTRE
Fochabers, Grampian

On A96 1m W of Fochabers.
Mar–Dec, Mon–Fri 1000–1630; Easter, May–Sept, Mon–Fri 1000–1630, Sat 1100–1730, Sun 1230–1630. D (P) (0343 820393).

Visitors can tour the factory where the famous soups, preserves and other foods are made and see a reconstruction of the original Baxter family shop in Fochabers and of a Victorian kitchen. There are a restaurant, picnic areas, a gift shop, and woodland walks are laid out, one leading to a viewpoint looking to the estuary of the River Spey.

BEAULY
Highland

On A862 11m W of Inverness.

From Inverness the A862 runs along the southern shore of the Beauly Firth, passes the turnoff to Moniack Castle, crosses the Beauly River and turns north to the town named 'Beau Lieu' (beautiful place) by the Valliscaulian monks from France who founded the Beauly Priory here in about 1230. At the priory entrance is the shaft of the old mercat cross. Beauly has close links with the Lovat family, chiefs of Clan Fraser, whose seat is the 19th-century Beaufort Castle, two miles south of the town (not open to the public). In the town square is a monument marking the raising of the Lovat Scouts to serve in the Boer War. To the south-west is Aigas, with a field study centre and a practising silversmith.

BEAULY PRIORY
Beauly, Highland

Apr–Sept, Mon–Sat 0930–1900, Sun 1400–1900. D (P).

The priory's most notable features are the lovely 13th-century triangular windows in the south wall, and the west doorway of the south transept, also 13th century. The north transept, restored this century, is the burial place of the Mackenzies of Kintail.

BEINN EIGHE
Highland

Visitor centre at Aultroy, on A832 2m N of Kinlochewe. May–Sept, daily 1000–1700 (044 584 254).

Beinn Eighe, a vast sprawl of a mountain with half a dozen separate tops, is owned by Scottish Natural Heritage (formerly the Nature Conservancy Council) and is one of Scotland's premier national nature reserves, noted not only for the magnificence of the mountain scenery but also for the Caledonian pine forest on the lower slopes and for the wildlife ranging from eagles to pine martens. The reserve, which borders the National Trust for Scotland's **Torridon** estate, has won awards, including the Diploma of the Council of Europe, for the excellence of its management. It covers 12 000 acres in total, of which SNH own 10 500 acres. Beinn Eighe (file mountain) is quartzite, giving it the distinctive grey-white appearance that can almost look like snow from a distance. Two trails have been laid out for visitors, and excellent interpretive booklets are available. Both start from a car park

by Loch Maree, four miles north of Kinlochewe, and both go through Coille na Glas Leitire (wood of the grey slope), the most important pine wood.

BENBECULA
Western Isles

Reached by regular car ferry from Oban to Lochboisdale in South Uist or from Uig on Skye to Lochmaddy on North Uist, or daily direct flight from Glasgow.

The island of Benbecula sits between **North Uist** and **South Uist** and is linked to both by road causeway. As with other Hebridean islands, its character is sharply divided between the low machair coast on the west, with magnificent beaches and a profusion of summer flowers, and the rugged east side, hilly and with myriad blue lochans. From South Uist the causeway reaches Creagorry. A left turn on to the B892 passes the modern school at Lionacleat, and a diversion can be made to the ruin of Borve Castle, a Clan Ranald stronghold. At various points the road can be left to go down to the shore and walk, in summer, among the splendour of the machair flowers, a carpet of colour on the springy turf. The road turns east past the ruined chapel of Teampall Challuim Chille dedicated to St Columba. From here Balivanich, the main settlement serving the airport and military base, can be reached. The A865 is rejoined near the causeway to North Uist, beside a vast area of sandy flats rich in birdlife. Benbecula is a Catholic island and on Rueval (hill of miracles) is Hew Lorimer's statue of the Madonna and Child, known as Our Lady of the Isles. It was erected in 1957 with contributions made by Catholic communities all over the world. Benbeculas's **Museum Sgiol Lionacleit** is of interest.

BENBECULA, MUSEUM SGIOL LIONACLEIT

At Lionacleit School. All year. Mon–Fri. Free (0870 2211 extn 137).

The museum stages exhibitions of island life and history and also hosts travelling exhibitions.

BENNACHIE
Grampian

Car park off B9002 1m W of Oyne, 8m W of Inverurie.

Bennachie holds a very special place in the affection of Aberdeenshire folk: for many it is 'their' hill. Though it is not particularly high or wild it is a notable landmark, the eroded tors on its summits of Watch Craig, Oxen Craig and the Mither Tap standing out from the surrounding countryside. Mither Tap has an ancient fort on its summit. Alone among Scottish hills, it has its own very vigorous pressure group, the Bailies of Bennachie, who work to conserve the hill, maintain its public amenity, and guard against unwanted development. The hill can be climbed from several places; the car park near Oyne gives access to the tops through woodland. Leaflets are available and there is a map at the car park, which has toilets and picnic areas. The ascent is not difficult – the paths are well maintained – and the views over

the countryside of Gordon District are splendid.

BEN NEVIS
Highland

5m E of Fort William.

Britain's highest mountain is usually climbed either from Achintee in Glen Nevis or from the youth hostel further up the glen. There is a path all the way, but the climb should never be underestimated: the return trip is an arduous ten miles, and good equipment including boots is a prerequisite. The summit area – under snow for up to ten months of the year – includes the remains of the former observatory, which operated here for 20 years until 1904; the weather readings taken then are still being analysed today. The staff lived here all year round, with supplies coming up the same path used today. The famous Ben Nevis Race is held on the first Saturday in September. Up to 500 runners set off from Town Park, the winner returning in only 90 minutes. Because it is Britain's highest mountain at 4406 feet, Ben Nevis is often used for charity climbs; cars have been up, as have pianos and other musical instruments, people have walked up backwards, and so on. The cliffs on the north-east side contain many hard rock climbs.

BEN NEVIS DISTILLERY
near Fort William, Highland

At junction of A82 and A830 2m N of Fort William. Easter–Oct, Mon–Fri 0900–1800. D (P) (0397 700200).

The distillery, closed for some years, resumed production in 1990 after being bought by Nikka Whisky Co of Japan, and a visitor centre opened in summer 1991. The distillery is producing a single malt and two blends under the name 'Dew of Ben Nevis', and a humorous audio-visual show explains the connection between Ben and Dew, featuring the giant Hector MacDram, who uses Ben Nevis as a footstool and is credited with discovering the Dew. Distillery tours can be taken, followed by a tasting, and there is a café and gift shop.

BEN NEVIS EXHIBITION AND CRAFT CENTRE
Fort William, Highland

High Street, Fort William. May–Sept, daily 0900–1730 (to 2200 in Jul/Aug); Mar, Apr, Oct, Mon–Sat 0900–1730 (0397 2504).

The exhibition features the topography, history and legends of our highest mountain with contour model and film. There are crafts on display with goods for sale.

BERRIEDALE
Highland

On A9 10m N of Helmsdale.

Inland from the A9 north of Helmsdale, the distinctive conical hill shapes of Morven and the smaller Maiden Pap can be seen. This area is known as Langwell Forest, from the Duke of Portland's estate centred on Langwell House at Berriedale. The Berriedale Water joins Langwell Water to rush into the sea past the scant remains of

an earlier stronghold of the Earls of Caithness. Langwell House is not open to the public, but the gardens sometimes are, with a garden centre for the sale of plants. Power is generated by a wind turbine. The **Kingspark Llama Farm** nearby can be visited.

BETTYHILL
Highland

On A836 10m E of Tongue.

The village of Bettyhill is named after Elizabeth, 1st Duchess of Sutherland. It sits at the east side of Torrisdale Bay, which has fine sands. Here the River Naver meets the sea, and Invernaver is a national nature reserve. Because of its exposed position, mountain plants occur here almost down to sea level, and there is a fine raised beach with a number of important archaeological sites. On the east side of Farr Point, not easily accessible, is the ruin of Borve Castle, a former Mackay stronghold. In Bettyhill is the **Strathnaver Museum**.

BIRDS, see **HIGHLAND BIRDS** panel p136.

BLACK ISLE
Highland

From Inverness via the A9 over the Kessock Bridge.

The large promontory known (although it is not an island) as the Black Isle juts out between the Cromarty and Moray Firths. The area is well wooded in its centre, with a fine coastal strip offering good beaches and outstanding wildlife. From the A9, the B9161 leads to Munlochy, above the long inlet of Munlochy Bay, a bird reserve noted for its waders. A car park has information boards. The road continues, meeting the sea at Avoch, burial place of Sir Alexander Mackenzie (1735–1821), a noted explorer and the discoverer of the river in Canada which bears his name. A circular walk from Avoch to **Fortrose** along the shore, returning inland, can be followed.

The road continues through Fortrose and **Rosemarkie**, after which a minor road nearer the shore can be taken as an alternative. From Eathie a path goes down to an old fishing station and along the shore to Eathie Gorge, investigated by Hugh Miller (see **Cromarty**). The A832 is rejoined near Cromarty, from where the south side of the Cromarty Firth is followed by the B9163. A stop can be made at Udale Bay, a nature reserve with superb sands and more excellent birdlife. St Michael's Chapel, Balblair, is tenth century; from here there is a walk beside the bay and back through Balblair village, where the devil is said to have appeared several times at the Balblair Inn. Just inland, Jemimaville and Poyntzfield owe their names to a former landowner who married a Dutch lady called Jemima Poyntz. At Culbokie a forest walk can be taken, and from here minor roads lead to the forested interior of the Black Isle. From this side of the peninsula oil rigs can often be seen 'parked' for maintenance in Nigg Bay. The A9 is rejoined near Dunvornie.

BLAROUR NURSERY
Spean Bridge, Highland

All year. Daily 0930–1730. Free.

Interpretive panels make up an exhibition called 'Lochaber – Its Land and People', showing the geology of the area, its flora and fauna, and its long history including clan battles.

BOAT OF GARTEN
Highland

Off A95 or B970, 8m N of Aviemore.

The village of Boat of Garten, named for a long-defunct ferry across the River Spey, has become associated in recent years with the regular appearance of ospreys in summer at the RSPB reserve at **Loch Garten**, two miles to the east; indeed, from **Aviemore** on the A9, road signs actually say 'ospreys' when the birds are in residence. Boat of Garten itself has plenty of accommodation and offers good **fishing** and golf; it is also the northern terminus of the **Strathspey Railway**.

BONAR BRIDGE
Highland

On A836 26m N of Dingwall.

At Bonar Bridge the Oykel river meets the Dornoch Firth. The first road bridge was built by **Thomas Telford** in 1812; it was rebuilt after a flood in 1892 and has since been widened. This has long been an important staging-post for travellers. From Bonar Bridge, roads head north-west through **Lairg** into

Sutherland and through Strath Oykel to the west coast. The vast pile of Carbisdale Castle nearby is now a youth hostel.

BRAEMAR
Highland

On A93 50m N of Perth, 60m W of Aberdeen.

From its summit at over 2100 feet on the Tayside/Grampian Regional boundary beside the Cairnwell ski grounds, the A93 skitters down beside the Clunie Water to Braemar, where it turns east to follow the River Dee towards **Aberdeen**. Despite the road's loss of 1000 feet, it is still passing through one of the highest villages in Scotland. Braemar owes its establishment to its strategic position at the confluence of hill passes from Strathspey and the south, and there has been a settlement here for over 1000 years. The ruins of Kindrochit Castle, by the Glenshee Road car park, date back to the 14th century. Just across the road is the cottage where, in 1881, R.L. Stevenson wrote the first draft of *Treasure Island*. From here walks lead through woods to **Braemar Castle** or, by a sharp scramble, to the summit of Creag Choinnich (Kenneth's Crag), a superb viewpoint.

The Invercauld Arms Hotel is on the site where the Earl of Mar raised the standard to start the Jacobite Rising of 1715. The Stuarts failed in their attempts to win back the throne, and the line continued down to the present royal family, who attend the famous Braemar Gathering at the Duke of Fife and Princess Alice Memorial Park on the first Saturday in September each year. On the western edge of

Braemar is the Morrone National Nature Reserve, noted for its birch woods. A minor road runs west by the Dee, a noted salmon river, for six miles to Linn o'Dee, where the river wrestles its way through a narrow channel. One final statistic of which Braemar is proud: it jointly holds the British record for the lowest recorded temperature, at -27.2°C.

BRAEMAR CASTLE
Highland

On A93 1m E of Braemar.
May–Sept, daily 1000–1800. D (P)
(03397 41219).

A multi-turreted stronghold, the castle we see today was rebuilt in 1750 after being sacked by Farquharson of Inverey, and was then garrisoned by Hanoverian troops. There is much to see, including towers climbed by spiral stairs, an underground prison, and historical relics. It has a shop and a tearoom.

BROCHS, see panel p88.

BRODIE CASTLE
near Nairn, Grampian

Off A96 6m E of Nairn.
Easter–end Sept, Mon–Sat 1100–1800,
Sun 1400–1800; Oct, Sat 1100–1800, Sun
1400–1800. Grounds open daily all year. D
(P). NTS (03094 371).

Brodie is a superb example of a Scottish fortified house, built on a basic Z-plan, with later additions. The earliest parts date from the 16th century, and it has been the home

Brochs

Brochs are circular double-walled drystone fortifications, concentrated in their distribution on the west coast of Scotland and the islands, in Caithness, and in both Orkney and Shetland. It is generally accepted that they date from around the first century BC and were used until about AD200. The name derives from an Old Norse word meaning a strong place – apt indeed when you look at any well-preserved broch.

Who built the brochs? How did the design evolve? When were they abandoned, and why? The answers to these questions are still sought by archaeologists, and may indeed never be found. We can visit brochs today and wonder at their sophistication and strength.

In their construction, brochs follow a pattern. The outer walls have a definite inward curve as they get higher, known as a 'batter'; the same shape is seen in cooling towers at power stations and factories today. The twin walls totalled probably 15 feet in thickness, making the broch almost impossible to destroy from outside.

The interior is usually 30–40 feet in diameter, on several levels with 'galleries' reached by stairways. It is possible that a turf or thatch roof was added to some brochs, with an opening for smoke from the fire to escape. Quite a number of people could thus have survived inside, and excavation has indicated that animals were also kept in brochs: bones of cattle, sheep and pig have been found. Nor were the finer points of life forgotten: artefacts and ornaments of deerhorn, stone, bronze and pottery, and even dice and counters, have been recovered from brochs.

Among the best surviving brochs are those in Gleann Beag, near **Glenelg** (Dun Telve and Dun Troddan); at Struanmore on **Skye** (Dun Beag); and Dun Dornaigil near Loch Hope in Sutherland. There are many brochs in **Orkney** and **Shetland**, most notably perhaps **Midhowe** on **Rousay**, **Clickhimin** near **Lerwick** and **Mousa**, one of the finest of all. There are also smaller remains in central and southern Scotland, including Tirefour on the island of Lismore, near Oban; Coldoch, north of Stirling; and Edinshall, near Stow in Berwickshire.

Brochs are identifiably Scottish buildings, although they are also found in Ireland. They are very special and exciting places, the more so for the mystery that surrounds them.

of the Brodies of Brodie ever since:
the present chief, Ninian Brodie,
still lives there. The castle contains
many exquisite pieces of furniture,
porcelain (English, European
and Chinese), paintings including
Dutch 17th-century masters and
French Impressionists, armour,
weaponry and much else. The
extensive grounds have woodland
walks, a large pond with nature
trail and wildlife hide, gardens,
children's adventure playground,
picnic areas and a campsite. There
is a gift shop and tearoom.

BRORA
Highland

On A915 15m N of Dornoch.

Brora is a neat, pleasing place.
There are good sands, a golf
course and fine **fishing** on the rivers
that tumble down from the hills
behind the town: Brora also has
its own station on the line from
Inverness to **Wick** and **Thurso**. Once
it had a busy harbour, but few
vessels are to be seen here now.
Industry continues at the woollen
mill (which has a shop) and at
Clynelish Distillery, which makes
its own distinctive malt as well as
contributing to blended whisky.
The distillery dates from 1819. Coal
was mined here, starting in 1598
and continuing erratically until as
recently as 1974, when the mine
was reopened during the Middle
East oil crisis. Three miles north of
Brora is Cinn Trolla, a fine **broch**.

BUCKIE
Grampian

On A990 15m E of Elgin.

The A990 coast road leaves the A98
east of Fochabers to run through
Buckie, **Findochty** and **Portknockie**,
small towns of individual character
clinging to the Banffshire coast.
Buckie is an open, breezy place still
very much oriented to the sea: some
houses in the old Seatown have
their gable-ends facing the water
so that boats could be drawn up
between them. Buckie's fortunes
improved with the start of the
herring boom in the 1840s. The fish,
known as 'the silver darlings',
brought prosperity to the town;
the harbour was improved and
expanded, and now serves vessels
which range as far afield as Iceland
and Cornwall. The large twin spires
of the Catholic Church of St Peter
almost give it the appearance of
a cathedral. In West Cluny Place
(the name recalling the landowner
Gordon of Cluny who prospered
here in the 19th century) is the
Maritime Museum, which gives a real
feel for the town's long association
with the sea.

BULLERS OF BUCHAN
Grampian

Off A975 5m S of Peterhead.

Just north of **Cruden Bay** are the
cliffs known as the Bullers of
Buchan, renowned for the birdlife
that crams and crowds them all
year round, screaming and calling
incessantly. Every ledge and
cranny, it seems, holds a bird
or a pair, and nests cling to the
most improbable sites. Gannets,
kittiwakes, fulmars, shags,
cormorants: all are here in great
profusion, especially in the spring
and early summer months when
they are breeding and raising

young. A good footpath leads down to the Bullers. The cliffs themselves plunge several hundred feet into the North Sea, riven by wave incuts, fretted by the never-ending action of the water.

BURGHEAD
Grampian

On B9089/B9103/B9040 10m E of Forres.

From **Findhorn** the long sweep of Burghead Bay curves north-east, backed by dunes and the forest of Roseisle, to reach Burghead itself, on a promontory above sandstone cliffs. There was an ancient Pictish fort here, taken over by Norsemen, who called it Torfness. Their underground well can still be seen: it may have been used for baptismal ceremonies. On the mound above can be seen the site where the Clavie (a tar-filled barrel) is burnt each year on 11 January in one of the highlights of Burghead's year. This is most probably a legacy from an ancient Norse fire festival held to placate the gods for the New Year. Burghead has a neat harbour used by fishing boats and yachtsmen; and a huge grain store on the landward side, used by whisky producers.

CAIRNGORM MOUNTAINS
Grampian/Highland

Straddling the area between Strathspey and Deeside, this vast upland mass presents a solid mountain wall to the roadside observer. It is the greatest expanse of ground in Britain over 3000 feet, a plateau riven by corries of unsurpassed grandeur and cut through by two major hill passes. The area contains four summits over 4000 feet including Cairn Gorm itself and Ben Macdui, second only to Ben Nevis in order of height. The interior, a place of supreme wildness and unfettered beauty, is attainable only by a long march: it should be no other way, and the rewards more than compensate for the effort.

Much can be seen and enjoyed on the fringes of the range, however. From **Aviemore** the Cairngorm ski road passes through **Rothiemurchus** to stop in Coire Cas: the buildings and ski-tows (considered by some to be unsightly) do provide all-year facilities including cafés and toilets. From the **Braemar** side good tracks lead to Derry Lodge and White Bridge from where the mountains can be viewed, or climbed by those with the necessary equipment and experience. These are not hills to be trifled with: the climate is sub-arctic, and summit winds of over 100 mph are far from rare. Much of the area is designated a national nature reserve, the largest in Britain at over 625 000 acres: as would be expected, the flora and fauna are superb, though great concern exists over the poor state of the remnant Caledonian pine forest. There is an exceptional range of literature on the area.

CAITHNESS GLASS
Wick, Highland

Harrowhill, Wick. All year Mon–Fri 0900–1700, Sat 0900–1300 (Apr–Sept, Sat to 1600). D (P). Free (0955 5200).

Visitors can take factory tours to see glass blowing (weekdays only), and there is a shop with a wide range of products and a café. The facilities are expected to improve in 1992 with the opening of new premises.

CALEDONIAN CANAL, see
panel p92.

CANDACRAIG GARDENS AND GALLERY
Strathdon, Grampian

On A944 18m W of Alford. Apr–Oct, daily 0900–1900. D (P).

This Victorian walled garden includes a lovely old summer-house with displays of paintings, a rose garden, and a fountain. There is a visitor centre, tearoom, and plants are for sale.

CANNA, see SMALL ISLES.

CANNICH
Highland

On A831 12m W of Drumnadrochit.

The Caledonian Canal

To build a navigable passage linking the lochs of the Great Glen by stretches of canal, cutting out the long and hazardous sail round the west and north coasts of Scotland, was at the same time an obvious and an extraordinarily bold idea. Conceived 200 years ago and supported by the great engineering brains of the time including John Rennie and James Watt, the task of overseeing the construction was given to a man whose service to the Highlands was immense: **Thomas Telford** (1757–1834).

Designer of roads, bridges and buildings, Telford faced perhaps his greatest challenge with the canal. He had to overcome difficult terrain, impossible weather, intractable landowners and the usual reluctance of government to pay up on time. He had worthy lieutenants, but the enormity of the task wore even them down, so that in 1922, 18 years after work started and shortly before it was due to finish, John Rickman, Secretary to the Canal Commissioners, wrote: 'It has come to the birth but whether strength will be afforded to bring it forth – to open it throughout – I am not confident.'

Happily, his fears were groundless. The great work was completed in the autumn of 1822 and the canal has been regularly used ever since. It still provides a very important 'short cut' for fishing boats travelling from the west coast to the North Sea. Today use of the canal as a recreational area is rising. During the summer of 1991 the graceful vessels in the Tall Ships Race passed through, south to north, en route to Aberdeen.

The canal links Loch Lochy, Loch Oich and **Loch Ness**. Up to 1400 men were employed in its construction; there are splendid flights of locks at Corpach (called Neptune's Staircase), **Laggan**, **Fort Augustus** and **Inverness**.

The canal offers a remarkable sailing experience, particularly through the long trench of Loch Ness with all its stories of monsters, and also provides splendid walking along its towpath, from Fort Augustus, Corpach and Laggan.

The roads through Strath Glass and Glen Urquhart converge at Cannich, a small settlement with hotel, guest houses, youth hostel and shop. From here minor roads lead through two long and beautiful glens, with **hydro-electric** power providing a link between them. West is Glen Cannich, extending for nine miles through forests to the dam at Loch Mullardoch, one of the largest in Scotland. The loch – much enlarged through the power scheme – sits amid superb mountain scenery. From the Mullardoch dam, water is piped to Loch Beinn a'Mheadhoin in **Glen Affric**, which runs south-west from Cannich. Before the glen proper is reached, the Fasnakyle power station is passed. Opened in 1952, the buildings are of a tawny sandstone, to lessen their impact on the scenery. Display boards give information on the power scheme.

CAPE WRATH
Highland

Minibus service from ferry at Keoldale, 1½m W of Durness, May–Sept, daily – for times enquire locally.

The north-western tip of Scotland ends abruptly at cliffs over 500 feet high, topped by a fine Stevenson lighthouse, built in 1828 and still manned. Although the name 'Wrath' may often seem appropriate, its origin is in fact a Norse word meaning a turning point. The minibus goes 12 miles across the uninhabited moorland called the Parph, once noted for wolves, to reach the cape: a diversion can be made on foot to Clo Mor, the highest cliffs on

mainland Britain. In summer the area has superb flowers.

CARDHU DISTILLERY
Knockando, Grampian

*On B9102 6m W of Aberlour.
Easter–Oct, Mon–Sat 0930–1630
Nov–Easter, Mon–Fri 0930–1630
(03406 204).*

The original Cardhu distillery (the name means 'black rock') was founded in 1824, but the one visited today dates from 1885, and was acquired by the Johnnie Walker company in 1893. There are displays, an audio-visual show, distillery tours, tastings, a café, gift shop and picnic area.

CARRBRIDGE
Highland

On A838 7m N of Aviemore.

Carrbridge is an attractive alternative for visitors to Strathspey not wishing to stay in **Aviemore**. Smaller and more homely, it offers a good range of accommodation and has its own station. The notable old bridge dates from 1717; it was damaged in the exceptional floods of 1829. Nearby to the east is Duthill, with the mausoleum of the Grant family. For many people, the main attraction at Carrbridge is the **Landmark Centre**.

CASTLE FRASER
near Kemnay, Grampian

Minor road off A944 10m W of Aberdeen.

93

Jul–Aug, daily 1100–1800; May–Jun, Sept, daily 1400–1800; Oct, Sat–Sun 1400–1700. Garden: all year daily, 0930–sunset. D (P). NTS (03303 463).

The castle, which belongs to the same architectural period as **Craigievar** and **Crathes**, was started about 1575 but not completed until 1636. It takes the form of a large, fortified Z-plan tower-house with courtyard ranges. The round tower, which has a fine balustraded top, survived attacks by Royalist forces in 1638 and 1645. There is a good formal garden and also an adventure playground, picnic area, tearoom and shop.

CASTLE TIORAM
near Acharacle, Highland

At end of minor road, 4m N of Acharacle.
All year. Daily, at low tide. Free.

Castle Tioram (the name means 'dry castle') is on a small island in Loch Moidart, linked to the mainland by a causeway. This pentagonal 14th-century stronghold, seat of the MacDonalds of Clanranald, was in use until 1715, when it was burned to prevent an invading force of Campbells occupying it. The castle can be visited at low tide.

CATTERLINE
Grampian

Off A92 5m S of Stonehaven.

The small coastal village of Catterline, a peaceful place with its neat natural harbour nestling under low cliffs, is especially associated with the artist Joan Eardley, who

drew much inspiration for her land- and seascapes here.

CAWDOR
Highland

On B9090 5m S of Nairn.

For most people, Cawdor equals Macbeth, who in Shakespeare's play is greeted as 'Thane of Cawdor'; and tradition has it that King Duncan was murdered at **Cawdor Castle**. There has certainly been a settlement here for a very long time. The church is 14th-century and has an unusual tower, with a corbelled parapet topped by a pyramid. Parts of the old mill of 1635 also survive. There are other castles nearby: a mile or so west is Kilravock, seat of the Rose family, started in 1460 with later additions, and south of Cawdor is Dalcross Castle, a Lovat foundation of 1620, later the home of the Mackintosh chiefs.

CAWDOR CASTLE
Highland

Off B9090 5m S of Nairn.
May–Sept, daily 1000–1700. D (P) (06677 615).

This has been the home of the Earls of Cawdor for over 600 years. The central tower dates from 1372 and was fortified in 1454. Most of the surrounding buildings are 16th century. There are fine gardens and extensive grounds with woodland walks, plus a nine-hole pitch and putt golf course and a putting green. There are also picnic areas, a restaurant and snack bar and a shop. Although Macbeth became

Thane of Cawdor, the existing castle has no connection with the hero of Shakespeare's play.

CLAN CAMERON MUSEUM
Achnacarry, Highland

On minor road off B8004 at Gairlochy. Easter–Oct, daily 1400–1700. D (0397 7473).

A reconstructed croft house is home to an exhibition on the long history of Clan Cameron. The Camerons supported Prince Charlie in the 1745 Rising, and there are mementos of this period, and of the then chief, known as 'the gentle Lochiel'. There are also displays on the commandos who used the area during 1942–5 and on the Queen's Own Cameron Highlanders regiment.

CLAN MACPHERSON MUSEUM
Newtonmore, Highland

In Newtonmore. May–Sept, Mon–Sat 1000–1730, Sun 1430–1730 (05403 332).

Relics include a letter from Bonnie Prince Charlie to his father, the clan's green banner (which it is said has never witnessed defeat in battle), James MacPherson's fiddle and many other interesting exhibits.

CLAVA CAIRNS
near Inverness, Highland

Minor road off B851 or B9006, 5m E of Inverness. All reasonable times. Free.

From **Culloden** a minor road plunges into the valley of the River Nairn. Unobtrusive signs point to the site of Clava Cairns, a group of chambered cairns with a powerfully evocative atmosphere. The cairns, possibly dating back 4000 years, show the great significance attached to burial sites and rituals at the time. The work involved in constructing them, over the grave passages they contain, was very substantial. The cairns have surrounding low stone circles, and several of the stones bear the mysterious cup-and-ring markings whose full meaning is still unknown.

CLEARANCES, see panel p97.

CLOVERLEAF FIBRE STUD
near Aberchirder, Grampian

Off A97 at Bridge of Marnoch, 2m S of Aberchirder. Guided tours at 1100 and 1430 daily, all year.

Llamas, guanacos, alpacas, goats and rare sheep are bred for their fleeces which are made into garments, sold at the stud's own shop. There are also reindeer.

COCK BRIDGE
Grampian

On A939 10m SE of Tomintoul, 15m NW of Ballater.

For motorists in Scotland, hearing the name Cock Bridge on radio or TV means the coming of winter: the road from here to **Tomintoul**, which reaches a height of over 2000 feet at **The Lecht** ski centre, is usually the first to be closed by snow. This has been a through route for many centuries, commanding the mountains to either side, hence the siting of **Corgarff Castle** here; General Wade used it for one of his **military roads** in the 18th century, which led to the newly built **Fort George** near **Inverness**. Contraband whisky also passed this way. Both south and north of Cock Bridge the line taken by the military roadbuilders varies from the modern road, and can be walked. The southern stretch, beside the River Don through Delachuper, is particularly good. Above Cock Bridge on the A939 are superlative viewpoints looking over **Strathdon** and Deeside.

COIGACH
Highland

W of A835, 5–10m N of Ullapool.

This large, roadless area includes Ben Mor Coigach, a complex mountain rising to 2450 feet. It has sea-cliffs at its western end and further high crags to the east, the most dramatic being Sgurr an Fhidhleir (peak of the fiddler) above Lochan Tuath. A little north is Beinn an Eoin (hill of the birds), another finely shaped mountain. Ben Mor Coigach can be climbed from the small car park at Blughasary, off the A939 seven miles north of **Ullapool**, from where there is also a demanding coastal walk to **Achiltibuie**.

CONON BRIDGE
Highland

On A862 2m S of Dingwall.

The original bridge here is a **Thoma. Telford** design, and dates from 1809. The new bridge carrying the A835 a mile to the north-east was opened in the 1970s and has itself been largely superseded by the A9 Cromarty Firth crossing. The railway bridge – by another great engineer, Joseph Mitchell – is notable. Mitchell himself called it 'a Thomas great triumph'. It is 'skewed' across the River Conon at an angle of 45 degrees, and the south side is 300 feet higher than the north. Mitchell's bridge was opened in 1862 and cost over £11 000.

CORGARFF CASTLE
Grampian

Off A939 at Cock Bridge.
Apr–Sept, Mon–Sat 0930–1900, Sun 1400–1900; Oct–Mar, Mon–Sat 0930–160¢ Sun 1400–1600 (apply to keykeeper in winter months).

Corgarff was built by the Elphinstones in 1537, passed to the Forbes, and was severely damaged by a raiding party in 1571. It was restored only to be burned again by Jacobites in 1689. It was later garrisoned by government troops both to control local rebellion and to try to capture whisky-smugglers The castle has been extensively restored in recent years.

CORRIESHALLOCH GORGE
Highland

At junction of A835/A832, 12m S of Ullapool. All times. Free. NTS (031–226 5922).

This is one of the finest examples o a box canyon in Britain. The River

The Clearances

After the Jacobite defeat at **Culloden**, many Highland chiefs went into exile, their estates forfeited by the crown. In 1784 they were allowed to return, but the situation had changed: their need now was for money, not the service and loyalty of their clansfolk. Experiments by 'improvers' had shown that the glens could support hardy breeds of sheep such as the recently developed Cheviot. Sheep produced income, from wool and mutton; but the animals needed space, and that space was occupied by people living, as they always had done, on hundreds of small crofts. For the landowners, there was only one answer: the people had to go.

The first major Clearances were in 1792 in Sutherland, on land owned by Sir John Sinclair and by Lord Stafford (later the 1st Duke of Sutherland). That year became known in Gaelic as *Bliadhna nan Caorach*, the Year of the Sheep. The people were moved, against their will, to new settlements on the coast, where they had to learn to work the sea and try to scrape a subsistence from often hopeless soil.

Estate factors such as the hated Patrick Sellar carried out their masters' orders with no regard for the well-being of the people, and in the early 19th century the evictions became more and more cruel, with houses burned even as the people struggled to remove a few belongings. In the strath of Kildonan there were at one time nearly 2000 people; all were cleared. The pattern was repeated in other parts of Scotland, notably on the west coast and the islands. There were some small revolts, but if necessary the lairds and sheriff officers simply called in troops to quell these risings.

Unable to survive, thousands emigrated to Canada, the United States and later to Australia. The bad harvests of 1835–6 and the dreadful potato blight of 1846–7, ruining the staple diet and reducing many to starvation, accelerated the emigration process.

The 1st Duke of Sutherland, whose land saw so much clearance, stands today in stone effigy on the summit of Ben Bhraggie, above **Golspie**. Perhaps fittingly, his back is to the empty glens. The full story is well told in John Prebble's book *The Highland Clearances*, in the museum at **Bettyhill** and at the coastal crofting village of **Badbea** in Caithness.

Droma plunges 150 feet over the Falls of Measach into the canyon, which can be viewed from a suspension bridge dizzily spanning the gorge. There is also a viewing platform further down the canyon. The suspension bridge was built in 1867 by Sir John Fowler, one of the designers of the Forth Rail Bridge, who was at the time owner of the Braemore estate, which included the canyon. The span is 82 feet and although the bridge may appear light, it is a very strong structure and a fine piece of engineering.

CORRIEYAIRACK PASS
Highland

Between Fort Augustus and Laggan, Strathspey.

The Corrieyairack was one of the finest of all General Wade's road-building achievements. Completed in 1732, it rises to a summit of 2500 feet. Over 500 men were employed in its construction, and the original line can still be followed: it makes a superb walk. Either side of the summit there are carefully graded zigzags, those on the east being especially fine. There are several original bridges: one, at Glen Shira, stands abandoned in a field, but that at Garvamore is still in use. It was Wade's first double-span bridge.

CRAIGELLACHIE
Highland

On A95/A941 4m NW of Dufftown.

Craigellachie lies at an important junction of rivers as well as roads:

here the Fiddich, rushing down from the hills beyond **Dufftown**, bursts impatiently into the Spey. The village has a Victorian feel to it with fine villas and substantial hotels, and was indeed a favoured place for holidays in the 19th century. It is still used by fishermen and walkers: the Speyside Way path passes through the village. Craigellachie means 'strong rock' and the tough gneiss of the cliff across the Spey provided one anchor for **Thomas Telford**'s bridge of 1814. This is a masterpiece: the oldest iron bridge in Scotland, designed to make the very best use of the new material in a light, graceful yet very strong structure. The iron was cast in Wales by William Hazledine, known as Merlin because of the magic he wrought. The bridge sustained heavy traffic until 1973, when the new road bridge was opened. The poet Robert Southey celebrated the bridge in verse and the noted local fiddler Will Marshall composed a dance tune called Craigellachie Brig in its honour. There is a distillery in Craigellachie (on the Dufftown road) and another above the village, across the Spey, where the well-known Macallan malt is produced.

CRAIGIEVAR CASTLE
Grampian

Off A980 25m W of Aberdeen.
May–Sept, daily 1400–1800. Grounds: all year, daily 0930–sunset. D (P). NTS (03398 83635).
Visitor numbers may be restricted.

Craigievar is just how a child draws a castle, with high battlemented towers, small windows, and an air

Crofting

Crofting has changed, and is experiencing something of a revival. Up to the end of the 19th century, it was a way of life. The crofter held a small amount of land and sustained himself and his family by keeping cattle and sheep and growing potatoes and other produce. Byproducts such as wool and hide were also put to use. After the Clearances, many crofters were forced to move to the coast and had to learn a new way of existence, with fishing the main activity, supported by whatever could be grown on the poor land they were given.

In the latter part of the 19th century, there were a number of uprisings as crofters protested against their treatment at the hands of landowners and estate factors. These risings culminated in the 'Battle of the Braes' on the island of **Skye**, which was thought (potentially at least) so serious by the government in London that a force of Marines was despatched to quell the riot.

Lord Napier was then asked to head a commission to look into the situation in the crofting areas. His report, combined with the campaigning efforts of the Highland Land League, which successfully sponsored several MPs, led to the 1886 Crofting Act, which gave crofters security of tenure and other rights.

In the 20th century, crofting alone has not been able to provide a livelihood: other employment has had to complement crofting. Crofters do all manner of jobs, from manual to highly skilled labour, but the croft is crucial to their way of life.

There were 'land raids' after both World Wars when returning servicemen tried to claim what they felt they had been fighting for, but in general it can be said that for much of this century crofting went through a period of quiet decline. In recent years there has been a vigorous revival, spearheaded by a small number of men who established the Scottish Crofters Union in 1986.

Dr James Hunter, the union's first director, has written several books about crofting, and is a passionate advocate of the crofting way of life. He (and others) feel that crofting has much to offer, providing secure tenure on a small amount of land and ensuring that land is kept in good heart, while the crofter contributes to the local economy both by the produce of the croft and by the work he carries out as his main occupation.

(continued)

Crofting *(continued)*

The traditional crofting areas are the western and northern Highlands and the islands, particularly the Hebrides. These are still crofting's heartland, but the edges are beginning to spread out a little with signs that crofting may be gaining a foothold in Argyll and some of the eastern counties. The SCU now has several thousand members and has negotiated further improvements in the legal position of crofters.

The basic croft consisting of a house with a long, thin strip of land behind it can still be seen, especially on the islands. Agricultural development programmes in the Hebrides and elsewhere have been careful to conserve the nature of crofting while enabling crofters to make improvements. Tree-planting on crofts is becoming more common. Trees, even if planted by the crofter, were formerly the possessions of the landlord, this is no longer the case, and crofters can harvest timber crops themselves.

Highlands and Islands Enterprise continues the work of its predecessor, the HIDB, in supporting crofting as an integral part of the Highland way of life, and the croft seems set not just to survive but to flourish in the 21st century.

---

of impregnability. It is perhaps the best of all the Aberdeenshire tower-houses, and was built by William Forbes, known as Danzig Willie because of the extent of his trade with that Baltic port. The castle stayed in the Forbes-Sempill family until 1963. Inside, there are superb plaster ceilings, a long gallery, and much fine furniture and ornament. The extensive grounds contain picnic areas and woodland walks. There is a café and shop.

CRAIGSTON CASTLE
near Turriff, Grampian

On B9105 4m NE of Turriff. Open occasionally in summer: enquire locally or telephone (08885 228).

The castle has been an Urquhart seat since it was built in 1607. It ha fine woodlands around it.

CRATHES CASTLE
Grampian

On A93 15m W of Aberdeen.
Easter–end Oct, daily 1100–1800. Gardens and grounds: all year, daily, 0930–sunset.
D (P). NTS (033 044 525).

Crathes was built by and was for centuries owned by the Burnetts of the Leys, whose original home was on an island in Loch of the Leys (long since drained). The move to Crathes was a slow one, starting in the 1560s but not completed for over 40 years, due mainly to the death of two lairds in quick succession. The castle's noteworthy features include ceilings both of painted wood and of plaster. In the Muses Room, the Seven Virtues grace the beams. A prized relic is the Horn of Leys, said to have been given to Alexander de Burnard by Robert the Bruce. The extensive grounds have topiary yew hedges, walled gardens, woodland walks and nature trails (one for the disabled). Among regular summer attractions are ranger-led expeditions to hear the 'dawn chorus'. Crathes has a visitor centre with exhibitions, restaurant, shop, play areas and a dog trail.

CREAG MEAGAIDH
Highland

Access from Aberarder on A86, 17m E of Spean Bridge, 20m W of Newtonmore.

The Creag Meagaidh massif was bought by the Nature Conservancy Council (now Scottish Natural Heritage) in 1985 to stave off threatened large-scale commercial afforestation. The national nature reserve extends to 10 000 acres taking in birch woodland, a fine high corrie and superb mountains. The hills rise from the shores of Loch Laggan. There is a small visitor centre at the former farmhouse of Aberarder, the main point of access for the range. A path leads up through the birch woods into Coire Ardair (corrie of high waters) with its loch and cliffs, noted for their winter climbing, and beyond to the notch in the ridge above known as the Window, which gives access to the surrounding summits. Across Loch Laggan is Ardverikie, once

visited by **Queen Victoria** and Prince Albert in Scotland with a view to purchase. Their time here was marred by poor weather and persistent midges, and they turned east to Deeside instead.

CROFTING, see panel p99.

CROICK CHURCH
Highland

Minor road for 10m W from Ardgay on A836. All reasonable times. Free.

From **Ardgay**, a narrow road winds up Strathcarron into increasingly lonely country. The area was once well populated, but was cleared in the mid 19th century. Some of the people of Glen Calvie took refuge in the small church at Croick in 1845 during a **Clearance**, and scratched a number of poignant messages on the window glass, which can still be seen today. Unusually, the church, which is modest enough, was designed by none other than **Thomas Telford**, the engineer much better known for bridges, roads and canals. Just outside the churchyard are the remains of a **broch**.

CROMARTY
Highland

On A832 24m NE of Inverness.

Cromarty, at the east end of the **Black Isle**, was once a royal burgh and a thriving port, but its fortunes declined in the 17th century. Later George Ross established clothing factories and a brewery here, and more recently it has become a holiday centre. There are a number of fine old houses and the Court House, built by George Ross in 1782, has a cupola with clock. The parish church features three 18th-century lofts, and the gaol has been turned into a visitor attraction. Cromarty was the birthplace, in 1802, of Hugh Miller, who attained fame as a pioneering geologist and was also a noted theologian. **Hugh Miller's Cottage** can be visited.

CRUDEN BAY
Grampian

On A975 8m S of Peterhead.

Cruden Bay has a good sandy beach with a golf course behind it on the dunes. To the east is the small harbour of Port Erroll, named for the Earls of Erroll, for centuries lairds in these parts. The 9th Earl built New Slains Castle on the cliffs here in about 1600; later, the lexicographer Dr Samuel Johnson was entertained here. It has been suggested that the novelist Bram Stoker based Dracula's Castle on Slains, after staying in Cruden Bay. At Cruden Bay the pipeline from the North Sea Forties oilfield comes ashore, starting its land journey to Grangemouth. Just to the north are the noted sea-bird cliffs of **Bullers of Buchan**.

CULLEN
Grampian

On A98 20m E of Elgin.

Cullen is known as 'the pearl of the Banffshire coast'. Clustered around the harbour is the old Seatown,

where many cottages have been restored. The upper town is divided from it by huge railway viaducts, no longer carrying trains but still a notable landmark. Designed by Patrick Barnett, they were built in 1884 because the then Countess of Seafield refused permission for the line to run further inland, near Cullen House. Similarly, the present town of Cullen is sited where it is because, in 1822, the Earl of Seafield felt the village was too close to the house, so had it demolished and re-sited further away. The town has spacious streets and a fine square, with the cross which the villagers brought with them when they were forced to move. The Auld Kirk can still be seen on the original site. Much of it is 14th century; inside, the Seafield Loft dates from 1602. From Cullen a fine coast walk leads east to the ruin of Findlater Castle, an Ogilvie stronghold precariously sited on a promontory. Care is needed when exploring here: there are steep, sudden drops.

CULLODEN
Highland

On B9006 5m E of Inverness.
Visitor centre: Jun–mid Sept, daily 0900–1830; Apr–May, mid Sept–Oct, daily 0900–1730; Feb–Mar, Nov–Dec, daily 1000–1600 (closed Christmas). Battle site: all year, daily. D (P). NTS (0463 790607).

On bleak Drumossie Moor the last hopes of the Jacobites seeking to re-establish the Stuarts on the British throne were extinguished on a cold April day in 1746. It was not so much a battle as a débâcle. Everything was stacked against the Jacobites: the site was (from their angle) poorly chosen; the government forces under the Duke of Cumberland were superior in numbers and equipment; and the Jacobites were tired and hungry after a forced night march. There could be only one outcome. After the defeat Prince Charlie, no longer Bonnie, became a hunted fugitive, narrowly evading capture time after time until he finally escaped to France, never to return. The visitor centre has full interpretive displays, an audio-visual show, café and shop. The battlefield is itself evocative, with its many cairns and memorials to the clansmen who fell here. Culloden village is largely a dormitory suburb of **Inverness**. Another impressive site, **Clava Cairns**, is nearby.

DALLAS DHU DISTILLERY
near Forres, Grampian

Off A940 2m S of Forres. Apr–Sept,
Mon–Sat 0930–1900, Sun 1400–1700. HS.

This little Victorian distillery
has been taken over by Historic
Scotland as a classic example of its
kind, and offers guided tours, a film
on the history of whisky- making,
an exhibition, café, picnic area
and a shop with 200 whiskies
for sale.

DALWHINNIE
Highland

On A9 45m N of Perth.

Dalwhinnie is on the northern side
of the Drumochter Pass, set at over
1100 feet at the head of Loch Ericht.
The most distinctive building is
Dalwhinnie Distillery. Dalwhinnie
means 'meeting place': through
ways from south, north and west
do indeed meet here, and the
cattle drovers, whisky-smugglers
and Jacobite renegades from earlier
times have been replaced by
tourists speeding up the A9, which
follows the line of General Wade's
road north towards Ruthven
Barracks (see **Kingussie**) and
Inverness.

DALWHINNIE DISTILLERY
Dalwhinnie, Highland

May–Sept, Mon–Fri 0930–1600
(05282 264).

The distillery, which was
founded in 1898 and claims
to be the highest in Scotland,

offers free guided tours plus
a malt whisky tasting. It
has a visitor centre and
shop.

DARNAWAY ESTATE
near Forres, Grampian

Off A96 3m W of Forres.

On its way to the sea, the River
Findhorn twists through the
Darnaway estate of the Earls of
Moray. The extensive forest, much
of it mature, was used for the
individual race in the 1976 World
Orienteering Championships,
and provided a tough test of
navigation and fitness. The work
of the estate today is explained in
the **Darnaway Farm Visitor Centre**.
Darnaway Castle is mostly an early
19th-century reconstruction on
the site of a much older building.
It has been a Moray home for
500 years.

DARNAWAY FARM VISITOR CENTRE
near Forres, Grampian

Off A96 3m W of Forres. Jun–mid
Sept, daily 1000–1700. Ranger-led
estate tours, including Darnaway
Castle, Jul–Aug, Wed, Thu, Sun
1300–1500.
D (P) (0309 72213).

The visitor centre has an
exhibition on the work of the
extensive **Darnaway Estate**,
with audio-visual presentation.
The milking parlour can be
seen and there are walks,
a tearoom and children's
play area.

DEER, see **RED DEER** panel p194.

DEER ABBEY
Old Deer, Grampian

On B9029 1m W of Mintlaw.
Apr–Sept, Thu–Sat 0930–1900, Sun
1400–1900. Free.

The abbey was founded in 1218 by William Comyn, Earl of Buchan, for Cistercian monks from Kinloss, on the site of an earlier Celtic monastery from which came the Book of Deer, a Latin manuscript of parts of the New Testament annotated in Gaelic. It is now in Cambridge University Library. Relatively little of the abbey survives, though its outline can be traced.

DELGATIE CASTLE
near Turriff, Grampian

Off A947 3m S of Turriff. Apr–Sept,
Fri–Sun 1400–1700 (08886 3479,
mornings only).

The tower home of the Hays of Delgatie, Earls of Erroll, dates back to the 13th century, though it has been much altered since, and has notable painted ceilings and a turnpike stair with 97 steps. Mary Queen of Scots stayed here in 1562.

DIABAIG
Highland

On minor road on N shore of Loch
Torridon, 20m W of Kinlochewe via A896.

The road through Glen Torridon passes under the magnificent mountains of **Beinn Eighe** and Liathach, and at **Torridon** village, a minor road takes off along the north shore of the loch, leading on past Inveralligin to twist its way over the very steep Bealach na Gaoithe (pass of the winds) to Diabaig (more correctly, Lower Diabaig). The village could hardly have a more inspiring setting, on its own small loch incut from Loch Torridon, looking across to the northern part of the **Applecross** peninsula. From Diabaig a fine coastal walk leads past the isolated Craig youth hostel to Redpoint.

DINGWALL
Highland

On A862 12m NW of Inverness.

The name means 'council place' in Norse and Dingwall, a Norse colony said to have been the birthplace of Macbeth, has been a royal burgh since 1226. It is still an administrative centre, holding the offices of Ross and Cromarty District Council. The Town House includes much on the life of the noted soldier Sir Hector MacDonald, also commemorated by the large monument on Mitchell Hill above the town. The obelisk near the church is somewhat different in character. It marks the burial place of the 1st Earl of Cromartie '3ft 6in to the S thereof' – reputedly to stop his wife from dancing on his grave. The railway divides here, branching west to **Kyle of Lochalsh** and north to **Wick** and **Thurso**.

DOLLS MUSEUM
Strathpeffer, Highland

Spa Cottage, The Square. Easter–Sept, Mon, Wed–Sun 1400–1800 (0997 21549).

A private house holds a small but appealing exhibition of dolls and other memorabilia.

DORNIE
Highland

On A87 9m E of Kyle of Lochalsh.

Where three lochs – Duich, Shiel and Long – meet, the small settlements of Dornie and Ardelve have grown up. Offshore are two islands. Eilean Tioram (dry island) is linked to the shore at low tide. The other is linked at all times, by the bridge which leads to the famous castle, **Eilean Donan**. From Dornie the minor road beside Loch Long leads to Glen Elchaig, one of the starts for the walk to the **Falls of Glomach**.

DORNOCH
Highland

On A949 (off A9) 6m N of Tain.

The opening of the Dornoch Firth bridge has cut 20 miles off the southern approach to Dornoch and made the historic old town that much more accessible. Crossing the firth, wide expanses of sand on either bank are visible, where Dornoch has a links golf course. The town has been a royal burgh since 1628 and was formerly the seat of the Bishops of Caithness, whose palace is now a hotel.

The square contains the **Dornoch Cathedral** and a craft centre in the old jail. Dornoch claims the dubiou distinction of having burned the las witch in Scotland, in 1722.

Nearby are two castles with similar names but very different histories. Skelbo, six miles to the north, is a ruin dating from the 13th century, the name meaning 'place of shells'. Skibo, west of Dornoch, is a vast early 20th-century pile buil by the steel millionaire Andrew Carnegie. It is not open to the public. On a minor road four miles north of Dornoch is Embo, a fishing village and holiday resort with extensive sands.

DORNOCH CATHEDRAL
Highland

Dornoch Town Square. All year. Daily, 0900–dusk. D (P). Free (0862 810325).

Founded in 1224 by Gilbert de Moravia, Bishop of Caithness, the cathedral was fired in 1570 during a clan feud between Murrays and Mackays, and has been restored several times since. It has fine 13th-century stonework.

DOUNREAY
Highland

On A836 6m W of Thurso.

The name of Dounreay is inextricably associated with nuclear power, due to the siting here of the prototype fast reactor station, which resulted in a considerable influx of people to the **Thurso** area. The 'golfball' dome, though familiar from photographs, still comes as a urprise when seen. The **Dounreay Visitor Centre** is attached to the power station. The chief of Clan Mackay, Lord Reay, takes his name from the settlement here (two miles west of the power station) where the 1739 church has an interesting external stairway. Sandside Bay is well named: it has a lovely beach with flower-rich dunes.

DOUNREAY VISITOR CENTRE
Highland

On A836 6m W of Thurso. Easter–Sept, daily 0900–1630. Free. (0847 62121 xt 656).

An exhibition shows how nuclear power works and why the station here was established, and conducted tours of the plant are offered each afternoon (over 12s only, no dogs). There is a picnic area, tearoom and shop.

DRUM CASTLE
near Peterculter, Grampian

On minor road off A93 10m W of Aberdeen. May–Sept, daily 1400–1800; Oct, Sat–Sun 1400–1700. Garden: Jul–Sept, daily 1000–1800; Oct, Sat–Sun 1400–1700. Grounds: all year, daily 0930–sunset. D P). NTS (03308 204).

This is one of the oldest tower-houses in Scotland, dating from 1286, and is the only one to have remained very largely in the original state. In the early 17th century an Irvine laird added a court and mansionhouse with two square towers. Further additions took place in the 19th century.

There is a walled garden containing fine historic roses.

DRUMBEG
Highland

On B869 35m N of Ullapool.

Leaving the A894 just south of the Kylesku Bridge, the B869 dips and rises sharply several times before reaching the crofting village of Drumbeg on Eddrachillis Bay. It commands superb seaward views north to Scourie and inland soar the ridges of Quinag ('the milking pail', an odd name for a mountain). The road continues westwards with more magnificent views through Clashnessie and Clashtoll to **Lochinver**. A diversion leads to Culkein and the walk to the Point of Stoer, just west of which is the isolated rock stack known as the Old Man of Stoer, a challenge to climbers.

DRUMNADROCHIT
Highland

On A82 15m S of Inverness, 20m N of Fort Augustus.

Halfway up the west side of **Loch Ness**, the road takes a substantial diversion around Urquhart Bay to reach the village of Drumnadrochit ('bridge on the ridge', or possibly 'back bridge'). It is notable for having not one but two Loch Ness exhibitions, the **Loch Ness Lodge Visitor Centre** and the **Official Loch Ness Monster Exhibition Centre**. South of the village on the lochside is **Urquhart Castle**, a favourite 'monster watching' point. A little further south is a memorial to John Cobb, who lost his life on the loch in 1952 trying to break the world water speed record.

DUFF HOUSE
Banff, Grampian

Off A98 at S edge of Banff. Apr–Sept, Mon–Sat 0930–1900, Sun 1400–1900. D (P).

William Adam's baroque masterpiece, said to have been modelled on the Villa Borghese in Rome, was never completed but is still a rich example of his work. Commissioned by the 1st Earl of Fife around 1735, the design included an impressive façade resembling that of Hopetoun House near Edinburgh. The building has seen various uses in recent years and is still being restored. Its original cost was £70 000, an enormous sum for 1740. There is a fine walk up the Deveron River to the Bridge of Alvah from the house, passing the Duff family mausoleum.

DUFFTOWN
Grampian

On A941 17m S of Elgin.

It used to be said that: 'Rome was built on seven hills, Dufftown stands on seven stills' and certainly **whisky** is an important business hereabouts, each distillery claiming special properties for its product. As you enter Dufftown from the west you pass three in a row, including **Glenfiddich Distillery**, which has full visitor facilities. In its grounds is **Balvenie Castle**, whose long history is surpassed by that of Mortlach Church; the original

foundation here was by St Moluag in 566. The present T-shaped church has interesting stained-glass windows, one showing a locomotive and another rubber-tapping in Malaysia. By the River Dullan is the Battle Stone, marking a victory of Malcolm II over Norse invaders in 1040. Dufftown was largely planned in the early 19th century by James Duff, Earl of Fife; the four main streets meet at the Town House of 1836, which houses a local museum.

DUFFUS CASTLE
near Elgin, Grampian

Off B9012 5m NW of Elgin. Apr–Sept, Mon–Sat 0930–1900, Sun 1400–1900; Oct–Mar, Mon–Sat 0930–1600, Sun 1400–1600. Free.

Though ruinous, Duffus still makes a dramatic impression as it rises from the coastal plain. Freskin de Moravia started the fortification here in the 12th century; the substantial tower was added by Nicholas Sutherland in the 14th century. The moat is still filled with water. Nearby is the ruined 13th-century Duffus Old Church and St Peter's Cross, a medieval mercat cross.

DUNBEATH
Highland

On A9 16m N of Helmsdale.

The A9 bypasses Dunbeath but the short diversion into the village is well worth taking. The neat harbour is still used by fishing boats and has splendid birdlife. Offshore is the Beatrice oilfield, the only North Sea field visible from the mainland. It can be viewed through binoculars from the **Dunbeath Heritage Centre**, opened by the Queen Mother in 1989. A heritage trail has also been set up, going inland up the strath past a meal mill, **broch** and other interesting sites. Dunbeath was the birthplace of the author Neil Gunn in 1891. Its 17th-century castle, much altered, has been renovated and is lived in. Two miles north is **Laidhay Croft Museum**. On the moors some six miles west, a cross marks the place where the Duke of Kent was killed in a plane crash in 1942. Dunbeath estate has a large flock of cashmere goats, breeding the animals for their fine wool.

DUNBEATH HERITAGE CENTRE
Dunbeath, Highland

Jun–Sept, Mon–Sat 1000–1700, Sun 1100–1800; May, Mon–Fri 1000–1300, 1400–1700, Sat 1400–1700, Sun 1100–1800; Apr, Mon–Fri 1000–1300, 1400–1700. D (P) (05933 233).

Tableaux show Dunbeath's history from earliest times to the present day with soundtrack effects. There is an audio-visual programme, and displays on geology and wildlife.

DUNCANSBY HEAD
Highland

Minor road off A9 2m E of John o'Groats.

On a clear day, the rewards for taking the road that winds across moorland from **John o'Groats** to the lighthouse at Duncansby Head are great. The lighthouse itself is relatively recent, dating only

from 1924; it is manned and is not open to visitors. The view is very extensive, taking in much of the Caithness coast and a fair panoply of **Orkney** islands, pointed out by a viewpoint indicator. But the real riches lie a little south, gained by a short walk along the coast and round the deep and impressive Sclaites Geo, noisy with both waves and sea-birds. Soon enough the Duncansby Stacks come into view: towering pyramidic rock pillars in the sea, they make an unforgettable impression.

DUNDONNELL
Highland

On A835 20m SW of Ullapool.

Dundonnell is in an enviable situation at the head of Little Loch Broom. There are only a few buildings: a hotel, a youth hostel, and the Smiddy, a climbers' hut which was indeed converted from an old smithy, and won an award in 1975. Dundonnell House dates from 1769 and its Japanese gardens and aviary are occasionally open. Dundonnell's name is known to thousands of climbers and hill-walkers, for above it towers the superb mountain An Teallach (the forge). Its ridge is magnificent, providing scrambling as well as superlative views.

DUNNET
near Thurso, Highland

On A836 6m E of Thurso.

Driving east from **Thurso**, the road sweeps round the glorious expanse of Dunnet Bay with its extensive sands and rich birdlife. At its western end is Castletown, a 19th-century settlement which thrived on the production of flagstones from local quarries; many can still be seen in use as field boundaries. Dunnet village has a fine old church, parts of which are 14th century; its saddleback tower is a notable feature. Timothy Pont, a famous mapmaker, was minister here from 1601 to 1608. Minor roads lead north past St John's Loch to Dunnet Head, the most northerly point of the British mainland, from where the views are magnificent. The cliffs are over 300 feet high, but even so the lighthouse (an 1831 Robert Stevenson design) has had windows shattered in winter storms by sea debris hurled up by wind and waves. The Queen Mother's Scottish home, the Castle of Mey, is five miles to the east. The castle, which was originally called Barrogill, dates from about 1600. It is not open to the public.

DUNNOTTAR CASTLE
near Stonehaven, Grampian

Off A92 2m S of Stonehaven.
Apr–Oct, Mon–Sat 0900–1800, Sun
1400–1700; Nov–Mar, Mon–Fri 0900–1600
(0569 62173).

You could hardly imagine a more perfect site for a castle than this: atop cliffs on a promontory jutting into the wild North Sea. Little wonder that the director Franco Zeffirelli chose it in 1990 for his film version of *Hamlet*. Dunnottar dates back at least to the seventh century; the earliest parts left today are 13th century, most dating from the late 16th or early 17th centuries. It was besieged by Montrose in 1645 and

in 1652 saw the Scottish crown jewels and other treasures – sent there for safe keeping – smuggled out during another siege, by Cromwell's troops. The regalia went to **Kinneff**, just down the coast. In 1685 over 100 prisoners died here after being crammed into a small space for two summer months. There is a very good walk from **Stonehaven** along the cliffs to Dunnottar, which can be continued to the RSPB reserve of **Fowlsheugh**.

DUNROBIN CASTLE
near Golspie, Highland

On A9 2m N of Golspie. June–mid Sept,
Mon–Sat 1030–1730, Sun 1300–1730.
Gardens: all year, daily 0930–sunset, free
when castle is closed. D (P) (04083 3177).

Dunrobin, which is still lived in, has the appearance of a fairytale castle with its tall turrets and towers. The home of the Dukes of Sutherland for centuries, the castle has grand state rooms with magnificent furniture and ornaments. The extensive grounds, running down to the sea, contain woodland as well as fine formal gardens. The museum is a former summer-house which contains many interesting exhibits, rightly described in the castle's own brochure as 'a unique and eccentric collection' accumulated by the family.

DURNESS
Highland

On A838 22m W of Tongue.

The small town of Durness sits on an outcrop of limestone that has led to the relative fertility of the soil and also to the coastal formations including Smoo Caves, east of the town (open all year). There are three caves, of which the outer is most easily seen: it is very impressive, being 200 feet long and 30 feet high. To the north of Durness, the walk out to Faraid Head reveals fine coastal scenery and a rich variety of plants. From Keoldale the ferry crosses to the minibus for **Cape Wrath**. A little to the west of Durness is Balnakiel. The name means 'church homestead' and it is said that St Maelrubha founded a church here in the early eighth century. The present building is from 1619 but has not been used for worship for over a century. The grave of

Rob Donn, 18th-century poet, may be seen here. Balnakiel has a thriving craft village, housed in unpretentious former military buildings.

DYCE
Grampian

On A947 5m NW of Aberdeen.

Dyce, a large and rather sprawling suburb of Aberdeen, is the site of the airport for the area. From here helicopters shuttle out to the oil rigs of the North Sea and back. The old church of St Fergus holds two fine Pictish stones.

EAS COUL AULIN
near Kylesku, Highland

At head of Loch Glencoul, 3m E of A894.

This wild, uninhabited place would scarcely be visited were it not for statistics which tell us that the Eas Coul Aulin, sliding over the Leiter Dubh (dark slope) on its way to Loch Beag, an inlet from the larger Loch Glencoul, is the tallest waterfall in Britain, with a measured drop of 685 feet. It can be approached either from the A894 near Loch na Gainhmich, a rough moorland trek of three miles, or by boat from **Kylesku** in summer into Loch Beag, which still means a walk of a mile or so to see the falls.

ECHT
Grampian

On B9119 12m W of Aberdeen.

This odd little name may simply mean 'hilly place'. The small village does have hills around it, notably the Barmekin of Echt to the north-west, the summit of which has extensive Iron Age fortifications. To the east is a good stone circle at Cullerlie. There are further standing stones to the west at Midmar, where the 17th-century church has its own stone circle in the churchyard. Midmar Castle (not open to the public) is late 16th century; above it rises forestry and then the Hill of Fare, site of the Battle of Corrichie in 1562, at which the Earl of Huntly's forces were defeated by those of Mary Queen of Scots.

EIGG, see SMALL ISLES.

EILEAN DONAN CASTLE
Dornie, Highland

On A87 9m E of Kyle of Lochalsh. Easter–Sept, daily 1000–1800 (0599 85202).

Eilean Donan, on an island reached by a bridge, is one of the best-known of all Scottish landmarks. The original castle was established in 1230. Mackenzie lords added a large tower-house in the 14th century before moving east and leaving Eilean Donan to the Macraes, who made further additions. In 1719, during a curious episode in which Spanish ships sailed up Loch Duich in support of the Jacobite cause and a skirmish took place on the **Kintail** hills, the castle was bombarded by English forces. It remained ruined until Colonel John Macrae started extensive restoration work earlier this century, finishing the work in 1932 and leaving the castle which is so admired today. Realignment of the A87 nearer the lochside has taken away the former 'surprise view' of the castle coming over the brae from Inverinate; the old road can still be walked to enjoy the view. The castle has displays, mementos of Clan Macrae and a gift shop.

ELGIN
Grampian

On A96/A941 12m E of Forres, 17m W of Keith.

Elgin (the name derives from a Celtic term meaning 'little

reland') is the largest town in Morayshire, with a population of about 16 500. Modern planners have preserved the heart of the old burgh, including the cobbled market place, the Plainstones. Lady Hill, once a motte (fortified mound), now holds a large statue of the Duke of Gordon. The main street was notable for its arcaded passages; few have survived. Tower House and Thunderton House (now both inns) are 17th century; Bonnie Prince Charlie stayed in the latter before the Battle of **Culloden**. There are several fine classical 19th-century buildings including St Giles Church (designed by Simpson, 1832) with its large Greek portico and Dr Gray's Hospital (Gillespie Graham, 1819). But the main glory of Elgin is the ruined **Elgin Cathedral**, called the 'lanthorn of the North'. An interesting town trail can be followed on foot. Elgin, which enjoys a mild climate, is a prosperous place today, with good shops and other facilities, and is a centre for tourism in the area. Whisky is distilled at the Glen Moray Distillery in Bruceland Road.

ELGIN CATHEDRAL
Grampian

Elgin. Apr–Sept, Mon–Sat 0930–1900, un 1400–1900; Oct–Mar, Mon–Sat 030–1600, Sun 1400–1600. D (P).

The great twin towers of Elgin Cathedral dominate the town. This was once the most splendid cathedral in Scotland but due to neglect in the 16th and 17th centuries, it fell into disrepair. Building started in the mid 13th century and additions continued for three centuries. The cathedral was not used for services after about 1560 and was plundered for lead and building stone. What remains is still impressive.

ELLON
Grampian

Off A92 16m N of Aberdeen.

Ellon, now partly a commuter town for **Aberdeen**, is an ancient settlement at an important crossing-point on the River Ythan; the fine 18th-century bridge has been superseded by a modern road bridge. West, towards **Pitmedden**, is the Prop of Ythsie, a large stone tower erected in memory of Lord Aberdeen, who was Prime Minister from 1852 to 1855. It commands an extensive view over the fertile farmlands of Buchan.

ERIBOLL
Highland

On A838 20m W of Tongue.

It is said that naval crews stationed here in World War II called the place 'Loch 'Orrible'; it can certainly be wild, but to most eyes it is beautiful rather than the reverse. The long, sheltered loch is ringed by hills, and the lower ground is fertile. On the roadside at Eriboll is the last telephone in Britain using the old 'push button A' method; left here almost by accident, it is now carefully preserved. To the north is Whiten Head, one of the few British breeding places of the grey seal. Access by foot is difficult, but there are summer boat trips from **Durness**.

ERISKAY
Western Isles

Car ferry from Ludag on South Uist,
Mon–Sat all year.

Eriskay is remembered for three
things: the landing of Bonnie Prince
Charlie on 23 July 1945 – his first
touch of Scottish soil; the wreck of
the SS *Politician* in 1941, inspiring
Compton Mackenzie's novel *Whisky
Galore*; and the 'Eriskay Love Lilt',
one of many folk tunes collected
on the islands by Mrs Marjory
Kennedy Fraser. Eriskay ponies,
only 12 hands high, are still used to
carry peats and seaweed.

Eriskay today holds a community
of about 200. Modern fishing
vessels operate from the sheltered
harbour, and a unique pattern of
knitwear is made here and exported
far afield. A new pub called, after
the famous wreck, Am Politician,
opened in 1988. Eriskay is a
Catholic island, and the Church
of St Michael's has an altar made
from the bow of a lifeboat and a bell
taken from a German battleship.

EVANTON
Highland

On A9 7m NE of Dingwall.

Above the small village of Evanton
is the remarkable Black Rock
Ravine, a two-mile gorge in places
200 feet deep and only 12 feet
wide, cut by the River Glass. The
minor road up Strath Glass leads
in a mile to a path and footbridge
spanning the gorge, which is as fine
as **Corrieshalloch** but much less well
known. General Sir Hector Munro,
who lived at Novar House, erected
the odd Indian temple on Knock
Fyrish, north of the village. It is
based on the gateway of a town in
India captured by troops under his
command in 1781.

FALLS OF GLOMACH
near Morvich, Highland

Access by path from either Glen Elchaig or Dorusduain, both off A87 at Dornie and Morvich respectively. NTS (031–226 5922).

The dramatic falls, 370 feet high, are remote from any road, and the walk in needs good footwear and a stout heart; by the shortest way from Dorusduain, it is a ten-mile round trip. The Glen Elchaig approach is longer – seven miles each way – and is a demanding but rewarding full-day excursion.

FASQUE HOUSE
near Fettercairn, Grampian

On B974 1m N of Fettercairn.
May–Sept, daily except Fridays 1330–1730.
Ͻ (P) (05614 201).

The house, a Gladstone family home for two centuries, has public rooms on view and also a 'below stairs' section of kitchens, pantry and other rooms. It is surrounded by a large deer park. There are mementos of the life of William Ewart Gladstone (1809–98), who was Prime Minister no fewer than four times: first from 1868 to 1874; again from 1880 to 1885; briefly in 1886–7; and again from 1892, only resigning from office in 1894 at the advanced age of 85 years.

FEARN
Highland

On B9166 6m SE of Tain.

The village of Fearn is at the centre of the large promontory separating the Dornoch and Cromarty Firths.

It is richly fertile land with high sunshine figures. Fearn Station is nearly two miles from the village, which is notable for its abbey, the earliest parts of which are 14th century. The nave and choir are still used as the parish church. To the east, the coast at Balintore and Shandwick has good beaches.

FETTERCAIRN
Grampian

On B996/B974 4m W of Laurencekirk.

Queen Victoria and Prince Albert were here in September 1861, at the end of a typically long day from **Balmoral** over Mount Keen. Their visit was unannounced, and in the late evening they 'went out and walked through the whole village, where not a creature moved'. The turreted arch at the entry to the village was erected later to mark their visit. Fettercairn is still a quiet place, backed by hills and forests and looking out over the rich farmland of the Howe of the Mearns. The annual show, in early July, is one of the best of its kind, with varied livestock and entertaining stalls. **Fettercairn Distillery** where Old Fettercairn malt is produced can be visited, as can **Fasque**.

FETTERCAIRN DISTILLERY
Grampian

Off B974 just W of Fettercairn village.
All year. Mon–Fri 1000–1600. Free
(05614 205).

Fettercairn claims to be Scotland's second oldest distillery, dating from 1824. W.E. Gladstone was one of

Fish Farming

With the energetic support of the Highlands and Islands Development Board (now Highlands and Islands Enterprise), fish farming showed dramatic growth through much of the 1970s and 1980s. From three experimental units in the late 1960s, at **Lochailort**, Otter Ferry on Loch Fyne and Ardtoe in **Ardnamurchan**, the industry expanded to over 300 farms 20 years later.

The west coast lochs, and the islands, have proved an ideal environment for fish farming. Both fresh and sea water are present in abundance, and are clean. For the time when the young fish are in the loch cages, a good tidal flow is an advantage, as is reasonable protection from storms.

Fish farming has provided substantial employment, often in remote areas. By 1988 the industry was supporting 1335 full-time and 400 part-time jobs, while downstream activity such as packing, despatch and the production of nets and cages was said to support a further 5000 jobs. Salmon continues to be the dominant species but trout, turbot and halibut have also been farm-produced.

Fish farming has been especially successful in Shetland. The first unit was only established in 1982 but ten years later there were 60 salmon farms producing between them about a quarter of the total Scottish production of 20 000 tonnes of farmed fish.

Shellfish farming has also been a great success, especially in providing crofters with a second string to their economic bow. Oysters, mussels and scallops are produced on ropes suspended in the water. They require relatively little attention and are in demand from the catering trade. Clam production has been tried on an experimental basis.

Fish farming suffered something of a downturn in the early 1990s when the market was overloaded with fish from Norwegian producers. A number of Scottish farms were closed, but it is clear that the industry has a strong future, under proper control. Environmental concerns have also been expressed, both about the effect of fish farms on the wider marine environment, and on the intrusive nature of farms and cages on a wild and beautiful landscape.

Both these problems are being addressed. Much research has taken place on fish diseases, and this is continuing, and greater control is now being exercised to limit the number of farms in sensitive locations.

e founders. It has a visitor centre
th audio-visual show and gift
op. Distillery tours can be taken,
ter which the produce may be
mpled.

NDHORN
ighland

n B9011 4m N of Forres.

ndhorn, on its lovely bay, is the
ird village on this site, its two
edecessors having been largely
estroyed by storms in 1694 and
'01 respectively. The small resort,
ith superb sands curving east
wards Burghead, is best known
day for the **Findhorn Foundation**.

NDHORN FOUNDATION
ighland

*l year. Findhorn Bay Caravan Park.
on–Sat 0900–1700, Sun 1400–1700.
iided tours May–Sept at 1400. D (P)
309 30311).*

he Foundation is a community of
eople drawn together by spiritual
ad artistic links and devoted to a
eaceful way of life in harmony
ith nature and the planet. It is
ted, ironically, next to a large
AF base. The residents live in
ergy-efficient buildings and use
ind power. There is a visitor
entre with displays, weaving and
ottery workshops, gardens, café
ad a bookshop.

NDOCHTY
rampian

n A942 2m E of Buckie.

This small, neat fishing village is
set on the west side of a natural
harbour between **Buckie** and
Portknockie, but retains its own
definite identity. It has entered the
tourist business, a little cautiously.
The name often trips up unwary
visitors: it's pronounced 'Finechty'.

FISH FARMING, see panel p116.

FISHING, see panel p118.

FLOW COUNTRY, see panel
p119.

FOCHABERS
Grampian

On A96 10m E of Elgin.

When the 4th Duke of Gordon
rebuilt Gordon Castle (largely
demolished in 1955) on a grandiose
scale in 1776, he had the nearby
village rebuilt and replanned a
mile away on the present site of
Fochabers. Most of the streets are
in a grid pattern, and the main
street still has charm despite the
heavy traffic thundering through.
Interesting buildings include the
Bellie Kirk, with classical portico
and spire; Milne's School, gifted to
the village by Alexander Milne, a
Fochabers man who made a fortune
in New Orleans; and the Gordon
Chapel of 1834, which originally
had a private entrance for the
ducal family at the rear. The former
Pringle Church houses a splendid

Fishing

S cottish rivers and lochs offer exceptional sport for the fisherman in search of salmon and trout. The fishing is varied: from town beats within the boundaries of **Inverness** to remote Highland and island rivers, and from quiet ponds to wild lochs reached only after a hard tramp.

Major fishing rivers include the Spey, Dee, Don and Findhorn. The salmon fishing season runs from either January or February to October, the season for brown trout starting a little later in March. Most early fishing is done by spinning as the water at this time is high, coloured and cold. Later on, when the water is both lower and warmer, 'flies' (brightly coloured baits) are used.

Spinning rods are up to ten feet in length; fly fishing rods are longer, between 12 and 17 feet. Casting is a skill acquired after some practice, and there is great debate amongst anglers about both baits and methods of casting. Flies are also used for trout, whether fishing from the bank or out in a boat on one of the many trout lochs.

Fishing is not just a sport practised and enjoyed by many thousands of people, it is a major income earner for the Highlands and Islands. Many hotels offer special fishing holidays, and the best 'beats' on prime rivers are now frequently sold on a 'timeshare' basis, the beat being purchased by a syndicate in one- or two-week periods for 25 years or longer.

Fishermen seem cheerfully oblivious to the weather or other distractions such as midges; there are of course idyllic days by the river or drifting in a boat on a loch surrounded by majestic scenery, but there are also many days of wind and rain when nothing bites and only the thought of the comfort of the hotel or fishing lodge at the end of the day sustains the angler.

Salmon runs, in particular, have declined in recent years. The full reason for this is still sought but net fishing at the estuaries is thought to be one factor, and a number of net fisheries have been closed or bought out by fish conservation bodies in an attempt to conserve the wild stock and allow it to build up again – essential if the high reputation of Scottish fishing is to be maintained.

Fishing is enjoyed by members of the royal family on exclusive beats and by ordinary people (and many visitors) on beats for which licences (usually sold at tackle shops) still cost only a few pounds. They all dream of catching a really big fish. The Scottish record for a salmon is a fish of 67 pounds caught by a girl of 22 on the River Tay in the 1920s. It seems unlikely that monster will ever be bettered.

The Flow Country

The term 'Flow Country' is used to describe the very large area of Caithness and Sutherland covered primarily by blanket bog. The true 'flows' are in west Caithness and east Sutherland, a flat landscape of pool systems stretching for many miles. The whole peatland area of the two counties extends to 4 000 000 hectares –over 1500 square miles – the largest expanse of blanket bog in Europe.

Peat forms over a long period of time in flat or very gently sloping areas where the climate is cool and wet and the ground remains largely waterlogged. This stops the plant remains from decomposing. The most important peatland plants are the sphagnum mosses, described as the 'powerhouse of the bog'. They keep the surface moist and also contain acids which contribute further to the slowing-down of plant decay.

The peatlands of Caithness and Sutherland can be said to form a near-natural landscape. Scientific investigation has shown that there has been no real tree cover here for several thousand years, and the area is ecologically of international significance.

The Flow Country houses significant populations of rare birds such as the greenshank, hen harrier and merlin. Two-thirds of all Europe's greenshank breed here as do 35 per cent of Europe's dunlin. There are otters, wildcats, rare types of dragonflies, and many very special plants. Much of the area is under conservation designation.

The stability of the flows has, despite all this, been severely threatened in recent years by extensive conifer planting, grant-aided by government. Considerable drainage and deep ploughing were required before the trees could be planted. There is also concern over the growing use of peat for gardening, which has led to mechanized extraction. The traditional small-scale peat-cutting for fuel does not harm the flows.

After a period of great controversy and conflict, policies for the Flow Country are being established by the agencies concerned – principally Scottish Natural Heritage, the Forestry Commission and Highlands and Islands Enterprise – which, it is hoped, will safeguard the core of the peatlands and also allow controlled development to take place.

The Flow Country can be seen from the A895, A897 or B871 roads or from the train between Kinbrace and Georgemas Junction.

local museum. Just west of the village, across the River Spey, is the plant and visitor centre of **Baxters**, the well-known food manufacturers and preservers.

FORRES
Grampian

On A96 10m E of Nairn.

Forres, on the River Findhorn, has the distinction of being named on the first map of Scotland, made by Ptolemy, where it appears as 'Varris'. Today Forres is a pleasant town, population about 8000, with good shops in its busy main street, off which are narrow wynds. The Town House, in Tudor-Gothic style, is 19th century and the Falconer Museum, named after Dr Hugh Falconer, a noted fossil collector, is in golden Moray stone. The wooded Cluny Hill is crowned by the Nelson Tower, an 1806 memorial to the victor of Trafalgar which is an excellent viewpoint for Findhorn Bay and the coast. Just north of Forres is Sueno's Stone, a carved Pictish monolith 23 feet high. Two miles south of Forres is **Dallas Dhu Distillery**.

FORT AUGUSTUS
Highland

On A82 35m S of Inverness.

Fort Augustus was chosen as a Highland strongpoint by General Wade in 1725 because of its strategic location, at the junction of routes from all the compass points and at the south end of Loch Ness. The village was formerly called Kilcumein, and the old Cille-chumein burial ground can

still be seen a mile south of the village off the A82. Little is left of the 18th-century fort; the remains are incorporated into St Benedict's Abbey School. There is a good walk beside the **Caledonian Canal** south from Fort Augustus, and the locks always provide interest. Loch Ness cruises are available in summer. East of Fort Augustus, the finest of Wade's **military roads**, the **Corrieyairack Pass**, rises to 2500 feet on its way to Strathspey.

FORT GEORGE
near Inverness, Highland

On B9006 off A96 10m E of Inverness. Apr–Sept, Mon–Sat 0930–1900, Sun 1400–1900; Oct–Mar, Mon–Sat 0930–1600, Sun 1400–1600. D (P). HS (031–244 3101).

Fort George survives much as it was built, and provides a notable illustration of military life in the 18th century. Constructed between 1748 and 1763, it commands the entrance to the Moray Firth, and thus to **Inverness**, from its promontory site. It replaced an earlier fort badly damaged by the Jacobites in 1746. It contains the regimental museum of the Queen's Own Highlanders.

FORTROSE
Highland

On A832 14m NE of Inverness.

This small town on the **Black Isle** is dominated by the sandstone **Fortrose Cathedral**, late 14th century in origin. The chapter house is even older. Fortrose is a pleasant resort looking across the entrance to the Moray Firth towards **Fort George**. Its golf course shares with **Dornoch** the claim to have seen the burning of the last witch in Scotland; a stone marks the spot where the deed was done.

FORTROSE CATHEDRAL
Fortrose, Highland

Apr–Sept, Mon–Sat 0930–1900, Sun 1400–1900; Oct–Mar, Mon–Sat 0930–1600, Sun 1400–1600. HS (031–244 3101).

The south aisle is the earliest part of the cathedral, dating from the late 14th century. The church was completed in 1485 by Abbot Fraser, who had travelled here from Melrose in the Borders; 200 years later it was pillaged by Cromwell for stone needed for his fort in Inverness. A more modern steeple sits oddly against the mellow old ruins. The Chapter House beside the cathedral is 13th century.

FORT WILLIAM
Highland

On A82 12m N of Ballachulish, 8m S of Spean Bridge.

Fort William is the West Highlands' major tourist centre. The fort of the name, dating from 1690, is gone, its site taken by the railway station. There are summer steam excursions along the line to Mallaig. Traffic bypasses the long main street, which has rather uninspiring architecture. It holds the **West Highland Museum** and the **Ben Nevis Exhibition and Craft Centre**.

The town's fortunes declined when the pulp mill at nearby Corpach had to shed many workers, but it is making a determined effort to become a year-round resort following the opening of the ski centre on Aonach Mor, four miles north of the town, in 1989. At the junction of the A82 and A830 is the visitor centre at the **Ben Nevis Distillery**. Fort William lies in the shadow of the great bulk of **Ben Nevis**, best viewed not from the town but from Corpach. The road up **Glen Nevis** through fine mountain scenery ends at a car park from where a short walk leads through a magnificent gorge to the alpine meadow at Steall, with a lovely waterfall. It should be said that Fort William lies in an area of high precipitation: the winter snows which are attracting skiers are matched by summer rains. April to June tends to be the driest period.

FOWLSHEUGH
Grampian

Off A92 6m S of Stonehaven.

Fowlsheugh is a reserve in the care of the Royal Society for the Protection of Birds. There is a small car park at Crawton, with information boards, and a path leads along the cliffs. The best time to visit is from May to mid July when the place has been aptly described as a 'sea-bird city'; up to 150 000 birds pack on to the cliffs, occupying every possible space to breed. Thousands of pairs of kittiwakes, razorbills and guillemots come here together with smaller numbers of fulmar, shag, and puffins.

FOYERS
Highland

On B852 12m NE of Fort Augustus.

The Free Church and the 'Disruption'

Throughout the 18th century there was great debate and dissent in ecclesiastical circles in Scotland. This arose partly from the Jacobite Risings, which were aimed at restoring the Catholic Stuarts to the throne of Britain instead of the Protestant line established with William and Mary in 1688, and partly from the debate about the 'true covenant'. Patronage – the granting of parishes to ministers without reference to the parishioners – was also greatly resented.

Many new movements arose during this time. In 1743 the Reformed Presbyterian Church proclaimed itself the 'only true Kirk'; the following year the Secession Church was formed, in defiance against the imposition of ministers by the General Assembly of the Church of Scotland, its ruling body. By the end of the century there were also the Relief Church, the Auld Lichts, the New Lichts, and evangelical groups following the teachings of John Wesley. The situation was extremely complex.

Discontent and division continued into the 19th century. In 1834 the Evangelicals obtained control of the General Assembly for the first time. There followed what became known as the 'Ten Years Conflict', centring on the issue of patronage. It led to the Disruption of 1843; in that year over 400 ministers left their manses and livings and set up the Free Church of Scotland.

The new movement received remarkable support. By 1847 it had over 700 churches of its own, and had set up New College in Edinburgh to train ministers. When it appeared that schoolmasters who supported the new Church might be dismissed from their posts, Free Church schools were set up – more than 500 by 1869. At the same time, other dissenting groups combined to form, in 1847, the United Presbyterian Church of Scotland (often called the UP).

The two new churches combined in 1900 to form the United Free Church of Scotland, with a total of 1700 congregations. A minority of ministers and supporters of the Free Church resisted the union, claiming that fundamental principles on which their Church was founded had been violated, and split off to maintain their own Free Church, often referred to as the 'Wee Frees'.

These Churches survive today. The 'Wee Frees' have their stronghold in the islands, particularly the Hebrides. They maintain strict observance of the Sabbath, and in recent years have forcibly opposed the introduction of Sunday ferries, for example. Their services are plain, and in some areas are still conducted in Gaelic.

After leaving **Fort Augustus** the road following the line taken by General Wade climbs into Stratherrick, with wide views, and then plunges down through woodland to regain the lochside at Foyers. This was the site of the first development of **hydro-electric power** in Scotland, in 1896, when the British Aluminium Company (now British Alcan) harnessed the power of the Falls of Foyers to produce electricity. The original turbine and wheel remained until 1970, and now Scottish Hydro-Electric has a major pumped storage scheme operating using water from Loch Mhor, which was formed for the scheme. The river that flows into its south end is called simply the E – the shortest name in Britain. The falls can still be viewed. A little north of Foyers, on the way to **Inverfarigaig**, is Boleskine House, once lived in by Aleister Crowley, the self-styled 'Great Beast' who dabbled in the occult.

FRASERBURGH
Grampian

On A92/A98 18m N of Peterhead.

Fraserburgh, or the Broch as it is known (a local word for burgh), is a major fishing port, handles much other trade in the harbour, and also has oil-related industry. Fraserburgh Bay has fine sands and a links golf course. The castle on Kinnaird Head was built to guard against Viking incursions – it did better when converted to a lighthouse in 1786). There are plans to convert it into a national lighthouse museum. East of Fraserburgh are the attractive twin fishing villages of

Cairnbulg and Inverallochy, and a little way inland is Cairnbulg Castle (not open to the public), seat of the chiefs of Clan Fraser for centuries. Started in 1380, it was extensively altered by Sir Alexander Fraser (who founded the town) in the mid 16th century and restored in 1896–7 by shipowner John Duchie. The Frasers took it over again in 1915. The Fraser mausoleum can be seen in Saltoun Square in Fraserburgh.

FREE CHURCH, see panel p122.

FYVIE
Grampian

Off A947 10m N of Oldmeldrum.

Fyvie is most notable for **Fyvie Castle**, which has witnessed so much of Scotland's historical pageant, but the village itself, on the River Ythan, is not without interest. There was a priory here in the 13th century, marked by a cross standing in a field near the church, which itself has very old Pictish stones embedded in the chancel wall. Inside are the coat of arms of Alexander Seton, the 1st Lord Dunfermline, dated 1603, and a notable modern window of the Archangel Michael, designed by the American Tiffany who perfected a unique type of stained glass called Favrile.

FYVIE CASTLE
Fyvie, Grampian

Jun–Aug, daily 1000–1800; Easter–end May, Sept, daily 1400–1800; Oct, Sat–Sun

1400–1700. Grounds: all year, daily
0930–sunset. D (P). NTS (06516 266).

It is said that Fyvie's five towers
represent five centuries of Scottish
history: each is named after a family
who owned the castle – Preston,
Meldrum, Seton, Gordon and Leith.
The Preston Tower dates back to
the late 14th century; the Leith
Tower was added by Alexander
Forbes-Leith less than a century
ago. Inside there are many superb
treasures in the form of furniture,
artefacts, armoury and paintings.
There is an exhibition on the Castles
of Mar, a lochside walk, picnic area,
tearoom and shop.

GAELIC, see panel p127.

GAIRLOCH
Highland

On A832 20m NW of Kinlochewe.

Gairloch, superbly sited looking south to the **Torridon** mountains and west to **Skye**, has been a holiday resort since Victorian times. After the railway reached **Achnasheen** in 1868, there was a regular horse-drawn connection. Industry has long included **fishing** and agriculture, as well as the iron smelting on Loch Mareeside in earlier times. Today Gairloch spreads round the bay to take in Strathy; it is still a very popular base for holidays. To the north, a minor road runs up past the well-named Big Sand, an extensive beach, to Melvaig and on to the lighthouse at Rubha Reidh, built in 1912 to the design of David Stevenson. West of Gairloch, the drive to Red Point offers glorious seaward views. From the car park near the end of the road you look out on a scene of matchless beauty, over **Raasay** and Rona to the hills of Skye and, on clear days, the Outer Hebrides. From Red Point a long coastal walk leads south to **Diabaig**. Near Gairloch are the **Inverewe Gardens**.

GAMES, see **HIGHLAND GAMES** panel p138.

GARVE
Highland

On A835 14m W of Dingwall.

The small village of Garve (meaning 'rough', applied to the rugged landscape) has the feel of a gateway. Here the road divides, the choice being west through Strath Bran to **Achnasheen** or north-west over the moors and down to **Ullapool**. There is a station on the **Kyle of Lochalsh** line. Northward, the scenery is dominated by the great bulk of Ben Wyvis where there have been proposals, so far unrealized, for skiing development. To the east are the Rogie Falls, viewed from a suspension bridge.

GLEN AFFRIC
near Cannich, Highland

Minor road off A831 at Cannich.

Surrounded by superb hills and blessed with one of the few substantial remnants of Caledonian Pine forest in Scotland, Glen Affric is one of the most beautiful of all Highland glens. Long and of increasing wildness as you travel west, here as in few other places you find the natural progression from mature forest on the lower slopes through more scattered trees higher up to the bareness of the hilltops. There are parking places at Dog Falls and Loch Benevean (more properly Beinn a'Mheadhoin, 'loch of the middle hill') with marked walks available. From the road-end one of the great through walks in Scotland leads past lovely Loch Affric and more scattered groups of pines to the small, remote Alltbeithe youth hostel (no road

Gaelic

G aelic had been supplanted by Scots as the dominant spoken tongue of the ordinary people of Scotland east and south of the Highland Line (with the exception of Galloway) by the end of the 14th century. In the Highlands and Islands it retained its dominant position for much longer: visiting Torridon in 1877, Queen Victoria could record that she 'spoke to a woman, but she could not understand us, only knowing Gaelic'.

The decline of the language coincided with the decline of the population as many thousands emigrated: concern arose for the future of the old tongue, and in 1891 an association aimed at ensuring its continuity, An Comunn Gaidhealach, was formed. The following year the first national Gaelic festival, or Mod, was held in Oban. The Mod is now a week-long celebration of Gaelic in verse and song, and as well as the national festival (held each October) other smaller Mods are held in many parts of the country.

Gaelic's decline continued into recent years, but a revival is now under way. Considerable sums of money have been allocated to the development of Gaelic radio and TV programmes, and the language is offered to secondary school pupils as an option not just in the Highlands and Islands but in many Lowland schools as well. At the very important younger end, Gaelic playgroups have been a notable development, giving small children a grounding in the language through play.

The Gaelic heartland remains in the islands: from **Lewis** down to **Barra** it is still used in everyday speech. Gaelic thrives in poetry through the work of such writers as Sorley Maclean of **Skye**. In music, Gaelic has moved rapidly into the modern era with the huge popularity of Runrig, a rock music group who mix Gaelic and English.

Gaelic is a rich, expressive tongue. When applied to the landscapes of the Highlands and Islands it is capable of great beauty. As with connected tongues such as Welsh, Gaelic has not found it altogether easy to adjust to the technological age, but it is making progress. It is right that such a lyrical language should not be lost to us: those who kept its flame alive, if sometimes only flickering, over the past 50 years can begin to see that flame becoming more vigorous at last.

access: the name means 'stream of birches') and into **Kintail**.

GLENCOE
Highland

On A82 20m N of Tyndrum, 15m S of Fort William. NTS.

The A82 makes Glencoe one of the most accessible of all Scotland's glens: it is famous both in terms of scenery and history. From the south, the traveller crests the summit of **Rannoch Moor** to be greeted by the powerful pyramid of Buachaille Etive Mor (the Great Herdsman of Etive), the mountain that guards the entrance to both Glencoe and Glen Etive. Passing the Kingshouse Hotel (one of the oldest in Scotland) the road twists through the narrow part of the upper glen and then straightens out to drop nearly 1000 feet towards **Ballachulish**. On either side majestic peaks and buttresses rise: to the south the Three Sisters and Bidean nam Bian, to the north the Aonach Eagach (notched ridge), a classic scramble for the experienced walker. Glencoe is one of Scotland's finest rock climbing areas, and there is skiing on Meall a'Bhuiridh opposite the Kingshouse (not strictly speaking in Glencoe).

Glencoe is often called 'gloomy' or 'forbidding'; certainly the mountains rise steeply from the floor of the glen, which is flat and pastoral, carrying several farms, but the scene surely inspires awe rather than gloom. The National Trust for Scotland, which owns much of Glencoe and Glen Etive, 14 200 acres in all, has the **Glencoe Visitor Centre** in the lower glen. Many books have been written about Glencoe and its history, and

especially the notorious Massacre of February 1692. The **Glencoe and North Lorn Folk Museum** can be visited. Glen Etive is also well worth exploring. A single-track road runs down the glen for 15 miles to Loch Etive.

GLENCOE AND NORTH LORN FOLK MUSEUM
Highland

In Glencoe Village (minor road off A82). May–Sept, Mon–Sat 1000–1730.

Thatched cottages hold displays on the history of the area and particularly its people, with domestic and agricultural implements, toys, photographs, clan and Jacobite mementos.

GLENCOE VISITOR CENTRE
Highland

On A82 at lower end of glen. Jun–Aug, daily 0930–1830; Easter–end May and Sept–Oct, daily 1000–1730. D (P). NTS (08552 307).

The National Trust for Scotland visitor centre has displays on the landscape, wildlife and history of the area, a snack bar and shop.

GLENELG
Highland

On minor road 10m W of A87 at Shiel Bridge.

The village with the palindromic name (it probably means Irish glen, indicating early settlement) is reached by a steep, twisting climb over the Mam Ratagan pass. At the top of the pass there is a superb view back to the Five Sisters of **Kintail**. The road continues, to reach the sea at Glenelg, a small, attractive village looking across the Sound of Sleat to **Skye**. Cattle were at one time swum across the sound on their way to the markets of the south, and later a fort was established at Bernera to guard the crossing. South of Glenelg in Gleann Beag are Dun Telve and Dun Troddan, two of the finest **brochs** on mainland Scotland. Southward, the road runs past Sandaig to **Arnisdale**.

GLENFARCLAS DISTILLERY
near Aberlour, Grampian

Off A95 17m NE of Grantown-on-Spey, 6m SW of Aberlour. Jun–Sept, Mon–Fri 0900–1630, Sat 1000–1600, Sun 1300–1600; Oct–May, Mon–Fri 0900–1630. D (P) (08072 245 or 257).

The distillery was first opened in 1836. It was sold to the Grant family in 1865 and remains in Grant ownership today. The stills are gas-fired and the all-important water is taken from the Green Burn. Glenfarclas is bottled as a single malt in various strengths up to the cask strength 105 – a fiery dram indeed. The visitor centre, opened in 1973, has fine wood panelling taken from the liner SS *Australia*. There is a whisky exhibition in four languages, distillery tours, gift shop, audio-visual show and picnic area.

GLEN FIDDICH
near Dufftown, Grampian

From the very top of Glen Fiddich the view extends over a wide expanse of whisky country, with Glen Livet directly below to the south and the distilleries of **Dufftown** away to the north. The glen itself offers fine, wild scenery. The river crosses the A941 at Bridgehaugh and runs past the remains of Auchindoun Castle, a massive ruin on a hill previously crowned by a prehistoric fort. The castle was built for King James III in the 1470s by Robert Cochrane, who was also responsible for the Great Hall at Stirling Castle. Three miles below Auchindoun, the river twists suddenly westward to reach Dufftown, passes below several distilleries and **Balvenie Castle**, and runs on to meet the Spey at **Craigellachie**. The former railway along this stretch has been converted to a spur of the Speyside Way footpath, and makes a pleasant walk.

GLENFIDDICH DISTILLERY
Dufftown, Grampian

On A941 1m W of Dufftown. All year. Mon–Fri 0930–1630 (closed Christmas and New Year); Easter–mid Oct, Sat 0930–1630, Sun 1200–1630. D (0340 20373).

This is the only Highland distillery where malt whisky is bottled on the premises. The visitor is shown a film on the history and present technology of the plant and a guided tour follows, with a sampling. There is a gift shop and picnic area.

GLENFINNAN
Highland

On A830 18m W of Fort William.

The raising of the Stuart standard here in August 1745 has ensured that Glenfinnan will always be linked with the Jacobites and the Rising that ended so disastrously at **Culloden**. The village lies at the head of Loch Shiel, which runs for over 20 miles between the hills of **Moidart** and Sunart to **Acharacle**. Above it is the glen itself, reached by walking under the viaduct carrying the railway to **Mallaig**. This is the longest concrete railway bridge in Scotland; it has 21 arches in 416 yards, and was built in 1901.

From the viaduct you look down on the village and the famous Glenfinnan Monument, erected in 1815 by Macdonald of Glenaladale, a descendant of the man whose support for Bonnie Prince Charlie was crucial at the start of the Rising. Glenaladale, on the west side of Loch Shiel, produced 100 men in August 1745: it is deserted today. The figure at the top of the monument is not the prince, as is often supposed, but simply a Highlander. The monument is now floodlit at certain times. There is a **Glenfinnan Visitor Centre**.

GLENFINNAN VISITOR CENTRE
Highland

On A830 18m W of Fort William. Jun–Aug, daily 0930–1830; Easter–May, Sept–Oct, daily 1000–1300, 1400–1730. D. NTS (039783 250).

The visitor centre tells the story of the 1745 Rising, the raising of the standard, the campaign, and the final defeat of Bonnie Prince Charlie and his supporters at Culloden, with a commentary in four languages. There is a snack bar and gift shop.

GLEN GARRY
Highland

On A82 W of Invergarry (15m N of Spean Bridge).

The A87 runs alongside the short River Garry (from *garbh*, meaning rough), and one and a half miles from Invergarry passes the burial ground at Cill Donnain near Munerigie Farm. A minor road on the left then runs down Glen Garry. This was the original road to **Kyle of Lochalsh**, superseded when Loch Loyne was enlarged for **hydro-electric power** generation. In the river is Eilean na Cloinne (island of the children), recalling a tale that seven children were abducted by a 'water-bull' here. The road passes the old inn at Tomdoun and continues to Loch Quoich (*cuaich*, a cup), a hydro-enlarged loch, as is Loch Garry, and beyond to Kinlochhourn; the longest 'no through road' in Britain. There is fine mountain scenery all around, especially at Loch Quoich looking towards **Knoydart**. Iron was smelted in Glengarry for a time in the 18th century. Today it is heavily forested.

GLEN GRANT DISTILLERY
Rothes, Grampian

Easter–Sept, Mon–Fri 1000–1600. D (P) (03403 413).

Founded in 1840, the distillery soon established a reputation for its whisky, maintained today with its well-known Glen Grant products,

including a single malt. There is
an audio-visual presentation and
distillery tours are offered, with a
tasting afterwards. There is also a
gift shop.

GLEN LIVET
Grampian

On B9008 5m S of Bridge of Avon.

The River Livet rises in the Ladder
Hills and runs swiftly down to join
the Avon near Glenlivet village, in
the glen of the same name. This
is prime **whisky** country, and two
distilleries associated with the
glen can be visited, including the
Glenlivet Distillery. The Speyside
Way footpath passes through
Glenlivet on its way to **Tomintoul**.
Much of the land is owned by the
crown. **Glen Livet Estate** can be
visited by guided tour.

GLENLIVET DISTILLERY
Glen Livet, Grampian

*On minor road off B9136 near junction with
B9008. Easter–Oct, Mon–Sat 1000–1600. D
(P) (08073 427).*

In 1824, when the laws were
changed to cut out whisky
smuggling, this became the first
licensed distillery in the Highlands.
It is the only one entitled to call
its product 'The Glenlivet'. It was
founded by George Smith, who
had changed his name from Gow
because of the Jacobite connections
of his given name. The malt whisky
produced here is among the most
famous in the world. There is an
audio-visual show, tours are offered
with a tasting, and the distillery has
a coffee shop and gift shop.

GLEN LIVET ESTATE
Grampian

*Easter–Oct, Mon–Sat 1000–1700
(08074 285).*

This large crown estate offers
guided tours by Land-Rover to
show the history, landscape,
wildlife and land management.
There are many waymarked walks.

GLENMORANGIE
DISTILLERY
near Tain, Highland

*Off A9 1m N of Tain. Visits possible
Mon–Fri (not Jul–Aug); telephone first
(0862 3054).*

This is the only distillery in
Scotland producing solely its
own-brand single malt whisky.
The distillery has distinctive tall
stills which may contribute to the
whisky's special taste.

GLENMORE
Highland

*By the Cairngorm ski road leaving B970
at Coylumbridge; Glenmore is 7m E of
Aviemore.*

Passing through **Rothiemurchus**, the
road to the Cairngorm ski grounds
reaches Loch Morlich in the large
Glenmore Forest Park. There is an
information centre in the village
of Glenmore, with details of the
many different walks laid out in
the area. The forest has fine old
pines and is home to deer, pine
marten, wildcat and many different
birds. Among the more unusual
wildlife is the Cairngorm herd of

eindeer, introduced in 1952 and still thriving. The reindeer centre at Glenmore is open all year round. For a fee you can even 'adopt' a reindeer for a year. The Glenmore Lodge Outdoor Centre runs courses on mountaineering and hillcraft, skiing, canoeing and other outdoor activities.

GLEN NEVIS
Highland

By minor road 1m N of Fort William on A82.

This is a lovely glen. In seven miles it changes in character from the broader, wooded lower parts to the dramatic gorge at the road-end. To the north rises **Ben Nevis**, Britain's highest mountain, usually climbed from Achintee, while to the south are the peaks of the Mamores. The glen itself holds much of beauty, the river turning in slow loops between trees. The walk from the car park at the road-end up through the gorge to Steall, with its meadow, climbers' hut and waterfall, is rightly renowned. Here, the West Highland Way path ends its 95-mile journey from just north of Glasgow. There is an information centre with ranger service in the lower glen.

GLEN ROY
Highland

Minor road from A86 at Roy Bridge, 13m NE of Fort William.

Much of Glen Roy is a national nature reserve, one of the most interesting features being the

'parallel roads' clearly visible on the hillsides flanking this long glen. They mark the successive shorelines of an ancient lake formed when the entrance to the glen was blocked by ice during the last ice age some 12 000 years ago. A parking place partway up the glen has a viewpoint indicator and information boards. Glen Roy is an ancient through route from upper Strathspey: Montrose's troops cut over the hill from **Fort Augustus** into Glen Roy in a forced winter march before their success at the Battle of Inverlochy in 1645. The walk through to Loch Spey, over the main watershed of Scotland, and down to meet the **Corrieyairack Pass** at Melgarve, is a fine expedition today.

GLEN TANAR ESTATE
near Aboyne, Grampian

Off B976, 3m SW of Aboyne.
Visitor centre: Apr–Sept, daily 1000–1700 (03398 86072).

The visitor centre in Glen Tanar has displays on the landscape and wildlife of the area and on estate management. There is a picnic area plus hill and riverside walks from the centre; rangers take guided walks by arrangement.

GOLSPIE
Highland

On A9 8m N of Dornoch.

On the way from **Dornoch** to the town of Golspie the A9 crosses the Mound, the outlet into Loch Fleet. Beside the new bridge, opened in

1989, is **Thomas Telford's** beautiful old bridge of 1816. Its arches are closed by non-return flap valves which allow the fresh water out but prevent the salt water flowing upriver. Before the bridge was completed the land immediately upstream was often flooded. Golspie lies on land long associated with the Dukes of Sutherland, as is plain from the immense statue of the 1st duke atop Beinn a'Bhragaidh (speckled hill). A track goes all the way to the top of this hill, and you can share the extensive views with the duke over his land and out to sea. Golspie has a fine beach and golf course, and you can visit the workshops of the Orcadian Stone Company where ornamental clocks, pens, lamps and other items are made. There is also a display of rocks and fossils: the whole area is rich in prehistoric remains.

A good walk leads up the gorge of the Big Burn above the town. Two miles north of Golspie is **Dunrobin Castle**, home of the Dukes of Sutherland; near here is Carn Liath **broch**. South of Golspie a minor road leads to Littleferry, where you can watch the varied birdlife on Loch Fleet.

GRAMPIAN TRANSPORT MUSEUM
Alford, Grampian

On A944 at Alford, 25m W of Aberdeen. Apr–Sept, daily 1030–1700, and first two weekends in Oct. D (P) (09755 62292).

The museum, which includes the Alford Valley Railway Museum, has extensive displays of vintage cars, commercial vehicles, old bicycles, a horse tram, and the 'Craigievar Express' steam car, built by a local

postman. Displays include a driving simulator and a video bus, and there are special events in summer.

GRANTOWN-ON-SPEY
Highland

On A95/A939 15m NE of Aviemore, 23m S of Nairn.

This is a planned town, laid out in 1776 by Sir James Grant, with a spacious main square and walks beside the River Spey. Grant intended to develop textile manufacture but the town became a popular touring resort in Victorian times, and remains so today, with **fishing**, walking and golf in summer and **skiing** in the **Cairngorms** in winter. Castle Grant, the founder's home, is not open to the public at present. Also of note are the Speyside Heather Centre at Skye of Curr – a riot of colour at all times of the year – Muckerach Castle near Dulnain Bridge (1598 but recently restored) and, six miles north, **Lochindorb** with its island castle. Grantown has a lively local heritage society with plans for a visitor centre in the town; and there is an adventurous scheme for the Strathspey Railway to be extended from **Boat of Garten** to Grantown.

GROAM HOUSE MUSEUM
Rosemarkie, Highland

In Rosemarkie. May–Sept, Mon–Sat 1100–1700. D (P) (0381 20961).

The museum concentrates on Pictish remains, with a fine 'symbol stone' found locally, hangings, photographs and other exhibits. There is a display on the life of the

Brahan Seer, a visionary who lived in these parts, and a gift shop.

GRUINARD
Highland

On A832 15m N of Gairloch.

Past **Aultbea** the road crosses a hill to reach Gruinard Bay, a large curve between the headlands of Rubha Beag (little headland) and Stattic Point. The road passes through the intriguingly named First Coast and Second Coast (from the Gaelic An t-Eirthire Bhos 'the nearer coast' and An t-Eirthire Sios 'the further coast') to reach the main part of the bay with its hotel and fine sandy beach. Before the descent there is a viewpoint with a magnificent panorama of hills and coast. Offshore in the bay is Gruinard Island, which gained notoriety due to the experiments in germ warfare carried out here in World War II, when the island was infected with anthrax. It has only recently been declared safe after intensive chemical cleaning. Gruinard means 'green firth'.

HADDO HOUSE
near Pitmedden, Grampian

Off B999 4m N of Pitmedden, 19m N of Aberdeen. Jun–Aug, daily 1100–1800; Easter–May, Sept–Oct, daily 1400–1800. Gardens and grounds: all year, daily 0930–sunset. NTS (06515 440).

Haddo House was built in the 1730s to a design by William Adam, father of the Adam brothers, for the 2nd Earl of Aberdeen. The house has been described as 'a masterpiece of symmetry'. It features long curving passages and a high central section with matching curved stairs up to a first floor balcony. There is a fine collection of portraits including the 4th earl, Prime Minister from 1852 to 1855, William Pitt, Wellington and Peel. The chapel was designed by G.E. Street in the 1880s – his last major work – and has stained glass by Burne-Jones. The extensive policies are run as a country park by Grampian Regional Council in co-operation with the National Trust for Scotland and include a tree trail, bird hide, woodland and lakeside walks.

HALKIRK
Highland

On B874 6m S of Thurso.

Halkirk was laid out on a gridiron pattern in the late 18th century by the noted reformer Sir John Sinclair. The village is by the River Thurso, renowned for salmon **fishing**; in fact all the surrounding country is excellent for anglers, with Loch Calder and Loch Watten famed for their trout. To the south the extensive **Flow Country**, scene of considerable conflict between conservation and forestry interests in recent years, extends for many miles, crossed by the thread of the railway which divides at Georgemas Junction, just east of Halkirk. East of the village is the ruined 14th-century tower-house of Braal or Brawl.

HANDA ISLAND
Highland

By ferry from Tarbet (on minor road 6m N of Scourie: operates May–July only).

Handa is a bird reserve, until recently operated by the Royal Society for the Protection of Birds but now managed by the Scottish Wildlife Trust. Cliffs reach over 400 feet in height at the north end of the island, attracting guillemot, razorbill, kittiwake and fulmar, with lesser numbers of puffin and shag. The interior has small lochans and pine woods; great and arctic skua nest here. There is a resident warden in the summer months and a marked trail leads round the island.

HARRIS
Western Isles

Car ferry from Uig on Skye and Lochmaddy on North Uist to Tarbert: passenger ferry from Newtonferry on North Uist.

Harris retains its identity despite being geographically part of the same island as **Lewis**: the division occurs, not at the narrow neck of land at Tarbert, as might be imagined, but further north, along a line roughly from Loch Resort to Loch Seaforth. North Harris is a wild, mountainous area. Clisham is the highest point at 2630 feet,

Harris Tweed

Tweed is widely known as a tough, hard-wearing wool cloth. The word is thought to be a corruption of 'tweeled' or twilled, a description of such a fabric in which the weft yarns are worked over one and under two or more warp yarns, producing a diagonal pattern of lines within the cloth. Such a cloth has been woven for domestic use in Scotland for centuries, but it is only in the last 100 years that Harris tweed has gained particular fame.

The Harris Tweed Association was formed in 1909 to protect the makers of the cloth in the Western Isles and to help with marketing. The association's orb trademark is famous, and no cloth without it can properly claim to be Harris tweed. It must also be made only from Scottish wool and woven on hand looms.

Despite its name, the centre of production is not **Harris** but **Lewis**. Since 1934, a factory in Stornoway has carried out much of the preparatory work of carding, spinning and dyeing, after which the prepared wool is delivered to the homeworkers for weaving.

There are over 600 hand-weavers on Lewis and Harris and they produce over four million yards of cloth a year. The power for the loom is provided by the legs of the weaver, and his or her hands are meantime operating the shuttles. Traditionally, the skill was passed down from one generation to the next, but it can also now be learned at Lews College in **Stornoway**.

The resultant cloth – warm, very hard-wearing and with excellent water-resistance – comes in rolls 38 'weaver's yards' in length. Each 'yard' is 72 inches, so the rolls are, in more normally used terms, 76 yards long. They are 28½ inches wide. Finished rolls are collected by van to be taken back to the factory for onward delivery to finishing firms and fashion houses throughout the world.

Some weavers will also take private orders for rugs or garments, and offer very good value for money. Sample swatches will be sent on request. It is also possible for visitors to go to weavers' homes to watch them at work. Local tourist offices will give details.

Hand-weaving at home allows crofters time to tend animals and land, and moves to get weavers into the factory have been resisted. Originally, the weaving was simply part of family life, the wool being died with 'crotal' – natural colours from lichen or other plants – over the peat fire before being spun and woven. Only one or two weavers still carry out the full process themselves, for Harris tweed production has become a multi-million-pound worldwide business, and is a vital part of the economy of the islands.

Highland Birds

For the ornithologist, there is a great deal to see and to enjoy in the Highlands and Islands. Smaller birds of particular interest include the tiny **St Kilda** wren, unique to those distant islands, and the Scottish crossbill, one of the very few birds considered as being truly native to Britain. The bird is well named: its bill is indeed crossed so that it can extract seeds from pine cones in the forests where it lives.

Smaller raptors frequently seen on lower ground include kestrels, sparrowhawks and owls. Rarer species include the beautiful peregrine falcon and merlin. Efforts are under way to try to establish the red kite (which has a fragile foothold in Wales) in Scotland also. The mewing of the buzzard is a common sound in Highland Scotland; this beautiful bird of prey is seen throughout the area.

The heather moorland that characterizes much of eastern Scotland also supports one of its best-known birds, the red grouse. Their whirring flight and harsh 'go back' call will accompany many hill and moorland walks. Grouse are shot each year in the autumn; moor management often includes heather burning in the spring, to encourage the growth of young shoots, on which the birds feed. The black grouse or blackcock is less common: the bird's 'lek' or mating display is a very special sight. It takes place in the very early morning in spring on low ground, and lekking sites are known to ornithologists and estates.

The larger relative of the grouse, the capercaillie or 'horse of the woods', is confined to a few areas in Scotland and is often heard before it is seen, as it crashes noisily through the undergrowth.

A great success story of recent years is the osprey, only reintroduced to Scotland in the 1950s at **Loch Garten** (now a Royal Society for the Protection of Birds reserve). From here ospreys have spread to a large area of the Highlands, and over 30 pairs return from Africa each spring to breed. The birds can be seen from public hides at Loch Garten.

Mountain birds include the lovely little snow bunting, plover, pipit, and the dotterel, which nests at a few sites on high ground in the eastern Highlands. Ptarmigan, those strange residents of the tops, are found in many areas, particularly in the central and eastern Highlands. White in winter and rock grey in summer, their camouflage is perfect and they are often heard making a harsh belching cough before being seen.

(continued)

Highland Birds *(continued)*

They seem unafraid of humans, which makes close sightings possible. The hen will put on a 'broken wing' sham to lead people away from chicks when they are newly hatched.

The soaring flight of our largest bird of prey, the eagle, is a spectacle that cannot fail to thrill. Golden eagles cover very large territorial areas. There are more in the west, but they can also be seen in central and eastern districts. The sea-eagle, extinct in Scotland since the early 1900s, has been successfully reintroduced, initially on the island of **Rum** by Scottish Natural Heritage, and now on other island and headland sites.

Scotland is very rich in sea-birds. In the winter, many thousands of geese come south from the Arctic to coastal and island sites, and all year round, the coastal reserves such as **Fowlsheugh**, **Forvie**, the **Bullers of Buchan** and **Handa** teem with guillemot, cormorant, gannet and puffin. **Orkney** and **Shetland** are both exceptionally good places for birdlife, and in the Western Isles the curious grating of the corncrake is heard, one of the few places where this increasingly rare bird can find a suitable habitat in Britain.

but there are many other fine hills for the adventurous walker, with ringing Norse names such as Uisgnaval, Stulaval, Ullaval and Oreval. At the north end of the Oreval-Ullaval ridge is the vast cliff of Sron Ulladale, which holds major rock climbs. A road clings to the coast, through the estate of Amhuinnsuidhe (leaping river). The hills gradually decrease in height as you go south through Tarbert, where the island is very nearly cut in half.

On the west coast are fine sands at Luskentyre, and the road continues to Leverburgh, the name marking Lord Leverhulme, who owned the whole island of Lewis and Harris in 1918 and tried to establish a major fish processing operation here. He built roads,

houses and a factory here and changed the name from Obbe to Leverburgh, but the project was short-lived. Lord Leverhulme died in 1925. The coastal part of South Harris is prime crofting country, and the west side holds a machair strip rich with summer flowers and even some trees, rare on these windswept islands. South of Leverhulme is Rodel, with the outstanding St Clement's Church. Dating from the early 16th century, it was built by Alasdair Crotach, 8th chief of Clan MacLeod, who is buried here. The church, in cruciform shape, is richly decorated, the inspiration, it is said, of craftsmen who worked on Iona.

A minor road runs up the east coast passing Lingerabay, where there are current plans for a

Highland Games

The Games that are a colourful feature of the Highland summer for visitors have their origin in trials of strength, speed and daring staged by chieftains to establish who amongst their men were the best warriors. Tradition dates this back to the 11th century with stories of such a contest held by Malcolm III at or near **Braemar** – the scene of one of the most famous Games today.

The Games gradually evolved from a combination of military contest and social gathering into the event we see today. Even now there is no set pattern; some Games place emphasis on solo piping and dancing, others feature pipe bands, others again make the athletic events, particularly the 'heavy' competitions, their centrepiece.

The latter contain traditional elements only found in Highland Games and requiring very special skills, as in the tossing of the caber. 'Tossing' is perhaps not quite the right word for an attempt to upend a treetrunk weighing over 100 pounds! The event demands a rare combination of strength, balance and timing. Other heavy events include the hammer throw, for which competitors wear shoes with steel spikes at the toe, and throwing the 56-pound weight over the bar.

In recent years, a professional 'heavy' circuit has developed. The athletes travel from one Games to the next throughout the summer in Scotland and also compete at Games abroad – for Highland Games are held in many countries, not just those such as the USA, Canada and Australia where there is a strong expatriate population but also in exotic places like Dubai and Jakarta. In Scotland, amateurs have their own, separate competitions in heavy events, and in the tug-of-war, where local rivalries are fiercely fought out by teams of eight on a rope trying to pull each other over.

There is often a delightful contrast between the 'heavies' at one end of the arena and the wee lassies (and laddies) in the dancing competitions at the other. Throughout the day of the Games the dancers come up on stage in twos or threes, in immaculate Highland dress, to perform in competition what they have spent many hours practising, to the accompaniment of a solo piper.

(continued)

Highland Games *(continued)*

Running and cycling events are often held, on a fairly rough grass track. Like the heavy athletes, these competitors are often professionals, competing at Games throughout the summer. Many Games also feature a tough hill race to a nearby summit and back.

Highland Games are an important feature of the Scottish calendar. The principal season is July to September, though a few are held as early as April. Many now put on additional attractions, perhaps a parachute drop or a mock battle staged by one of the specialist groups such as the White Cockade Society. There are sideshows and stalls and – given the all-important good weather – it's a great day out.

massive quarry to provide aggregate or mainland projects; if present plans are followed through, the hill here will become a hole and a new loch will be created. **Harris Tweed**, a gentler and older industry, is still important to the economy of the area.

HARRIS TWEED, see panel p135.

HELMSDALE
Highland

On A9 11m N of Brora.

Helmsdale, the dale of Hjalmund, named after its original Norse settler, marks the boundary between Sutherland and Caithness. Fishing vessels still operate from the harbour. The A9 cuts into Helmsdale directly, using a modern bridge over the river. As with so many places, sitting nearby is a bridge by **Thomas Telford**, built

in 1811 and clearly seen from the gardens of the **Timespan Centre**.

Neighbouring the bridge are an old ice-house and the village's striking war memorial. From Helmsdale the A897 and the railway head up Strath Kildonan, scene of the 'Highlands gold rush' in 1868–9. Some gold was indeed found here, and tiny grains can still be found, but the amount was never enough to warrant the numbers who came looking for a fortune. Baile an Or, the 'township of gold', was established briefly in the strath, which leads to Kinbrace, Strath Halladale and the north coast.

HIGHLAND BIRDS, see panel p136.

HIGHLAND FOLK MUSEUM
Kingussie, Highland

In Duke Street, Kingussie. Apr–Oct, Mon–Sat 1000–1800, Sun 1400–1800;

Nov–Mar, Mon–Fri 1000–1500. D (P)
(0540 661307).

The museum covers a considerable
area, and a considerable part of
Highland history. Inside you can
see clothing, domestic utensils,
musical instruments, farm tools,
furniture, spinning, kitchenware
and much more. Outside is a replica
blackhouse and 'clack mill', both
from Lewis, a Victorian salmon
smokehouse, and a herb garden.

HIGHLAND GAMES, see
panel p138.

HIGHLAND RAILWAY MUSEUM
Nairn, Highland

At Nairn Station. Jun–Sept, Mon, Wed,
Thu, Sun 1000–1730, Sat 1000–1700.

The museum has photographs
and mementos of the railway age
from the earliest times up to the
present day.

HIGHLAND WILDLIFE PARK
near Kingussie, Highland

Off B9152 2m SE of Kincraig. Apr–Oct,
daily 1000–1700 (closing time may be earlier
in spring and autumn). D (P) (05404 270).

Opened in 1972, the park aims to
show Scottish wildlife (past and
present) in as natural a setting as
possible. As well as the expected
deer, wildcats, otters and pine
marten there are drive-through
enclosures with bear and wolf.
Rare domestic animals include Soay
sheep and there are many species of

birds. The park has a visitor centre,
café, shop and a children's zoo.

HILL O' MANY STANES
near Lybster, Highland

Off minor road at Clyth, 2m NE of Lybster.
All reasonable times. Free.

In a field are almost 200 stones laid
out in 22 parallel rows. The stones
are only two or three feet high, and
their purpose, possibly astronomic
measurement or ritual, remains a
mystery. Interpretive panels explain
as much as is known.

HILL-WALKING, see panel
p223.

HONEYNEUK BIRD PARK
near Banff, Grampian

Off A947 4m S of Banff. May–Oct,
Wed–Sun 1200–1800. D (P).

Over 100 species of birds and
animals are to be found here in
one of Scotland's largest wildlife
collections, which is also a major
breeding centre for rare animals.
Facilities include a children's
playground, pets corner, tearoom
and picnic area.

HOPEMAN
Grampian

On B9012 2m E of Burghead.

Hopeman is concerned mainly
with the sea. The gridiron pattern
of its streets overlooks the harbour

Hydro-Electric Power

The first commercial hydro-electric plant was installed at **Foyers**, on the east side of **Loch Ness**, by the British Aluminium Company in 1896. It continued operating until 1970. There is now a much larger pumped-storage scheme at Foyers supplying up to 300 000 kilowatts to the national grid.

Until 1939 there was only limited further development, but with the outbreak of war, investigations began into the feasibility of supplying large amounts of electricity through hydro generation. The man providing the impetus was Tom Johnston, Secretary of State for Scotland, and under his guidance in 1943, the North of Scotland Hydro-Electric Board was set up.

The Board was given wide-ranging powers, including the authority to sell its electricity nationally, and it later used income from those sales to help finance the provision of mains electricity to many remote areas, thus combining, as Johnston had foreseen, a social function with its industrial one.

There are a number of large hydro schemes in the Highlands; they are often in areas of great scenic beauty and though the landscape can never remain unaffected by such a major development, care has been taken. In **Glen Affric** the buildings are faced with local stone, for example, and are screened by trees as far as possible; this practice has also been followed elsewhere, and at **Morar**, on the west coast, the power station was built underground. Some proposals, such as a major scheme for **Glen Nevis**, were so strongly resisted by public opinion that they were dropped. Fish ladders are commonly provided at dams so that salmon, in particular, can pass upstream to spawn.

The larger schemes, including Affric–Cannich, and Tay–Tummel further south, use long underground tunnels to take water from one reservoir or catchment to another, so that the flow can be controlled to best effect. Dams were major engineering feats; in several cases, lochs were greatly increased in size, incorporating other, smaller lochs and drowning buildings.

There have been no large schemes built in recent years, though interest has revived in hydro generation, and several estates (**Knoydart** and Ardverikie are examples) have funded their own small schemes to provide power for local use.

(continued)

Hydro-Electric Power *(continued)*

The major development has been in the use of pumped storage, in which water is held in an upper reservoir and pumped back up to it at night when demand is lowest, before being released again during the day.

The Hydro-Electric Board was privatized in 1991 and is now called Scottish Hydro-Electric plc. It continues to provide electricity to a very wide area (by no means all of it by hydro generation) but it would seem that the days of building dams and tunnels, diverting water and impounding lochs are most probably over.

---

backed by cliffs quarried for their fine sandstone, used in a number of notable local buildings. A golf course is situated on links east of the village, and there is a fine walk along the cliffs to **Burghead**. Hopeman has experienced tragedy several times in recent years when fishing boats from here have been overcome by the often savage seas. Two miles away to the south-east is **Duffus Castle**.

Duchess of Gordon founded the Gordon Schools, now Huntly Academy. Huntly is now bypassed by the main artery, the A96, making the town quieter and restoring the fine square to something like its original function as a meeting place. A town trail can be followed using a leaflet obtainable from the Tourist Information Centre. Three miles to the north-west is the **North-East Falconry Centre**.

HUNTLY
Grampian

On A96/A97 11m SE of Keith, 14m E of Dufftown.

Huntly received its charter in 1545, but the town we see today is mainly 19th century. Sited where the Deveron and Bogie Rivers meet, it is a market and shopping centre for a wide area. The ruined castle of the Gordons, **Huntly Castle**, who brought the name Huntly with them from Berwickshire, is a notable landmark; the famous Gay Gordons dance is also named for the family. In 1839 the then

HUNTLY CASTLE
Huntly, Grampian

Apr–Sept, Mon–Sat 0930–1900, Sun 1400–1900; Oct–Mar, Mon–Sat 0930–1600, Sun 1400–1600. HS (031–244 3101).

The imposing ruins of the Gordon castle show marks of its long history. A Norman motte-and-bailey stood on this site, and a 15th-century tower, the Auld Wark, but most of what remains is the work of the 4th Earl of Huntly, dating from the 1550s and based on chateaux he had seen in France. After the Battle of Corrichie in 1562, at which Huntly himself died, the castle was pillaged. It was restored by the 5th Earl, pillaged again, restored again in 1602 and finally abandoned in the mid 17th century. The walls are adorned with rich heraldic carving, and the castle stands in an attractive wooded park.

HYDRO-ELECTRIC POWER,
see panel p141.

HYDROPONICUM
Achiltibuie, Highland

In Achiltibuie. Apr–Oct, daily: tours at 1000, 1200, 1400 and 1700. D (P) (085482 202).

This is an extraordinary place to find in such a remote location: a 'space-age garden' where plants flourish without soil. Here in the north-west Highlands you will see bananas, figs, lemons, vines and much else more usually associated with warmer climates. The 90-minute tour tells how it came about and how it is done, and you can buy growing kits in the shop to try it for yourself.

INCHNADAMPH
Highland

On A837 25m N of Ullapool.

The small settlement of Inchnadamph (the name probably means 'meadow of oxen') sits at the heart of a superb wild landscape, of equal interest to the walker, angler and geologist. To the east is **Assynt** with its high hills and the limestone caves on the Tralgill River; much of this area is a nature reserve administered by Scottish Natural Heritage. West is Loch Assynt with **Ardvreck Castle** and the unmistakable Sutherland mountain shapes of Canisp and Suilven rearing abruptly from a flat plain dotted with myriad lochans, the latter a delight and a constant challenge for the serious angler chasing brown trout. Just north of Inchnadamph at Skiag Bridge, the coast road to **Lochinver** forks west; a cairn by the roadside commemorates the work of two pioneering geologists, Ben Peach and John Horne. The geological story is still unfolding. In this area several different rock types – Torridonian Sandstone, Lewisian Gneiss, Durness Limestone – come together in a complex jumble of strata caused by the earth movement named the Moine Thrust. The SNH visitor centre at Knockan (**Inverpolly**) gives further information.

INGASETTER
Banchory, Grampian

In Banchory. All year Mon–Fri 0900–1700; Jul–Sept, Sat 1000–1600. Free. D (P) (03302 2600).

The perfume and cosmetic makers use local lavender and other products. There is an optional guided tour and a shop. Lavender harvesting and distilling takes place in July and August.

INSCH
Grampian

On B992 25m NW of Aberdeen.

The area around the town of Insch (the name means 'an island') marks the boundary between the districts of the Garioch (to the south-east of Insch) and Strathbogie (to its north-west). Foudland slate, quarried nearby, was used for the roof of **Balmoral Castle** and the area was also noted for whisky production, both legal and illicit. A distillery called Jericho near Colpy was renowned for its products, using the railway station at Insch to deliver them to the outside world. South-west of Insch is Leslie Castle, a 17th-century tower-house that has been carefully restored in recent years. It is not open but can be viewed from the roadside. Further to the south rises the distinctive hill of **Bennachie**.

INVERBERVIE
Grampian

On A92 12m N of Montrose.

Inverbervie is the first town encountered after crossing into Grampian Region north of Montrose using the coast road. Local people call it simply Bervie, and although it is by the sea there is no fishing, for it lacks a safe anchorage. There were formerly lax and jute mills here. The Bervie Water is crossed by a notable curved bridge, beside which is an attractive rose garden with a memorial to Hercules Linton, a Bervie man who designed the famous clipper ship *Cutty Sark* (now preserved at Greenwich, London). Bervie is the 'Segget' of Lewis Grassic Gibbon's novels: the author is rather hard on the town, which seems undeserving of his calumny. A couple of miles up the Bervie Water is **Arbuthnott**. South of Inverbervie is Gourdon, an attractive fishing village with curing sheds on the quay and a jute mill.

INVEREWE GARDENS
near Gairloch, Highland

On A832 6m N of Gairloch.
Garden: all year, daily 0930–sunset. Visitor centre and shop: May–Aug, Mon–Sat 0930–1800, Sun 1200–1800; Easter–end Apr, Sept–Oct Mon–Sat 1000–1700, Sun 1200–1700. Guided walks with head gardener, daily Easter–Oct at 1330. Restaurant, gift shop, plant sales. Disabled access to much of garden and greenhouses. NTS (044 586 200 or 229).

Inverewe is a tribute to what man can achieve given determination and the will to succeed. When Osgood Mackenzie came here in 1862 there was nothing but rock, bog and peat-hags – and a single willow tree. For the next 60 years he worked to create an exotic, beautiful and varied landscape of trees, shrubs, water and flowering plants from all over the world, aided by the warming effects of the Gulf Stream which washes these coasts. All the topsoil had to be brought in. Planting started in 1865 after the area was fenced against livestock intrusion, a thick shelter belt of pine and fir providing some protection from the winds that scour the west of Scotland for much of the year. Over the years much else was added, and the garden gradually grew to its present size: a far cry from the bareness of Am Ploc Ard (the high lump) that Mackenzie took over. His work was continued by his daughter, Mrs Mairi Sawyer. Today it is a major visitor attraction, and a place of pilgrimage both for horticulturalists and for those who simply love beautiful places.

INVERFARIGAIG
Highland

On B852 15m N of Fort Augustus, 16m S of Inverness.

After leaving **Foyers** the road along the east side of **Loch Ness** continues to Inverfarigaig, a small village surrounded by large forests. In the Pass of Inverfarigaig, a narrow defile, is a forestry visitor centre with displays and walks, one leading to an excellent viewpoint looking out over the loch. North of Inverfarigaig is Dun Dearduil, which has a vitrified stone fort on its summit. The narrow road up the pass climbs to Errogie to meet the upper road from Strathnairn. In the pass is a stone memorial to James Bryce, a noted geologist who died after a fall here in 1877.

INVERGARRY
Highland

On A82/A87 16m N of Spean Bridge.

The village of Invergarry, on Loch Oich, marks the point where the

A87, the modern 'Road to the Isles', turns west, leaving the Great Glen. The local economy is largely based on forestry, the **fish farm** a few miles to the west, and servicing tourists. In the grounds of the Invergarry Castle Hotel are the ruins of Invergarry Castle itself, once the home of the Macdonalds of Glengarry. Attacked several times, it was finally damaged beyond repair by Cumberland's troops in 1746. It can be viewed from the outside. By Loch Oich (part of the **Caledonian Canal**) is the Well of the Heads (Tobar nan Ceann in Gaelic), marking the revenge murder of seven men of Keppoch in 1663. It bears an inscription in Gaelic, English, French and Latin.

INVERGORDON
Highland

On B817 12m NE of Dingwall.

Originally called Inverbreakie, the town got its present name from Sir William Gordon of Embo, who owned the area in the 18th century. Invergordon is at the west end of Nigg Bay, a natural anchorage, and this led to its being used as a naval base before and during World War I. In the 1920s and 1930s its prosperity declined until the outbreak of another war brought the naval vessels back. The naval base was closed in 1956, but when the Highlands and Islands Development Board (now Highlands and Islands Enterprise) was set up in 1965, this area was chosen for major industrial development. **Nigg** got the oil rig platform construction yard; Invergordon got a large

aluminium smelter, which closed a few years ago, depressing the area yet again. There are still plans for development, but along more diversified lines, a change from the heady days of the 1970s when there was talk of a 'linear city' stretching right round the shores of the Cromarty Firth.

INVERMORISTON
Highland

On A82/A887 6m N of Fort Augustus.

The small village of Invermoriston has been associated with the Grant family since the 15th century, when John Grant, known as 'the Bard', built the first Invermoriston House. Glen Moriston, which leads west from the village, has much forestry planting. The area has many connections with Bonnie Prince Charlie, who was protected by the Seven Men of Glenmoriston after his escape from **Culloden**. The crag above Invermoriston House, on modern maps as Creag nan Eun (crag of the birds), should actually be Creag Iain – John's crag, after another Grant, a Jacobite supporter who took refuge here in 1689 and again in 1716.

INVERNESS
Highland

On A9/A82/A96 at north end of Loch Ness.

Inverness is often called the 'capital of the Highlands'. Here are the headquarters of Highland Regional Council, Highlands and Islands Enterprise, the Red Deer Commission and many other bodies. Its strategic position at

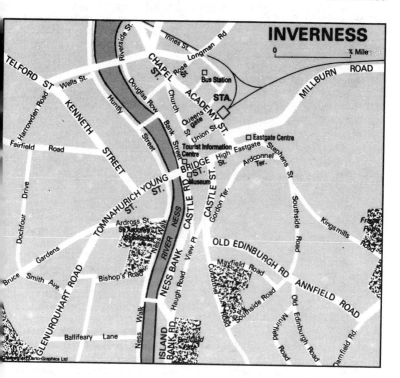

Town plan of Inverness

Island Life

Living on an island has a romantic feel to it, and there is indeed a very special atmosphere about the islands of Scotland, but in practical terms those who live on the islands, as distinct from just visiting them, have to be adaptable and resourceful.

Communication with the mainland is much more straightforward now than it was even 30 years ago. Ferries are larger, more comfortable and more frequent, and air services have developed to the point where even quite small islands have regular flights.

For the larger islands, the year divides into two distinct parts: tourist and non-tourist. It isn't quite as clear-cut as that, as there are always some visitors, even in winter, but in general terms, between June and September island populations are greatly swollen by visitors, and much of any island's activity is necessarily geared towards supplying the needs of those who come on holiday.

Bed and breakfast places reopen, as do visitor attractions, shops stay open longer and ferries run more frequently. The underlying agricultural and fishing activity goes on, of course, as it must, but it is important to maximize the income during that time.

Outwith the visitor season, the islands revert to a more normal social pattern. Winter months are the time for regular gatherings of clubs and societies of all kinds, for drama and music productions – and for making plans for the following year. With limited daylight and transport services reduced, travel is confined to shorter and more essential journeys.

The ferries and flights are a lifeline without which island communities would find it difficult to survive today. They bring essential supplies of consumer durables and other goods – and of course the post – and take out livestock going to mainland markets, and island produce bound for the wider world. Some of these transport services are part-subsidized by central government.

Each island, or island group, has its own character, and a recognizable 'feel' to it for those living there. There is a very special atmosphere about an island, coming from its intimate relationship with the elements, particularly the sea that surrounds it. Of its nature an island must be to some extent an enclosed community, but the Scottish islands have built on this as an advantage rather than letting it be a handicap. The recent exception is **St Kilda**, where the remoteness led to the islanders asking to be evacuated in 1930. Other small islands such as Fair Isle have shown population growth in recent years.

e north end of the Great Glen
nd of the **Caledonian Canal**)
d at the meeting of the Moray
d Beauly Firths has made it an
portant point of communication
r centuries; a market town, a
eeting place, and a major junction
r road, sea and rail travellers. The
wn received its charter as a royal
rgh from David I in the 12th
ntury. By then it had already seen
e castle rise and fall: three more
ere to suffer a similar fate before
e present castle was built in the
40s, not as a stronghold but as a
urthouse and jail. Outside it is a
atue of the Jacobite heroine Flora
acdonald. She looks across the
ver Ness with its many bridges to
 Andrew's Cathedral (1868) which
s a richly decorated interior. Next
 the cathedral is the Eden Court
eatre, which offers a year-round
ogramme of entertainment.
pleasant walk takes in these
ildings, the banks of the Ness
d the small islands in the river,
hich are wooded and feature
rious carved stone animals.
 One of the oldest buildings in
verness is the late 16th-century
bertarff House, formerly a Lovat
sidence, now the Highland office
 the National Trust for Scotland.
ore information on the town's
story can be found at the museum
 the 1880 Town House, where the
uncil Chamber has mementos of
cabinet meeting under the then
ime minister, David Lloyd George,
ld in 1921 – the first British
vernment cabinet meeting held
tside London.
 Today, Inverness is a major
opping centre with full
commodation facilities and links
 rail, road and air to every part
 Scotland and beyond. Cruises
 the Caledonian Canal and into
ch Ness are available in summer.

Two miles west of Inverness is
Craig Phadrig (Patrick's Crag), a
hill with an ancient fort, and a fine
viewpoint.

INVERPOLLY
Highland

*Information centre at Knockan on A835,
12m N of Ullapool. May–Sept, Mon–Fri
1000–1730. Free.*

The vast Inverpolly National Nature
Reserve (the name means 'mouth of
the peat moss') covers over 25 000
acres. It stretches from Elphin to
the coast at Enard Bay, north almost
to Inverkirkaig and south to Loch
Lurgainn. It takes its name from the
River Polly which runs into the sea
at Enard Bay and includes the fine
little peak of Stac Pollaidh, climbed
from a car park by Loch Lurgainn.
The interior of the reserve is largely
uninhabited, and supports a variety
of habitats and species, especially
birds. The geology is particularly
interesting, with mountains rising
abruptly from a flat, wet plain.
The information centre at Knockan
has displays on the rocks and their
formation, as well as a trail leading
to geological formations at Knockan
Cliff, which is owned by Scottish
Natural Heritage; the rest of the
area is managed by agreement with
the three large estates – Drumruine,
Eisg Brachaidh and Inverpolly –
which make it up.

INVERURIE
Grampian

Off A96 16m NW of Aberdeen.

Inverurie, the main town of
Gordon District, is sometimes

affectionately known as 'the capital of the Garioch'; it has long been an important meeting place and market town, and has been a burgh since medieval times. It is on the Aberdeen–Inverness railway, and once held the engineering works of the Great North of Scotland Railway Company. No sign remains, but their history is told in the town museum. Inverurie has a major paper mill – one of several on the Don, which river is here joined by the Urie of the town's name. At the south end of the town is Port Elphinstone, the birthplace of J. Pittendrigh Macgillivray, painter, sculptor and architect. Several of his works are in **Aberdeen** Art Gallery. The whole area is rich in prehistoric and Pictish remains, and south-east of Inverurie is the Bass, a large motte which once carried a fortified tower. To the west, at Aquohorthies, is a fine stone circle.

ISLA BANK MILLS (G AND G KYNOCH LTD)
Keith, Grampian

In Keith. Mill tours Tue and Thu 1430. Mill shop, Mon–Fri 0930–1215, 1330–1700.

The mill was established here in 1788 and produces fabric of high quality used by leading garment manufacturers.

ISLAND LIFE, see panel p148.

JACOBITE RISINGS, see
panel p152.

JOHN O'GROATS
Highland

On A9 17m N of Wick.

The A9, which starts in Edinburgh, ends its long journey at John o'Groats, looking over the wild waters of the Pentland Firth to Stroma and beyond to **Orkney**. The name comes from a Dutchman, John de Groot, who settled here in around 1500. It is said that he built an octagonal house with eight doors so that his eight sons each had his own entrance; another story says he provided an eight-sided shelter for travellers, so that whatever the direction of the capricious wind, they could find relief. There is now a large hotel, gift shops, and the much-photographed marker post giving the distance from Land's End in Cornwall. This near-1000-mile marathon is regularly undertaken by walkers, cyclists, people pushing prams and many other kinds of journeys, often for charity. Two miles to the east is **Duncansby Head**.

JOHNSHAVEN
Grampian

Off A92 7m N of Montrose.

Johnshaven is an odd mixture of old cottages in narrow lanes and modern council houses in rows. The fishing has declined since the high days of the 18th century, with only a few boats going out regularly. Also gone is the manufacture of sailcloth, but, down at the harbour, a large shellfish merchant supplies Johnshaven lobsters to many top-class restaurants. Just north of the village is Brotherton Castle, now used as a school.

The Jacobite Risings and the Stuart Pretenders

I n 1688, the Dutch William and his wife Mary were invited by the government to take the British crown. They were Protestants; the Stuart line which had led to James VII of Scotland and II of England was Catholic. William and Mary duly arrived and were crowned, and accepted in England, but Scotland was in ferment, and in the summer of 1689 that ferment was turned to action.

The pro-Stuart, Jacobite forces under Claverhouse – 'Bonnie Dundee' – and the English government troops under General Mackay met at Killiecrankie, south of Blair Atholl. The Jacobites were greatly outnumbered, but Mackay's troops had never faced a Highland charge before and as they struggled to fit their clumsy bayonets, Dundee's men were on them and through them, and the battle was turned into a rout, except for one thing – Dundee himself had been killed.

Without its charismatic leader, the rebellion lost momentum. Led now by Colonel Cannon, the Jacobites advanced to Dunkeld, where Cleland's troops fired the town and resisted the attack. The rising petered out until 1714, when George I, known as the 'German Lairdie' to Jacobites, took over the throne. By this time the Act of Union had been passed, in 1707, uniting the English and Scottish parliaments while granting Scotland some freedom in matters such as religion and the law.

The Jacobites rose again, under the Earl of Mar, known as Bobbing John for his unfortunate political vacillation. The field of battle this time, on 13 November 1715, was Sheriffmuir, near Stirling, which was a vital crossing-point on the route to Edinburgh. The battle was indecisive; neither side could claim victory, but the Jacobite advance was repulsed.

It rose again with Prince Charles Edward Stuart, son of James (the latter becoming known as the Old Pretender and Charlie as the Young Pretender) and grandson of James VII and II. Charles, the 'Bonnie Prince' of song and story, was young, fit and eager to claim the throne for his father. He was supported by the French, who saw Scotland as a tactical back door to gain influence, and ultimately power, in England. The rising was slow to develop, clan chiefs being reluctant at first, but it gathered momentum once the Stuart standard had been raised at **Glenfinnan** in August 1745.

(continued)

The Jacobite Risings *(continued)*

The London government sent an army north under Sir John Cope but the Jacobites evaded him and marched on, taking Perth, Stirling and Edinburgh without great difficulty. The two sides met on 21 September 1745 at Prestonpans, east of Edinburgh. It was a disaster for Cope, his forces taken unawares by the Jacobite advance under cover of mist. In half an hour it was all over, and now Charles and his Highland army were really on the march.

The Jacobites took Carlisle, Manchester and Derby. Panic was reported in the streets of London. But, far from home and on unfamiliar ground, doubts set in, and against his better judgment, Charles was persuaded by his senior officers to turn around and go back to Scotland, to hold what he had rather than risk losing all.

Historians have argued ever since about that decision: if it had gone the other way, would the government – and George – have fallen? We shall never know. The rest of the story is familiar. The Jacobite army went further and further north, government troops harrying them. There were victories at Clifton and Falkirk, but a major effort was under way to put this troublesome rebellion down, under the Duke of Cumberland; both sides were thus led by men in their mid 20s.

Drummossie Moor, better known to us as **Culloden**, is four miles east of **Inverness**. Here the Jacobite cause, so bravely pursued, finally drained away as, in a totally unequal fight, Charles's army, tired and hungry after an ill-advised night march, were cut down by Cumberland's fit, better-equipped troops.

It was Prestonpans in reverse, and those Highlanders who did not die on the field were ruthlessly pursued by Cumberland's troops. The 'Bonnie Prince' himself escaped and fled like a fox through the Highlands and Islands for five months, a price of £30 000 on his head, harboured and helped by his loyal supporters until he took ship for France, never to return. He died, a drunken old man, in Rome, and the Stuart cause was never to be fully revived.

Despite this, 'Bonnie Prince Charlie' has come to stand for a romantic dream of Scottish nationhood, and the idealized figure of the handsome young prince in his kilt leading his people against the 'Auld Enemy' persists in song and story today.

KEISS
Highland

On A9 7m N of Wick.

Situated at the north end of
Sinclair's Bay, Keiss is one of
several small villages between
Wick and **John o'Groats**. The main
street in Keiss is at right angles to
the A9, running both inland and
down to the sea at a small harbour
below Tang Head; just north are
the remains of two **brochs**, and a
further half-mile north on the cliff
edge is Keiss Castle, a small tower
built about 1600 for the 5th Earl of
Caithness but now ruined.

KEITH
Grampian

*On A96 17m SE of Elgin, 11m NW
of Huntly.*

Keith, centre of the farmlands of
Banffshire, divides into three. Old
Keith, by the River Isla, is medieval
in origin; New Keith, east of the
river, was planned and laid out
in the mid 18th century; and 'Fife
Keith', as it is known, west of the
river, was added in 1817. The oldest
building is Milton Tower in Station
Road, part of a castle built in 1480.
The Auld Brig, in Old Keith, dates
from 1609 and has steps up to its
crown. Also of note is St Thomas's
Catholic Church in Chapel Street,
New Keith, built in 1830 with a
façade modelled on Santa Maria
de Angelis in Rome. It has a fine
statue of St John Ogilvie; born
near Keith in 1580, he was not
canonized until 1976. There are
also good modern stained-glass
windows. Keith still produces
whisky and woollen goods and

the production of both can be seen
by visitors at **Isla Bank Mills** and
the **Strathisla Distillery**. It is a busy
market town and stages a major
agricultural show in early August
each year. Keith has a station on the
Aberdeen–Inverness line.

KEMNAY
Grampian

On B993 15m NW of Aberdeen.

The village of Kemnay has made
its name, and its fortune, from
granite, much of it taken from the
ironically named Hill of Paradise
nearby. The name Kemnay comes
from the 'kame' or ridge on which
it sits. Kemnay stone was used for
the Thames Embankment in London
(and five Thames bridges), the steps
of the Victoria Memorial outside
Buckingham Palace, the approaches
to the Forth Road Bridge, and
many other well-known public
places.

KILDRUMMY
Grampian

On A97 10m W of Alford.

The small village of Kildrummy,
above the River Don, was
originally Kindrummie,
'the end of the ridge'. Its
church (1805) is on a mound
of its own and, before the
area was properly drained,
was known as the Chapel
of the Lochs. A mile to
the south-west are the
large ruin of **Kildrummy
Castle** and **Kildrummy Castle
Gardens**.

KILDRUMMY CASTLE
Kildrummy, Grampian

On A97 11m W of Alford. Apr–Sept,
Mon–Sat 0930–1900, Sun 1400–1900;
Oct–Mar, Sat 0930–1600, Sun 1400–1600.

Dating back to the 13th century
when it was set up by Alexander
II to command the way from
Strathdon to Strathbogie,
Kildrummy had five large towers,
of which two remain in substantial
form. It was one of the main
strongholds of the Earls of Mar
until the 1715 Rising, after which
it fell into disuse. The ruins still
make a powerful impression, and
interpretive panels tell of the castle's
long and often turbulent history.

KILDRUMMY CASTLE
GARDENS
Grampian

On A97 11m W of Alford. Apr–Oct, daily
1000–1700 (09755 71264 or 71277).

A shrub and alpine garden, and
water gardens with a replica of
Aberdeen's Brig o'Balgownie, have
been created in an old quarry.
There is a shop with plants for sale,
woodland walk, play area and a
small museum (on request).

KINCARDINE O'NEIL
Grampian

On A93 27m W of Aberdeen.

Kincardine, a name occurring in
several parts of Scotland, means 'at
the head of the wood' – presumably
O'Neil's wood, in this case. There
was a settlement here at least
as early as 1231, when one Allan

Durward started the Church of St
Mary, the remains of which are still
to be seen. Alongside it he built a
hospice to serve travellers, for this
was an important crossing-point
on the River Dee, linking with the
ancient Cairn o'Mounth track from
the south. There was a bridge here,
then later a ferry, which operated
until **Thomas Telford's** bridge at
Potarch, two miles downstream,
opened in 1812. Kincardine O'Neil
is a quiet village today, the growth
that has occurred at **Banchory,**
Aboyne and **Torphins** (three miles to
the north-east) having passed it by.

KINCRAIG
Highland

On B970 6m S of Aviemore.

Kincraig is best known for the
Highland Wildlife Park, a mile and
a half away towards **Kingussie**.
The village itself has an attractive
situation at the east end of Loch
Insh. It was originally called Boat
of Insh from a ferry which plied
here. Much of Loch Insh and the
often-flooded marshes west of it are
a nature reserve run by the Royal
Society for the Protection of Birds,
with viewing hides and walks. Loch
Insh is much used for watersports,
and has a training centre at its east
end. On a knoll above the loch, just
south of Kincraig, is Insh Church,
which claims continuous worship
since the seventh century. It has a
very old Celtic bell and a font said
to have been used by St Adamnan.
Between Kincraig and **Aviemore** is
Alvie, with another very old place of
worship. The church, substantially
restored in the late 19th century,
is dedicated to St Drostan, another
Celtic saint, and has records going
back to the 14th century. On Tor

Alvie, the prominent wooded knoll well seen from the A9, are monuments to the last Duke of Gordon, to King George V, and to soldiers who died at the Battle of Waterloo.

KINGSPARK LLAMA FARM
Berriedale, Highland

½m N of Berriedale off A9. Open all year, daily (05935 202).

A herd of 16 llamas is an unusual sight on the Caithness moors. The gelded males are trained as pack animals, and visitors can go for a walk with the llamas carrying the picnic requirements. Prior booking is requested. The fleeces of both sexes are combed and the wool used for garments. Other attractions include peacocks, decorative fowl and chipmunks.

KINGUSSIE
Highland

On A86 10m S of Aviemore.

Kingussie means 'head of the pines' and is pronounced 'Kingoosie'. The modern village was established in 1799 by the Duke of Gordon. It had a thriving weaving and spinning industry but once the railway arrived in 1880 it became, and remains, a tourism centre.

Just off the main street is the **Highland Folk Museum**, Am Fasgadh, started by Dr Isobel Grant in 1935 and now reckoned to be the best museum of its kind in Scotland. Across the Spey are the gaunt ruins of **Ruthven Barracks**. Between Kingussie and the **Highland Wildlife Park** is Balavil, a name taken from

the French *belle ville*. It was the home of James Macpherson, a local schoolmaster who claimed in 1762 to have discovered and translated the works of the legendary Celtic bard Ossian. He was later discredited although he undoubtedly did translate very old Gaelic poems. He became MP for Camelford in Cornwall before returning to Badenoch in retirement.

KINLOCHBERVIE
Highland

On B801 20m SW of Durness.

This picturesque village, the last settlement of any size on the north-west coast, has developed into a very important fishing port. The harbour has been considerably developed in recent years, and Kinlochbervie is now one of the top five ports in the UK in terms of fish landed. From its onshore distribution plants, lorries leave for distant markets. A minor road continues to Sheigra, where there is a camping and caravan site and a fine beach: a further three miles north is Sandwood Bay, reached only on foot, a glorious sweep of sand with a rock stack, Am Buachaille (the herdsman) at its southern end.

KINLOCHEWE
Highland

On A832/A896 10m W of Achnasheen.

At the small village of Kinlochewe, roads divide to go north to **Gairloch** or west to **Torridon**, in either case amidst magnificent loch and mountain scenery. From

Kinlochewe a lovely walk can be taken along the Kinlochewe River to the end of **Loch Maree**: there was iron smelting in this area in the 18th century. The ascent of Slioch, a superb mountain well seen across Loch Maree, continues by the same path. West of Kinlochewe is the **Beinn Eighe** reserve, with a visitor centre at Aultroy.

KINLOCHLEVEN
Highland

On B863 7m E of Ballachulish.

At the head of Loch Leven you will find not an attractive Highland village but a small industrial town. Kinlochleven largely came into being in the early 20th century when the aluminium works was opened here, its power coming from the Blackwater reservoir four miles east. The power supply is all too obvious, with large pipes seen coming down the hill behind the town. It has received a boost in recent years with the opening of the West Highland Way path, which crosses from **Glencoe** via the Devil's Staircase (the old **military road**). Kinlochleven is the last settlement on the walk before its terminus in Fort William. Because of its setting deep in the hills, Kinlochleven gets no direct sunlight for four months of the year.

KINNEFF
Grampian

Off A92 2m N of Inverbervie.

A right turn off the main road just north of Inverbervie – or a bracing walk along the cliffs – leads to the small hamlet of Kinneff, above the inlet known as Little John's Haven.

The predecessor of the church seen today, most of which dates from 1738, played an important part in Scotland's history. When **Dunnottar Castle** was besieged in 1652 there was concern for the Scottish regalia, which had been taken to the castle for supposed safe keeping. Mrs Grainger, wife of the Kinneff minister, went to Dunnottar ostensibly to see the governor's wife but in reality to try to smuggle out the regalia. In this she was successful, hiding the crown in her copious apron while her servant-woman carried other parts of the regalia hidden in a basket.

KINTAIL
Highland

On A87 between Loch Cluanie and Shiel Bridge, 10–20m E of Kyle of Lochalsh.

The name Kintail is most often associated with the large estate on the north side of Glen Shiel, owned by the National Trust for Scotland and extending to over 17 000 acres. From Glen Shiel, the mountains forming the range known as the Five Sisters of Kintail rise very steeply to over 3000 feet. The ridge walk along them is one of the finest anywhere in Scotland; their crest is well seen from the summit of Mam Ratagan on the minor road to **Glenelg**. The Trust's estate includes the **Falls of Glomach** and there is a small seasonal information centre at Morvich. The hills on the other side of Glen Shiel are often known as the South Kintail Ridge; they contain in all no fewer than nine **Munros**, of which the easier eastern seven are usually taken together in one long day and the two at the western end, the Saddle and Sgurr na Sgine, in a separate expedition.

There was a skirmish in Glen Shiel in 1719 during a Spanish incursion in support of the Jacobite cause. The battle site is marked by a plaque, and it is also remembered in Coirein nan Spainteach (corrie of the Spaniards) in which some of the invading forces are said to have hidden while trying to escape. During this brief fight, **Eilean Donan Castle** was severely damaged by English forces.

KNOYDART
Highland

Passenger ferry from Mallaig to Inverie, all year Mon, Wed, Fri.

This large peninsula on the west coast, unconnected by road to the rest of Scotland, contains magnificent mountain scenery; its recent history has been turbulent and its future is still uncertain. In 1948 Knoydart was the scene of the last 'land raid' in Scotland, when six ex-servicemen unsuccessfully tried to claim croft land from the then owner, Lord Brocket. In 1982, in the aftermath of the Falklands conflict, the Ministry of Defence sought to acquire the whole 50 000 acres as a training area: resistance by conservation and mountaineering bodies prevented the acquisition. The estate has since been split into a number of smaller units. There is a small resident population, a remnant of the many hundreds who lived and worked here in past times. Foot access to Knoydart is usually from Kinloch Hourn by a path along Loch Hourn, or through Glen Dessarry, a very old trade and droving route. The fine mountain Ladhar Bheinn (claw hill) above Loch Hourn is now owned by the John Muir Trust, a conservation body dedicated to caring for wild land.

KYLE OF LOCHALSH
Highland

On A87 55m W of Invergarry.

Kyle of Lochalsh faces **Skye** across a narrow strait (Kyle meaning 'a narrows') over which the year-round ferry presently plies, taking visitors to the island. It is also a railway terminus: the scenic run from Inverness ends here. Kyle it is not especially attractive. Surrounding it is the National Trust for Scotland's **Balmacara** estate. The proposed road bridge, due to be built in the mid 1990s, would sweep past Kyle and touch down on the small islands of Eilean Ban and Eilean Dubh on its way to Skye.

KYLESKU
Highland

On A894 33m N of Ullapool.

Until recently travellers wishing to cross Loch Cairnbawn had to wait their turn at a small ferry; as the alternative was a detour of 100 miles, most were content to do so. Now, however, there are no delays, for a bridge was opened in 1984, sweeping across the loch in a long parabolic curve. The bridge has won praise for its design (by Ove Arup and Partners) and the way it complements its setting. On either side of the crossing are the small communities of Kylestrome and Unapool; boat trips are available in summer to see **Eas Coul Aulin**, Scotland's highest waterfall at the head of Loch Glencoul.

LAGGAN
Highland

On A86 8m SW of Newtonmore.

The name Laggan, meaning 'a hollow', occurs in several places in Scotland; here it is a scattered village at the east end of the **Corrieyairack Pass**, at an important crossing-point over the River Spey. There have been several bridges here, the present one, opened only a few years ago, was the first to take two lanes of traffic. It is not on the line of the military road, which comes down the south bank of the river and continues past Catlodge to Etteridge, on the A9. Laggan is Macpherson country, and a little to the east is that clan's Cluny Castle, an early 17th-century tower now incorporated into a 19th-century building (not open to the public).

LAIDHAY CROFT MUSEUM
near Dunbeath, Highland

On A9 2m N of Dunbeath.
Easter–end Sept, daily 0900–1700. D (P).

The longhouse (stable, dwelling house and byre under one thatched roof) is furnished in period style, with interpretive panels and displays, and a 'touch area' for the blind. There is a picnic area outside the museum.

LAIRG
Highland

On A836/A838/A839 11m N of Bonar Bridge.

'All roads meet at Lairg' is the saying; it is a significant junction, and also has a railway station. Not surprisingly, it has long been an important agricultural market, with a major sheep sale each August. To the north-west Loch Shin, a **hydro-electric** power reservoir as well as an excellent loch for angling, stretches away for nearly 20 miles. Near Invershin a footpath leads to the Falls of Shin, in a fine gorge where salmon may be seen fighting their way upriver. Lairg is a good centre for touring the areas to the north and west.

LANDMARK CENTRE
Carrbridge, Highland

On A838 7m N of Aviemore.
All year. Daily, Jul–Aug 0930–2000,
Apr–Jun, Sept–Oct 0930–1800, Nov–Mar
0930–1700. D (P) (047 984 614).

Landmark was one of the first purpose-built visitor centres in Europe. Its attractions include special exhibitions and displays on the landscape, wildlife and history of the Highlands; a 'timber tower' 70 feet high with a viewing platform at the top; walks including a 'treetop trail' which rises to 20 feet above the ground; a sawmill with steam engine and a nature centre. There is a restaurant, bar and gift shop.

LATCH OF COOK FARM PARK
New Byth, Grampian

Off A98 14m W of Fraserburgh.
Jul–Sept, Mon, Wed–Sun 1000–1800
(08883 419).

The park has many rare breeds on display including the almost extinct Bagot goats, and a herb garden.

LATHERON
Highland

On A9/A895 20m N of Helmsdale.

The roads from **Thurso** and **Wick** meet here, on a beautiful stretch of the Caithness coast. The much-photographed church in its lovely setting dates from 1735, and now houses a museum devoted to Clan Gunn. It has a separate belfry sited on a hilltop, so that the bells could be heard over the widest possible area. The small natural harbour of Janetstown, also known as Latheronwheel, is nearby.

LAURENCEKIRK
Grampian

Off A94 11m NE of Brechin.

Laurencekirk is the chief town of the Howe of the Mearns area. Founded in 1779 by Lord Gardenstone as a model village, it became a centre for linen weaving, and gained fame through Charles Stiven's beautiful snuffboxes. Lord Gardenstone (a snuff addict) brought Stiven here from Glenbervie. Laurencekirk is a market town, and a meeting place for people from the farming communities round about. It has a charming green.

LECHT
Grampian

On A939 8m SE of Tomintoul.

At the summit of the road from **Cock Bridge** to **Tomintoul** is the Lecht ski area. The hills rise barely 1000 feet from the road, so the runs are relatively short, and Lecht is generally known as an excellent place for beginners and intermediate skiers. The A939 follows the line of a **military road**, and a tough engineering job it must have been for the men of the 33rd regiment in 1754; their achievement is marked by a stone at Well of the Lecht, two miles north of the summit.

LEITH HALL
near Rhynie, Grampian

On B9002 10m S of Huntly.
May–Sept, daily 1400–1800; Oct, Sat–Sun 1400–1700. D (P). NTS (04643 216).

This attractive 18th-century mansion, built around an earlier tower-house, was the family home of the Leiths (later Leith-Hays) from 1650 until 1945. The house tells the family's story through furniture, ornaments and displays, including the document pardoning Andrew Hay after the Battle of **Culloden**. There is a tearoom and gift shop. The grounds include a fine 18th-century stable block, farmland (breeds include Soay sheep) and woodland with walks. There is a large informal garden and picnic area.

LEWIS
Western Isles

Car and passenger ferry, all year, from Ullapool to Stornoway; regular flights to Stornoway from mainland airports.

Lewis, with **Harris**, makes up the largest of the Western Isles. **Stornoway**, the island capital and its only real town, has a concentration of administrative services, shops, accommodation, harbour and airport. Once outside Stornoway you are into a rolling landscape of moorland and loch with small crofting communities. Industry includes **Harris tweed** production, **fishing**, and oil-related activities. The island retains a strong religious base and many people still strictly observe the Sabbath; moves to introduce Sunday ferries have been fiercely opposed.

There are four Lewis parishes. Point, the nearest to Stornoway, is a peninsula linked to the town by a causeway. The airport is here and nearby is the roofless 14th-century Church of St Columba. Barvas covers much of northern Lewis, taking in a number of small communities including Barvas itself and reaching the Butt of Lewis, the northern tip of the island. At Ballantrushal is Clach an Trushal, believed to be the tallest monolith in Scotland, and at Eoropie is the 12th-century Teamphull Mhor (St Moruag's Church). Uig was the scene of the discovery, in 1831, of the famous Uig Chessmen, a walrus-ivory set now in the British Museum. The parish also contains the standing stones at **Callanish** and the fine **broch** at Dun Carloway, nearly 30 feet high on one side. The final parish is Lochs, nearing Harris; its name is appropriate as the landscape is almost more of a waterscape. The alginate factory at Keose, north of Loch Erisort, supplied material used for fireproofing notepads taken by American astronauts to the moon.

LEWIS, ARNOL BLACKHOUSE

Off A858 12m NW of Stornoway. Apr–Sept, Mon–Sat 1000–1900; Oct–Mar, Mon–Sat 1000–1600.

This is a restored Hebridean 'blackhouse' built without mortar and roofed with thatch, with no chimney for the peat fire. Original furnishings and fittings have been retained.

LEWIS, CALLANISH

Off A858 15m W of Stornoway. All reasonable times. Free.

Callanish is the finest and in many ways the most mysterious group of standing stones in Scotland. Its powerful imagery is unquestioned: we may never know its original purpose, though a mix of astronomical mathematics and ritual seems probable. The main ring consists of 13 tall stones surrounding a central monolith 15 feet high with an avenue of 19 stones facing north. Other alignments conform to the cardinal compass points, giving rise to the theory that the stones were used for astronomical purposes. Research continues. There is a small seasonal tearoom, and a visitor centre is under discussion.

LEWIS, DUN CARLOWAY

On A858 16m W of Stornoway. All year. Free.

This is one of the finest remaining **brochs** anywhere in Scotland, reaching a maximum height of 30 feet, and all the more impressive for the isolation of its setting.

here, and the Sabbath is strongly observed.

LEWIS, MUSEUM NAN EILEAN

Point Street, Stornoway. Jun–Aug, Tue–Sat 1000–1230, 1400–1730; Sept–May, Tue–Sat 1400–1700. Free (0851 3773).

The museum has displays on various aspects of island life with sections on archaeology, agriculture, domestic life and the sea. A gallery stages special exhibitions.

LEWIS, STORNOWAY

With a population of 8000, Stornoway is the principal town and administrative centre for the Western Isles. It has a busy port with both commercial and leisure traffic and fishing vessels. Lews Castle, built for Sir James Matheson in the 1840s, is now a technical college teaching building, engineering, navigation and other skills. Its grounds hold the only substantial woodland on the island, though attempts are being made to encourage planting elsewhere. In St Peter's Episcopal Church is the prayerbook which David Livingstone took on his African travels. Martin's Memorial in Francis Street commemorates Sir Alexander Mackenzie, who made extensive explorations in northern Canada. Though not a particularly attractive town, Stornoway is a cosmopolitan community where you may well hear shopkeepers talking to their customers in Gaelic; the language is still widely spoken

LIGHTHOUSES, see panel p163.

LOCHAILORT
Highland

On A830 27m W of Fort William.

The small village of Lochailort, at the head of its eponymous loch, has a hotel and railway station on the Mallaig line. Here the A861 branches south to Moidart and **Ardnamurchan**. Bonnie Prince Charlie stayed at Kinlochmoidart House before rallying his followers at **Glenfinnan**. The area has excellent hill-**walking** and **fishing** on hill lochs; Loch Ailort holds a large **fish farm**.

LOCHALINE
Highland

On A884 32m SW of Corran Ferry.

An alternative route to Mull for travellers not in a hurry is to take the Corran ferry across Loch Linnhe then drive through Glen Tarbert and along the single-track road across **Morvern** to Lochaline, whence a small car ferry travels to Fishnish on Mull. The approach to Lochaline is over moorland and through forestry; a number of those evacuated from the islands of **St Kilda** in 1930 were settled here and worked in the forestry industry. Silica, used for high-quality optical glass, is quarried near Lochaline. At the head of Loch Aline is the ruin of Kinlochaline Castle, a 15th-century

Scotland's Lighthouses

The Commissioners of the Northern Lighthouse Board have been responsible for some of the most remarkable buildings to be found in Scotland. Lighthouses have a romantic air, but they are in reality totally practical buildings.

The Northern Lighthouse Board was formed in 1786. There were already a few lights around Scotland's coast (the first was erected on the Isle of May in the Firth of Forth in the 1630s) but with increasing trade it was clear that more were needed. The Commissioners concentrated on four sites – Kinnaird Head near **Fraserburgh**, **North Ronaldsay** in **Orkney**, Eilean Glas on **Scalpay**, off **Harris**, and the Mull of Kintyre.

Great ingenuity was applied, little time was wasted, and the Kinnaird Head light came into operation on 1 December 1787; all four were working by October 1789. Work continued at a steady rate, and in 1790 a 19-year-old apprentice lamp engineer started what was to be a long association between lighthouses and the Stevenson family.

Robert Stevenson was the first of the line. By 1800 he had become chief engineer. He was soon faced with the extremely difficult challenge of erecting a light on the Bell Rock off Arbroath on the east coast. The rock, a notorious hazard for sailors, is a reef, only above water at low tide, yet ways were found of overcoming all problems, and the light came into use in February 1811. Dubh Artach, south of Mull, and Skerryvore off Tiree presented similar difficulties. All these lights were manned until recent times.

Robert Stevenson was followed by his sons Thomas, David and Alan; the author Robert Louis Stevenson was Thomas's son and himself visited many lighthouses, writing graphically about them. These lights have become very familiar parts of the land- and seascape, at such places as **Duncansby Head**, **Dunnet Head** and Strathy Point on the north coast; Kinnaird Head and Buchan Ness in the east; Butt of Lewis, Mull of Kintyre and **Ardnamurchan** in the west. The lighthouse on Muckle Flugga is the most northerly building in Britain.

Some lighthouses can be visited, though few are manned now. The story of how they came to be built is an extraordinary one, peopled by dedicated men. The commissioners continue their work today from their headquarters in Edinburgh, ensuring that the mariner's way around Scotland's coasts is lit as it has been for 200 years.

Maclean stronghold captured by Macdonalds in 1644 which can be viewed from the outside only. On the shores of the Sound of Mull is another castle, Ardtornish, dating back to the 13th century. Here in 1461 the Lord of the Isles, Earl of Ross, plotted to divide up Scotland with the Earl of Douglas and Edward IV; a plan which foundered on the inability of factions to agree.

LOCHALSH WOODLAND GARDEN
near Kyle of Lochalsh, Highland

On A87 3m E of Kyle of Lochalsh.
Garden: all year, daily 0900–sunset.
Information kiosk and Coach House:
May–Sept, Mon–Sat 1000–1300, 1400–1800,
Sun 1400–1800. NTS (059986 207).

The National Trust for Scotland information kiosk and the Coach House have interpretive displays on the natural history and wildlife of the **Balmacara** estate. The gardens, with many fine trees, have woodland walks laid out.

LOCHCARRON
Highland

On A896 20m SW of Achnasheen.

Strung out along the north side of its loch, the village of Lochcarron was once a major centre for herring fishery; now it is a holiday centre with excellent hill-walking and angling. At North Strome, two miles to the west, are the scant remains of Strome Castle (NTS, all times, free). Lochcarron has an active environmental group which has produced an excellent leaflet of walks in the area.

LOCH GARTEN
near Boat of Garten, Highland

Off A95 or B970 8m N of Aviemore.
Information centre and hide: Apr–Aug, daily
1000–2000. The hide opens when the birds
arrive (0479 83694).

Ospreys nest at a number of sites in Scotland; most are known to only a few naturalists, but here and at Loch of the Lowes, near Dunkeld, viewing facilities are provided so that everyone can see these magnificent birds, which make the long trip from Africa each spring to return to their nest site in an old pine wood, and return to warmer climes in the autumn. The osprey is also known as the fish eagle, but they cannot be seen fishing from the Loch Garten hide. They have discovered instead a ready source of food from the **fish farm** at **Rothiemurchus** near **Aviemore**, and can sometimes be seen there grabbing a meal. The information centre and hide is the only access to the osprey area at the Loch Garten reserve, which is owned by the Royal Society for the Protection of Birds.

LOCHINDORB
Highland/Grampian

Off A939/B9007 10m N of Carrbridge.

This lonely loch, set in bleak moorland, is for ever associated with the 'Wolf of Badenoch', the son of King Robert II, who plundered the area in the late 14th century. The castle on its small island was a Comyn stronghold before that, captured and enlarged by Edward I in the early 14th century and not taken over by the Wolf as a base for his marauding exploits until 1372.

was largely destroyed by James 's forces in 1456. The castle can be een from the minor road running longside the loch.

OCHINVER
Highland

n A837 35m NW of Ullapool.

n attractive fishing village still with busy harbour, Lochinver is also n important holiday centre with ood sandy beaches at Achmelvich, lachtoll and Clashnessie. Inland the bare dome of Suilven, best een either from a boat (trips can e arranged) or from the road to verkirkaig, from where the fine alls of Kirkaig can also be visited. hese ancient hills, of Torridonian andstone resting on Lewisian neiss, are made up of some of the ldest rock anywhere in the world, nd form a quite unique landscape. here is a rich birdlife in the area, specially on the sea and coast.

OCH MAREE
Highland

y A832 between Kinlochewe and Slattadale.

rom Kinlochewe north, the road uns below the old Caledonian pine voods of the **Beinn Eighe** reserve; cross the loch rises the glorious eak of Slioch (spearhead), best een from the car park partway up ne lochside. Its lower flanks no onger hold extensive oak woods, s they once did; iron was smelted ere in the 18th century. Further orth are several islands, wooded nd rarely visited nowadays, and : Slattadale are the Victoria Falls, amed after **Queen Victoria** following

her visit here in 1877. The queen was rowed out to Isle Maree, on which St Maelrubha (after whom the loch is named) established a cell in the seventh century. Loch Maree and its surrounds are outstandingly beautiful, encompassing all that is best of the Highland scene.

LOCHNAGAR
near Ballater, Grampian

Access from Spittal of Glen Muick, 10m SW of Ballater.

The mountain of Lochnagar, on the royal estate of Balmoral, has been celebrated in literature by many writers including Byron, and more recently the Prince of Wales, in his short story *The Old Man of Lochnagar*. The mountain is most often climbed from Spittal of Glen Muick, where the Scottish Wildlife Trust has a small information centre. One route goes via Glas-allt Shiel, the lodge built by **Queen Victoria** as a retreat after Prince Albert died, on the shores of Loch Muick, Lochnagar has twin summits, Cac Carn Beag and Cac Carn Mor, and superb cliffs plunging down to the loch from which the hill takes its name (Lochan na Gaire, little loch of noise). There are major rock and ice climbs on these cliffs. Lochnagar is easily seen from the A93 Deeside road, rising above the Forest of Ballochbuie.

LOCH NAN UAMH
near Lochailort, Highland

On A830 30m W of Fort William.

This small sea inlet, meaning 'loch of the caves', saw both the start and the finish of the mainland adventures of Bonnie Prince Charlie. The prince landed here in August 1745 intent on restoring his father to the throne of Great Britain: the Prince's Cairn marks the spot where, just over a year later, he left for France, a dispirited refugee with a price of £30 000 – a vast sum at the time – on his head. The full story is told at the visitor centre at **Glenfinnan**.

LOCH NESS
Highland

Between Fort Augustus and Inverness.

Loch Ness was formed when the vast geological fault known as the Great Glen Rift was created, perhaps 350 million years ago, and is very deep, dropping to nearly 1000 feet below water level in places. The loch has never been known to freeze. Its narrowness, the steep surrounding hills, and the dark, peaty water would give it something of an air of mystery without the legend of its world-famous monster. The rumours started at least as early as the seventh century, when St Adamnan, Abbot of Iona, referred in his *Life of Columba* to an '*aquatilis bestia*' in the loch. Nothing certain has ever been found, despite extensive searches using modern equipment; the story of Nessie and the possibility of a sighting still draw many thousands of visitors each year to the loch and the surrounding area. Cruises can be taken on the loch from both **Fort Augustus** and **Inverness**; apart from these towns, other settlements on its shores include **Invermoriston, Foyers** and **Drumnadrochit**, where there are two 'monster' exhibitions the **Loch Ness Lodge Visitor Centre** and the **Official Loch Ness Monster Exhibition Centre**.

LOCH NESS LODGE VISITOR CENTRE
Drumnadrochit, Highland

In Drumnadrochit. Jun–Sept, daily 0900–2100; Oct–May, daily 0900–1800. D (P) (04562342).

The visitor centre has displays on local history and wildlife plus a large-screen cinema show on **Loch Ness** and the monster. Cruises on the loch can be arranged. There is a coffee shop and gift shop.

OFFICIAL LOCH NESS MONSTER EXHIBITION CENTRE
Drumnadrochit, Highland

In Drumnadrochit. May–Sept, daily 0900–2130; at other times check locally. D (P (04562 573 or 218).

The centre presents a 40-minute multi-media show telling the story of the monster and the many searches for it. There is a café and gift shop.

LOCH OF STRATHBEG
near Fraserburgh, Grampian

Off A952 5m S of Fraserburgh. Permits must be obtained in advance: contact the Warden, Loch of Strathbeg Reserve, Crimonmogate, Lonmay, Fraserburgh AB4 4UB.

This large, shallow loch less than half a mile from the coast is part of a 2500-acre RSPB reserve, and at times can carry as many as 20 000 wildfowl. Birds of prey include sparrowhawk, merlin and short-eared owl; in all nearly 200 species have been recorded in the past 20 years. Mammals include roe deer, badger and otter and the scavenging

nink, which preys on small birds.
The habitat ranges from dunes to
marshland with a correspondingly
rich variety of flora attracting good
numbers of butterflies. Access is
limited to a reception area and
observation hides.

LOSSIEMOUTH
Grampian

On A941 5m N of Elgin.

Lossiemouth was formerly the
port for **Elgin**, and still has a good
fishing industry, also found in
nearby Branderburgh, founded
by Colonel Brander in the 19th
century at the time of the herring
boom. The town looks to the air
as well as the sea nowadays, with
a large RAF base just to its west.
Between the airfield and **Duffus
Castle** is Gordonstoun School,
where several members of the royal
family were educated. The school
was set up by Kurt Hahn in 1934
on an estate formerly belonging to
the Gordons; the main house is a
classic building of the 1720s. No
1 Gregory Place, Lossiemouth,
was the birthplace of Ramsay
Macdonald, the first Labour Prime
Minister. There is a plaque outside
the house, and Lossiemouth
Museum in Pitgavenny Street has
a reconstruction of his study. He is
buried in the churchyard at Spynie,
between Lossiemouth and **Elgin**,
where the ruins of Spynie Palace,
formerly the seat of the Bishops of
Moray, can be seen.

LUMPHANAN
Grampian

On A980 10m NW of Banchory.

The small village of Lumphanan is
known for two things: the superb
Lumphanan Peel Ring, and the
possibility that Macbeth met his end
here in 1057. South of the village is
a ring of trees known as Macbeth's
Cairn, where, it is said, the king lost
out in hand-to-hand combat with
Macduff. There is also a Macbeth's
Cairn north of the village, but this
is prehistoric in origin. Lumphanan
means 'St Finnan's land', and
the village church is dedicated to
the saint.

LUMPHANAN PEEL RING
Grampian

*On minor road 1m SW of Lumphanan
village. All reasonable times. Free.*

This is a fine example of an
early medieval motte with walls,
earthworks and ditches. The wall
is probably 12th century but the
fortification was set up earlier. The
word 'peel' comes from paling, a
wooden defence which would have
predated the stone.

LYBSTER
Highland

Off A9 15m S of Wick.

The village of Lybster is spread
between the A9 and the sea,
terminating in an attractive harbour
below cliffs. The name may mean
'lee farm'. Lybster Church has
an inscribed Celtic cross by its
north wall. The area is rich in
prehistoric remains. Also of note
is the extraordinary little harbour
at Whaligoe, between Lybster and
Wick, reached by a flight of (it is
said) 365 stone steps down the cliff.

MACDUFF
Grampian

On A98, 1m E of Banff.

Smeaton's fine seven-arched bridge over the River Deveron separates **Banff** and the small town of Macduff, the latter owing its name to the 2nd Earl of Fife, not Shakespeare's character. Macduff now has the harbour serving both places; it was extended in 1966. The fish market, opened in 1964, handles an average of 10 000 boxes of fish a week. Nearby at Tarlair are open-air swimming pools, recalling the days when the town was a spa. The 1805 Italianate church stands at the brow of Doune Hill. The town's war memorial is even higher, commanding a splendid view of the harbour and a sweep of rocky coastline.

MALLAIG
Highland

On A830 45m W of Fort William.

Mallaig is at the end of the A830, and also of the scenic rail line from **Fort William**, along which steam-hauled excursions run in summer. Mallaig is an important harbour and port, used by many fishing vessels, pleasure-craft and ferries. The regular **Small Isles** run starts here, as does the car ferry to Armadale on **Skye** and the mail and passenger boat serving **Knoydart**.

MARITIME MUSEUM
Buckie, Grampian

In West Cluny Place. All year. Mon-Fri
1000-2000, Sat 1000-1200. D (P). Free (0309 73701).

The museum tells the story of Buckie's maritime history, how fishing vessels have evolved, and shows some of the tragedies that have inevitably occurred. It includes the Peter Anson Gallery, where a selection of this artist's work is on show.

MELVICH
Highland

On A836 18m W of Thurso.

Just north of the village of Melvich, the Halladale River empties into Morvich Bay, which has extensive sands: Portskerra nearby has a small, attractive harbour. A local legend tells how an old woman returning home from shopping was chased by the devil. She eluded him by running round and round a large boulder; in his fury the devil split it in two, but the woman escaped. The 'split stone' can still be seen, a mile east of Melvich. A few miles west is Strathy Point. From the end of the public road a short walk leads to the modern lighthouse (lit 1958) on cliffs rich with summer flowers and busy with sea-birds. The rare Scottish primrose is found here. An amusing touch is provided by the two small model lighthouses on the lochan reached just before the point.

MILITARY ROADS, see
panel p169.

The Military Roads

In 1724, the Fraser chief, Lord Lovat, sent a 'memorandum' to King George I in London in which he expressed concern at the poor state of roads and bridges in the Highlands, feeling this would hinder the government should there be further unrest. Major-General George Wade, a distinguished soldier but without a command at the time (he was in fact MP for Bath), was sent north to investigate.

Wade's report caused great alarm. He told the King that there were upwards of 12 000 men 'ready to rise in arms in favour of the Pretender' and that the main difficulty in opposing them was 'the want of roads and bridges'. Wade was immediately appointed Commander-in-Chief, North Britain, and £5000 – a very considerable sum – was voted for him to spend on improving barracks and lines of communications in the following year alone.

By 1740 the great network of roads he planned was well towards completion. **Fort William** to **Inverness**; **Fort Augustus** over the **Corrieyairack Pass** to Ruthven in Strathspey (perhaps his finest achievement); Dunkeld to Inverness; Crieff to Dalnacardoch – all were accomplished in a remarkable series of skilfully carried out exercises.

George Wade retired as a Field Marshal. His successor was Major William Caulfeild, who continued building until 1767, greatly expanding the network. He had worked with Wade and admired his predecessor to the extent of naming his son Wade Toby Caulfeild. Roads built under Caulfeild included the Rest and be Thankful in Argyll, Stirling to Fort William via **Glencoe**, and Fort Augustus to Bernera near **Glenelg** on the west coast.

The new roads helped government forces to travel more easily: they also helped the Jacobites, who used the Corrieyairack and other roads during the 1745–6 Rising. After 1746, government suppression ensured that the clans would not easily rise again, and the 'military roads' provided the means for linking all the main administrative centres in the Highlands.

Many of these roads can be traced today. They tend to be labelled on maps as 'General Wade's Military Road' regardless of who actually built them. Modern roads follow their line in many places, including the A9 from Perth to Inverness through the Drumochter Pass, reaching a height of over 1500 feet, and the A939 from **Cock Bridge** to **Tomintoul** reaching over 2000 feet at the **Lecht**. These roads are difficult enough for today's engineers; 250 years ago they must have been seen as miracles.

MILL OF TOWIE
near Keith, Grampian

On B9014 at Drummuir, 5m SW of Keith. Easter and May–Oct, daily 1030–1630.

This old oatmeal mill by the River Isla on the road between **Keith** and **Dufftown** has been restored to working order.

HUGH MILLER'S COTTAGE
Cromarty, Highland

Church Street, Cromarty. Easter–end Sept, Mon–Sat 1000–1200, 1300–1700, Sun 1400–1700. NTS (03817 245).

The cottage, built around 1710, contains an exhibition on the life and work of the eminent geologist, writer and theologian Hugh Miller, who was born here in 1802. Publications are on sale and there is a small garden.

MINTLAW
Grampian

On A950/A92 9m W of Peterhead.

The village of Mintlaw stands on an important road junction: north for **Fraserburgh**, east for **Peterhead**, south for **Aberdeen**. The place itself is small, in the agricultural heartland of Buchan. West is **Aden Country Park** and the village of Old Deer, with the ruin of **Deer Abbey**. The name 'deer' (see also **New Deer**) is believed to be from Gaelic *doire*, a forest, which would make the two nearby Forests of Deer actually 'Forest of Forest'. Three miles west of Mintlaw, off the A950, is the imposing stone circle of Loudon Wood.

MOIDART
Highland

Between Loch Ailort and Loch Shiel.

This wild, almost uninhabited area is a paradise for the adventurous walker and the naturalist. It is prime eagle country, as the birds are largely undisturbed by human activity. Among its principal mountains are Rois-Bheinn (hill of showers, an apt name here), and the two Beinn Odhars, Mhor and Bheag (big and little dun hill), on the west side of Loch Shiel. The road from **Lochailort** to **Acharacle** was only completed in 1966. It passes Kinlochmoidart House, where Bonnie Prince Charlie stayed in August 1745 before proceeding to **Glenfinnan**. A group of seven beech trees commemorates the Seven Men of Moidart who sailed up Loch Shiel with the prince. A walk leads from the minor road past the inn at Glenuig to the deserted village of Smearisary on the coast. The empty walls and overgrown crofts are a stark reminder of how the land has lost its people.

MONADHLIATH MOUNTAINS
Highland

Between Loch Ness and Strathspey.

The Monadhliath (grey hills) form a great block of wild country east of **Loch Ness**, almost roadless and virtually uninhabited, crossing the major river valleys of Dulnain and Findhorn to reach Strathspey. This is an area for the wanderer with a taste for isolation (except from August to October, when commercial stalking takes place).

he hills are largely rounded
nd undramatic – and frequently
yet underfoot – but the glens
re superb. The eastern part of
he area, above **Kingussie** and
Newtonmore, is better known, and
as easier access, and there is some
arming here. There have been
roposals for ski development, so
ar unrealized.

MONIACK HIGHLAND
VINERIES
Highland

Moniack Castle, off A862 7m W of
Inverness. All year. Mon–Sat 1000–1700. D
(P). Free (0463 83283).

At Moniack, wines are made from
unusual ingredients including birch
sap and country fruits. Tours show
he processes involved, with a
asting afterwards. There is a shop
nd café.

MONYMUSK
Grampian

On B993 15m W of Aberdeen.

The church in this quiet village
dates back to the 12th century.
Inside is an attractive modern
stained-glass window showing
a Culdee priest preaching with
Bennachie behind him. A large
Pictish inscribed stone stands in the
church entrance. The Monymusk
Reliquary, a casket said to contain
ne of St Columba's bones,
s in the National Museum of
Antiquities in Edinburgh. There
was an Augustinian priory here,
which was later fortified and is
now incorporated into Monymusk

House. In 1712 the Monymusk
estate was bought by Sir Francis
Grant (later Lord Cullen), a notable
agricultural reformer who planted
no fewer than 50 million trees. A
mile west of Monymusk is Pitfichie
Castle, a round tower attached to a
rectangular keep, recently restored
from ruin (not open to the public).

MORAR
Highland

On A830 5m S of Mallaig.

On its way to the village of Morar
from **Arisaig**, the A830 wriggles
tortuously along the coast, passing
a succession of rocky bays with
silvery-white sand. The sunsets,
looking out over the mountain
skyline of Rum, are rightly famed.
Nearing Morar, road and railway
meet to cross the River Morar,
a rapid stream of only a mile in
length but still enthusiastically
fished. It is the outlet from Loch
Morar, the deepest inland loch in
Britain, even deeper than **Loch Ness**,
dropping away to a glacier-gouged
maximum of 1060 feet below water
level. Like Loch Ness, it is said to
have a monster, a cousin of Nessie
called Morag, though there are
fewer reported sightings. Morar
itself is a small collection of houses,
a hotel and the railway station. On
the shore of the loch is a fine old
Catholic church. Morar Bay has
good sands and a glorious outlook.

MORVERN
Highland

Between Loch Linnhe, Loch Sunart and the
Sound of Mull.

The Munros

Sir Hugh T. Munro, Bt, of Lindertis (1856–1919), epitomizes the Victorian mountaineer. Well-travelled and of comfortable means, he was a founder-member of the Scottish Mountaineering Club in 1889 and its third president, from 1894 to 1897. Before then, he had undertaken the task which has secured his place in posterity, compiling the first accurate list of Scottish mountains over 3000 feet.

Munro's list, published in the *SMC Journal* in 1891, included 283 peaks which he felt should be classed as 'mountains' and a further 583 summits denoted as 'tops'. With such a list available, it was inevitable that people would try to ascend all the peaks named; and so the sport of Munro-bagging was born. In the century since then, it has given hundreds of hill-walkers pain, pleasure and a target in life.

It has also created considerable controversy, from the regular revisions carried out by the SMC. Some have become necessary as later and more accurate surveys have revealed certain peaks to be above 3000 feet, and thus worthy of promotion, and others to be, alas, a few feet below. The current list includes 277 Munros.

The first recorded Munroist is the Reverend Aeneas Robertson, who claimed completion on the Aonach Eagach, above **Glencoe**, in 1901. Robertson was a fine hillman who spoke Gaelic and was chairman of the Scottish Rights of Way Society for many years. He had ample leisure time to pursue his passion – a feature of the mountaineers of the time, when it must be remembered public transport in the Highlands was virtually non-existent and roads were of execrable standard.

After Robertson, there was a gap of 22 years before another completion was claimed, by Reverend A.R.A. Burn, who was the first to take in all the 'tops' as well. Since then, the list has grown more quickly, and in 1992 was nearing a thousand names.

Munro himself never quite managed to complete the list. It is known that he did not ascend the fearsome Inaccessible Pinnacle of Sgurr Dearg on **Skye** – but on his original list, that was a top and not a mountain. He had left the easy Carn Cloich-mhuilinn west of **Braemar** (now a Top of Beinn Bhrotain) for last, but it appears that another Deeside hill, Carn Ealar, also defeated him, despite several attempts.

(continued)

The Munros *(continued)*

It is remote, certainly, but of no technical difficulty. Munro suffered badly from rheumatism in later years, and this may have been a factor.

These details detract in no way from the measure of the man. He (and his contemporaries) went out in all weathers, in clothing which would nowadays be considered cumbersome and inadequate. His surveying work was remarkable, and his name has passed into common usage as a way of describing a very special part of Scotland's heritage. Blessed and cursed in equal measures by generations of hill-walkers, Munro will never be forgotten.

he mountainous peninsula known s Morvern is wild, very beautiful nd largely uninhabited. The A884 o **Lochaline** cuts across it: the only ther roads are a link to Kingairloch n Loch Linnhe and a road neandering along the north side f the Sound of Mull to Drimnin. rom Kingairloch a superb ridge valk around Glengalmadale can be aken, overlooking dramatic corries nd crags. South of here, visible rom the mainland, is the vast oastal super-quarry at Glensanda, vhich provides aggregate for se both at home and abroad. Around Loch Aline, especially to its vest, is much forestry, providing mployment. Here too is Fiunary, rom where Dr George Macleod 1895–1991), founder of the Iona Community, took his title when he vas ennobled. The road continues o Drimnin, passing the ruin of Caisteal nan Con (dog castle). rom Drimnin a track wanders ound to Rahoy: the estate here vas owned between 1977 and 991 by the Highlands and Islands Development Board in order to arry out experiments in deer

farming. The track continues to Glencripesdale, where a lodge has been turned into one of the most remote hotels anywhere on mainland Britain.

MUCK, see SMALL ISLES.

MUIR OF DINNET
Grampian

Off A93/A97 4m E of Ballater.

The national nature reserve at Muir of Dinnet incorporates woodland, heather moors, and notable landscape features formed towards the end of the last ice age. Lochs Davan and Kinord are 'kettle-holes', gouged out by ice; shallow, with rich flora including impressive water-lilies and an excellent winter birdlife. Otter are also found here. The woodland, on glacial moraines, mounds and ridges, holds lovely stands of silver birch and some Scots pine, and the heather moorland is beautiful in late summer and autumn. The best-known feature is probably the Vat, a huge pothole fed by the Burn o'Vat, which runs in a deep meltwater channel.

MUIR OF ORD
Highland

On A832/A862 15m W of Inverness.

With the rerouting of the A9 over the Kessock and Cromarty Firth bridges, the village of Muir of Ord has reverted to a quieter pace of life. For those not in a hurry, the route via **Beauly** and Muir of Ord to **Garve** and the west offers fine scenery. The **Ord Distillery** is open and a few miles to the west, in Strathconon, forest walks are laid out at Torrachilty.

MUNROS, see panel p172.

NAIRN
Highland

On A96 16m NE of Inverness.

Nairn, on a long, shallow bay looking across the Moray Firth, is vigorously promoting itself as a healthy holiday resort. The climate is generally dry and mild, and the town has excellent facilities for sport including golf, tennis, riding, walking – and cricket. The English game arrived here with the railway, which was built using labour from Yorkshire. The workmen were not to be denied their favourite sport, and Nairn still has a thriving club. Below Joseph Mitchell's 1857 railway viaduct is the old church of 1650, now a ruin. A new square-towered church (on the Inverness road) was completed in 1897. Nairn Court House dates from 1818, the steeple being added in 1860. In front of it is the 'Horologe', a sundial used for timekeeping before there was a town clock.

Nairn has long been a fishing port, and the Fishertown Museum in King Street is full of fascinating reminders of the times of the great herring fleet. An active reminder is the Nairn Fishermen's Society, founded in 1767 and thought to be the oldest society of its kind in Scotland. **Thomas Telford**'s 1821 harbour was replaced in 1932 by a larger harbour with better facilities. Nairn has plenty to offer the summer visitor: its own Highland Games, an agricultural show, and a country fair, the latter held in the park surrounding the mansion of Viewfield, where the town museum is housed. The **Highland Railway Museum** is in Nairn.

NAIRNSIDE FARM CENTRE
Cawdor, Highland

On minor road off B9090 at Cawdor. May–Sept, daily 1000–1700. D (P).

The centre offers farm tours and has a children's play area, video and shop. The farm breeds Friesland sheep for their milk and milking can be seen each afternoon. Sheep's milk, cheese and ice-cream are on sale. A collection of other rare breeds is being developed.

NETHY BRIDGE
Highland

On B970 5m S of Grantown-on-Spey.

The small town of Nethy Bridge stands at the north end of the large Abernethy Forest, much of which is run by RSPB as a nature reserve, including the famous **Loch Garten** osprey site. There are fine walks all around this area, and Nethy Bridge also offers golf. A mile north of the town, by the B970, is the ruin of Castle Roy (Red Castle), a Comyn stronghold and one of the oldest castles in Scotland. For much of the 19th century, there was considerable industry here as timber was floated down the River Nethy to the Spey then on to Garmouth on the Moray Firth in an enterprise started by Aaron Hill, playwright and entrepreneur. Today's commercial timber goes, less romantically, by lorry.

NEWBURGH
Grampian

On A975 12m N of Aberdeen.

Newburgh, a small, neat town, is on the estuary of the River Ythan (pronounced 'eye-than' and possibly meaning 'the talking river'). It has a good golf course. Here too is the Culterty Field Centre, part of Aberdeen University, where the rich birdlife of the estuary and the Sands of Forvie is studied. The sands hold the largest concentration of eider ducks in Britain, many terns, and in autumn and winter vast numbers of waders and wildfowl, the latter also using the farmland and Meikle Loch, a little way inland. Access to much of the reserve is restricted.

NEW DEER
Grampian

On A948 12m N of Ellon.

The 'new' villages of Aberdeenshire and Buchan were established in the second half of the 18th century, when 'improvers' like James Ferguson of Pitfour were driving turnpike roads through the countryside, introducing agricultural reforms, and trying to organize the production of linen, wool and other materials. Thus New Deer is half a dozen miles west of Old Deer, and within a relatively short compass you can find **New Pitsligo**, New Aberdour, New Leeds, New Byth and **Newburgh**. New Deer is a quiet place today, a small settlement in the rich Buchan farmland. Nearby is Maud, celebrated in two volumes of autobiography by the journalist Jack Webster (*A Grain of Truth* and *Another Grain of Truth*), which in turn led to TV documentaries about the farming life of the area.

NEW PITSLIGO
Grampian

On A950 12m SW of Fraserburgh.

New Pitsligo, sheltered by the Hill of Turlundie, has grown from the original 18th-century settlement into a sizeable village and a centre for the many farms round about it. The name comes from a Forbes laird who was created Lord Pitsligo in 1633. His grandson followed the Jacobites in 1715 and again, at the age of 67, in 1745, after which he was forced to hide in a recess still marked on maps as Lord Pitsligo's Cave, on the coast west of Rosehearty. The village gained a considerable reputation for lace-making in the 19th century, and the tradition continues, on a smaller scale, today. To the east is a commercial peat-cutting business which can be visited, and to the north is Northfield Farm Museum.

NEWTONMORE
Highland

On A86 15m SW of Aviemore.

Backed by the **Monadhliath Mountains** and facing the **Cairngorms**, Newtonmore has become a year-round holiday centre, catering for general tourists in summer, Cairngorm skiers in winter, and walkers in every season. In 1952 the first pony-trekking centre in Britain was set up here, at the Balavil Arms Hotel. Newtonmore is MacPherson country; it has the **Clan MacPherson Museum**, and in August each year the clan gathering and Highland Games take place. The town is also a famous shinty centre, and the

valry between it and Kingussie is
ntense. The **Waltzing Waters** show
s an intriguing new attraction.
Near the bridge over the Calder
s a notice in Gaelic saying, *An
Rathad Daingnichte le lach Gu Clach
Brighde* – 'the roadway established
y law to St Bride's graveyard'. It
marks the successful outcome of
a long legal battle by the people of
Newtonmore against a landowner
who tried to block traditional access
to the graveyard in 1875, and is a
reminder that Gaelic was then the
everyday language here.

OHN NICOLSON MUSEUM
Auckengill, Highland

*n Auckengill. Jun–Aug, Mon–Sat
1000–1200, 1400–1600. D (P) (0955 3761
xt 242).*

The museum includes many
interesting archaeological exhibits,
relics from Caithness **brochs**, and
details of the life and work of
John Nicolson, a noted Victorian
antiquarian who lived here. A prize
exhibit is a funeral beaker believed
to be 4000 years old.

NIGG
Highland

Off A9 20m NE of Dingwall.

Nigg has become a major industrial
centre, building and maintaining
the massive installations that serve
the North Sea oil production fields.
The platform construction yard
was established in the early 1970s,
and the great rigs can often be
seen in the bay. The industry has
brought considerable income to the
area, though it has gone through

periods of uncertainty. Over the
Hill of Nigg to the east, the other
villages of the **Fearn** peninsula
remain untouched by commercial
development.

NORTH-EAST FALCONRY VISITOR CENTRE
near Huntly, Grampian

*Off A96 3m NW of Huntly.
Apr–Oct, daily 1000–1800 (046 687 328).*

Visitors can see demonstrations
of falcons being flown at regular
intervals throughout the day. In
addition there are Highland cattle
and red deer. There is a café,
gift shop and picnic area. The
centre runs falconry courses with
hunting trips.

NORTH-EAST OF SCOTLAND AGRICULTURAL HERITAGE CENTRE
Aden, Grampian

*May–Sept, daily 1100–1700; Apr and Oct,
Sat–Sun 1200–1700. D (P) (0771 22857).*

The centre, in the restored Aden
Home Farm, has imaginative
displays on estate and farming life
from the 18th century to the present
day, using dioramas, audio-visual
techniques and sound effects.

NORTH UIST
Western Isles

*Car and passenger ferry from Uig (Skye) to
Lochmaddy.*

The large island of North Uist is
connected to **Benbecula** and **South**

Uist by causeways, but the usual arrival point is Lochmaddy on the east coast – one of the few settlements on that side of the island, which appears from the map to be a mass of lochs and lochans separated by small areas of land. Lochmaddy is 'loch of the dogs' from the shape of offshore rocks. It was an important fishing port, but that activity has declined. The island's population of about 1600 divides its activities between fishing (now based mainly at Grimsay), crofting, knitting and weaving, and the production of alginates from seaweed, with a factory at Sponish on Loch Maddy. In contrast with the islands to the south, North Uist is largely Protestant.

The west coast of the island has large expanses of sand, dunes and machair flowers in summer. Here is the Balranald Nature Reserve with a wide variety of birdlife including the rare red-necked phalarope. Off the coast, the Monach Islands are visible about ten miles away: they are noted for their population of seals. Historical sites include Dun Torcuill broch in the north-west of the island and Teampull na Trionaid (Church of the Trinity) in the south at Carinish, dating from about 1200. It is said that there was at one time something of a 'University of the Isles' here. From the very north of the island, at Newtonferry, a ferry crosses to Leverburgh on Harris.

OLD MANSE OF MARNOCH HERB GARDEN
near Aberchirder, Grampian

Off A97 10m S of Banff.
May–Oct, Mon–Sat 1000–1800, Sun
1300–1800 (04665 873).

The garden, beside the River
Deveron, grows culinary and
aromatic herbs, and the proprietors
run Scottish cookery courses.

OLDMELDRUM
Grampian

On A947 18m NW of Aberdeen.

Oldmeldrum (just 'Meldrum' to
locals) is an attractive small town
with narrow streets and lanes. In
the market square (a conservation
area), the former town hall of
1877, with ornamented chimneys
and wall decoration, is now a
library headquarters. Glengarioch
Distillery (pronounced 'Glengeeri')
was founded as far back as 1797.
A single malt is produced as well
as whisky for blends. The distillery
enterprisingly uses its waste hot
water to heat greenhouses growing
tomatoes, an innovation which
has become very profitable – well
over 100 tons are produced each
year. South of Oldmeldrum is Barra
Hill, site of a battle on Christmas
Eve 1307 when Robert the Bruce
defeated John Comyn.

ONICH
Highland

On A82 2m N of Ballachulish.

After crossing the **Ballachulish**
bridge northwards, the A82 passes
through the village of Onich. The
1875 church, by Alexander Ross,
replaced an earlier building erected
in about 1822 along with its manse,
which survives. These manses
were built to a standard design,
either single-storeyed, as here, or
for larger charges with two storeys.
They are solid, unpretentious
buildings but not without character.
By the shore is a large standing
stone, Clach a'Charra, dated to
about 1500BC. North of Onich
is Glen Righ, with forest walks
leading to a series of waterfalls (*righ*
is usually 'king' but is here more
probably *ruigh*, meaning 'glen on
the hill'), and beyond that is the
Corran ferry, crossing the narrows
of Loch Linnhe to **Ardgour**, **Morvern**
and **Ardnamurchan**.

ORD DISTILLERY
Muir of Ord, Highland

On A832 at W end of Muir of Ord.
Feb–Nov, Mon–Fri 0900–1200, 1400–1600.
Free (0463 870421).

The distillery was established in
1838. Guided tours are offered, and
there is a small reception area and
gift shop.

ORKNEY

Orkney consists of about 70 islands,
of which only a third are inhabited;
the total population is about 18 000.
Among the named islands are **Eday**,
Egilsay, **Flotta**, **Hoy**, **North Ronaldsay**,
Papa Westray, **Rousay**, **Sanday**,
Shapinsay, **South Ronaldsay**, **Stronsay**,
Westray and **Wyre**. Although
largely treeless, the islands are
generally green and fertile, giving

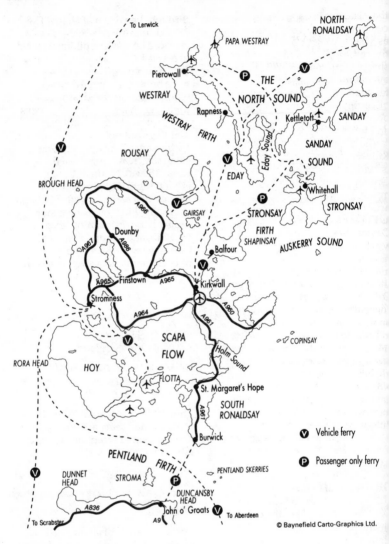

Orkney

e islanders the opportunity to ombine agriculture with **fishing** s a basis for their livelihood over e centuries. As well as excellent neep and cattle, Orkney produces notable cheese, and a whisky, lighland Park. There is a modern l terminal on Flotta, but it has een integrated into the community nd the landscape.

The administrative centre is irkwall, where an arts festival held at midsummer each year. rkney has a long tradition of nusic, literature and the other rts, maintained by such people s the composer Sir Peter Maxwell avies and the writer George lackay Brown. They, and others, ave found inspiration in the nagnificent land- and seascapes, ne wildlife, and the richness of rkney's history. There is a greater oncentration of prehistoric remains n these islands than anywhere else Britain, and such sites as **Maes owe**, **Skara Brae** and the **Stones of tenness** are awe-inspiring in their npact. The islands were under lorse rule for a long time, and still ave a strong Scandinavian feel to nem in place names and the local ialect and culture.

RKNEY, BIRSAY

n A967 11m N of Stromness.

irsay, at the north end of lainland, is notable for its istorical remains. The Earls of rkney built the **Earl's Palace** ere in the 16th century, and ubstantial ruins remain. Offshore n an island accessible at low tide **rough of Birsay**) are the remains f a Romanesque church and a lorse settlement. A superb coastal

walk can be started here, going south past Marwick Head and the Kitchener Memorial all the way to **Skara Brae**.

ORKNEY, BIRSAY, BROUGH OF BIRSAY

All year, at low tide (some winter closure – ask locally).

The Brough holds the remains of a Romanesque church, Norse dwellings and a small display of archaeological finds including a replica Pictish sculptured stone (the original is in the Royal Museum of Scotland in Edinburgh). Cheese-making can be seen at Swannay Farm and flour-milling at Boardhouse Mill.

ORKNEY, BIRSAY, EARL'S PALACE

All reasonable times. Free. HS (031–244 3101).

The extensive remains of the Earls of Orkney's large palace can be explored with the aid of interpretive panels.

ORKNEY, EDAY

Passenger ferry and flights from Kirkwall.

Eday, the central of the North Isles of Orkney, is about eight miles by one, with a pinched-in waist (the name means 'isle of isthmus'). It is fertile and holds about 50 farms, with a total population of about

200. Sea-bird colonies gather at Red Head, at the northern tip of the island, on the Calf of Eday, and on the small Mill Loch, which also has red-throated divers. There are chambered cairns in the southern half of the island, the best being at Huntersquoy. Carrick House is early 17th century. An artists' studio at Blett can be visited.

ORKNEY, EGILSAY

Car and passenger ferry from Tingwall or Rousay.

The small, flat island of Egilsay (possibly meaning 'holy island') lies off the east coast of **Rousay**, and has a population of about 40. The most notable historic building is the 12th-century St Magnus's Church, with an unusual round tower showing a distinct Irish influence. Earl Hakon had his rival, Earl Magnus, murdered at this site in 1115.

ORKNEY, FLOTTA

Car and passenger ferry from Longhope or Lyness.

Flotta lies in the eastern shadow of **Hoy**. It has seen considerable development twice this century. In World War II the army took most of the island over, building new roads and placing a gun-platform and searchlights at Stanger Head. More recently, Occidental Petroleum has built a large terminal to take crude oil from the Piper and Claymore fields in the North Sea. The company offers use of leisure facilities to the local people and has won environmental awards for the design and landscaping of the terminal. The indigenous population of about 150 is swelled by the Occidental workforce numbering up to 400.

ORKNEY, HOY

Passenger ferry from Stromness.

Hoy is the most mountainous of the Orkney islands. Its superb cliffs rise to 1140 feet at St John's Cliff, a vertical drop only exceeded by Conachair on **St Kilda**. Inland, the island rises gradually to Ward Hill at over 1500 feet. Longhope Bay is guarded by two Martello towers built in 1813–15, at a time when marauding American privateers frequented these waters. The Dwarfie Stone, two miles from Moness, is a large sandstone block carved out into a chambered tomb. Off the north-west coast is the Old Man of Hoy, a detached rock pillar 450 feet high and the scene of notable televised climbs in the 1960s.

ORKNEY, LAMB HOLM

On the tiny island of Lamb Holm, connected to Mainland by one of the Churchill barriers constructed in the 1940s, is a reminder of the many Italian prisoners-of-war held in Orkney during World War II. They transformed a corrugated iron hut into a Catholic chapel, with beautiful paintings and other decorations. The chapel was redecorated a few years ago by one of the prisoners who carried out the original work.

ORKNEY, MAINLAND, KIRKWALL

Car and passenger ferry from Scrabster to Stromness then 15m by road; regular flights from mainland airports.

Kirkwall is the administrative centre of Orkney, and the islands' principal town, with a population of about 7000. It has a long history: St Magnus Cathedral dates from 1137, the original castle from the 14th century, and Kirkwall has been a royal burgh since 1486. There are many other interesting and historic buildings, but Kirkwall looks forward as well as back, with thriving light industries and a busy tourist trade. From its harbour and airport ferries and flights go to many of the other islands. The annual St Magnus Festival, in June, offers two weeks of varied entertainment, but the artistic and social life is busy all year round.

ORKNEY, MAINLAND, KIRKWALL, BISHOP'S PALACE AND EARL PATRICK'S PALACE

Apr–Oct, Mon–Sat 0930–1900, Sun 1400–1900. HS (031–244 3101).

These two buildings are usually visited together. The Bishop's Palace is largely 16th century, on the site of a much earlier building. King Hakon died in the lower hall after his defeat at the Battle of Largs in 1263. The Earl's Palace was built for Earl Patrick Stewart by forced labour in 1600–7, and is a fine period building with castellation and a great hall. Earl Patrick planned to join the two palaces, but this plan was never realized.

ORKNEY, MAINLAND, KIRKWALL, ST MAGNUS CATHEDRAL

May–Aug, Mon–Sat 0900–1700. Free.

This massive cruciform building was started by Rognvald, nephew of Magnus: both are believed to be buried within the cathedral's pillars. Building went on into the 13th century, with an extension to the nave added later. There is much to see and admire in the grandeur of the cathedral.

ORKNEY, MAINLAND, KIRKWALL, TANKERNESS HOUSE MUSEUM

All year. Mon–Sat 1030–1230 and 1330–1730; May–Sept, Sun 1400–1700

Tankerness is a 16th-century merchant's house with courtyard and gardens, now containing a museum of Orkney life from prehistoric times to the present day. There are frequent special exhibitions.

ORKNEY, MAINLAND, MAES HOWE

Off A965 9m W of Kirkwall. Apr–Sept, Mon–Sat 1000–1900, Sun 1400–1900; Nov–Mar, Mon–Sat 1000–1600, Sun 1400–1600.

On a promontory between Loch of Stenness and Loch of Harray is what the author Eric Linklater described as 'the upturned green pudding-basin' of Maes Howe. The structure, an enormous megalithic sepulchre, has survived here for

3000 years. The walls of the main passage are formed of colossal stone slabs. This passage, which is only four feet high, leads to the large central chamber with a roof of overlapping courses of stone. Maes Howe was later used by Norsemen who left intriguing inscriptions, some romantic; one refers to the place as Orcahowe, 'orc' meaning a boar and giving a clue to the origin of the name Orkney.

ORKNEY, MAINLAND, STONES OF STENNESS

Off A965 8m W of Kirkwall.
All reasonable times. Free.

This impressive early stone circle originally had 12 uprights, of which four remain, the tallest rising to over 17 feet. The full circle measures over 100 feet in diameter and there is an encircling rock-cut ditch.

ORKNEY, MAINLAND, STROMNESS

On A965 15m W of Kirkwall.

An attractive village with a fine harbour, Stromness makes an immediate impression on the visitor arriving by ferry from **Aberdeen** or Scrabster. The picturesque main street grew from the prosperous times of the 18th and 19th centuries, when Stromness was a supply base for Hudson Bay ships and for whalers. Wynds between cottages lead down to the water. At the south end of the village is Login's Well, where ships formerly drew water: those recalled on its inscription include Captain

Cook's vessels of 1780 and the ships in which Sir John Franklin sailed in 1845 in an attempt to find the north-west passage round Canada. There is a golf course near the Point of Ness which looks out over **Scapa Flow**, and within easy reach are **Maes Howe**, the **Stones of Stenness** and Skara Brae. It is possible to walk all the way to the last-named along the cliffs.

ORKNEY, NORTH RONALDSAY

Weekly car and passenger ferry and daily flight from Kirkwall.

The most northerly of the Orkney islands, North Ronaldsay may appear to be a puzzlingly long way from **South Ronaldsay**. The names are in fact from different origins, the southern island from Rognvald, who settled it, and the northern from St Ringan, another name for St Ninian: North Ronaldsay was once known as Rinarsey. It is a flat island about five miles by one mile. A stone dyke runs round most of it: outside it you will find sheep happily chewing the seaweed. Orkney's first lighthouse was established here in 1789, replaced by a later structure of 1854 which, at over 130 feet, is the tallest land-based light anywhere in Britain. The Broch of Burrian was the origin of a stone inscribed with the celtic cross of Burrian, a design much used in modern jewellery.

ORKNEY, PAPA WESTRAY

Ferry by arrangement or daily flight from Westray.

Papa Westray holds the distinction of being the arrival point for the shortest scheduled air service in the world: two minutes from **Westray**, across the sound. The word 'Papa' indicates a religious house, in this case a small church dedicated to St Boniface and a ruined chapel dedicated to St Tredwell, who was said to have the power to restore sight. The island is fertile and has a population of about 120. It holds many interesting remains, most importantly the stone houses of the **Knap of Howar**. North Hill has colonies of terns and skua and is a nature reserve; Loch of Tredwell holds many waterfowl; but a less happy story is linked with Fowl Craig, where the last great auk was shot in 1813.

ORKNEY, PAPA WESTRAY, KNAP OF HOWAR

All reasonable times. Free.

These remains are believed to be of the oldest stone dwellings in north-west Europe, dating back to perhaps 3500 BC. Stone and bone axes, mallets and a spatula have been found, and the way of life is explained on interpretive panels.

ORKNEY, ROUSAY

Car and passenger ferry from Tingwall.

Rousay has a population of about 250, mostly living in the southern part of the island. The north and west are rugged, with fine cliffs, and the interior rises to over 800 feet at Blotchnie Fiold. As well as farming, there is a small factory processing crabs caught locally.

Rousay has many chambered cairns including the two-storeyed Taversoe Tuick and Knowe of Yarso, with four compartments, but the most famous site is **Midhowe**. Rousay offers excellent sport for the fisherman and a richness of birdlife for the ornithologist. On nearby Eynhallow (holy island) is a ruined 12th-century Benedictine church.

ORKNEY, ROUSAY, MIDHOWE

All times. Free.

At Midhowe, on the south-west coast of Rousay, are three **brochs**, one rising to 15 feet with a freshwater spring still flowing. Midhowe Cairn, known as the 'great ship of death' from its shape, is from the 4th millennium BC. The mound measures 106 feet by 42 feet and the inner chamber has 12 compartments.

ORKNEY, SANDAY

Car and passenger ferry, and flights, from Kirkwall.

Some 13 miles long but very narrow for much of its length, Sanday is in the Northern Isles and has a population of about 600. Its name is appropriate: there are fine beaches backed by dunes rich in summer flowers. The island has a flourishing knitting co-operative and a small electronics factory. Historic sites include Quoyness, a chambered cairn with an inner chamber reached through the roof and containing six cells. Quoyness (farm headland) is contemporary with **Skara Brae**. The lighthouse at

Start Point dates from 1806 but was automated in 1962.

ORKNEY, SCAPA FLOW

Between Mainland, Hoy, Flotta and South Ronaldsay.

The area of sea known as Scapa Flow, almost enclosed by islands, has strong links with the navy and with the two World Wars. From 1914 the British Grand Fleet sheltered here, and at the end of hostilities in 1918, German warships were escorted here. Many of them were scuttled by their crews in a gesture of defiance, and the wrecks provide a target for divers today. The British navy returned in 1939, but left after German action sank the battleship *Royal Oak*, with the loss of 800 lives. The fleet returned a year later after defences were strengthened. Over the next few years the Churchill barriers, now used as road causeways, were built to link **Mainland**, Burray and **South Ronaldsay**. Today Scapa Flow sees much ferry and commercial traffic; regular services pass through on the way to **Stromness**.

ORKNEY, SHAPINSAY

Car and passenger ferry from Kirkwall.

Shapinsay is the nearest island to **Kirkwall**, the ferry crossing taking 45 minutes. It is a fertile, low-lying island with a population of about 300, and is noted for the quality of its cattle. There are good sandy beaches. Shapinsay was the birthplace of the father of Washington Irving, the American author who created Rip Van Winkle. The principal building is Balfour Castle, a mansion built in 1847 for Colonel David Balfour, who energetically improved the island's agricultural production during his time there.

ORKNEY, SOUTH RONALDSAY

On A961 15m S of Kirkwall; summer ferry from John o'Groats.

South Ronaldsay, which is linked to Burray and **Mainland** by the Churchill barriers, is low-lying, nowhere rising to over 400 feet; even so it commands views of the other islands and seascapes. The island's long history includes notable Christian and Norse attachments. In the church of St Mary at Burwick is a large stone with two 'footsteps' in it, said to be those of St Colon, a disciple of St Columba, who preached from the stone. In another story the stone is said to be a porpoise which rescued a traveller called Gallus before being petrified. In the harbour village of St Margaret's Hope, the Norse fleet under King Hakon assembled in 1263 before sailing south to defeat at the Battle of Largs; this marked the end of Norse dominion over Orkney. Ships of a more modern kind are recalled in the Wireless Museum.

ORKNEY, SOUTH RONALDSAY, THE OLD SMIDDY

St Margaret's Hope. May–Sept, daily 1400–1700. Free.

The smiddy, which has been restored by the community council, has smiths' tools and other old agricultural implements.

ORKNEY, STRONSAY

Passenger ferry and flights from Kirkwall.

Looking like a twisted letter H, Stronsay is a low-lying, fertile island carrying a number of farms. It has a population of about 450. At one time Whitehall was a herring-fishing centre with hundreds of boats calling. Today it retains a fish-processing factory, though its future is uncertain as catch quotas and EC regulations hem the industry in. The island has a number of sheltered bays with sandy beaches; there is an impressive 'gloup' or holed rock at Kirbuster, in the south-east, and Rothiesholm Head is an excellent place for seeing sea-birds. Bay of Houseby has a **broch** at one end and a chambered cairn at the other.

ORKNEY, WESTRAY

Car and passenger ferry and flights from Kirkwall.

Westray, looking a bit like a booted leg reaching out to kick at **Rousay**, is a fertile island about ten miles long with a population of around 900. There are fine cliffs and good sandy beaches. As well as farming and fishing, crabs are processed for market at the harbour at Pierowall. Historical remains include two old churches. Westside, at the south of the island, is probably 12th century and is intact apart from the roof. St

Mary's, on Pierowall Bay, is 13th century, with later reconstruction. Half a mile west of Pierowall is **Noltland Castle**. Westray has much to offer the ornithologist with large colonies of sea-birds, waders, corncrake and many other birds.

ORKNEY, WESTRAY, NOLTLAND CASTLE

Apr–Sept, Mon–Sat 1000–1900, Sun 1400–1900; Nov–Mar, Mon–Sat 1000–1600, Sun 1400–1600. Free.

Noltland is a considerable stronghold with gun-loops, largely the work of Sir Gilbert Balfour, master of the household to Mary Queen of Scots. He was involved in the murders of Beaton and Darnley but was killed after plotting to overthrow the King of Sweden. There was a plan for Mary to go to Noltland after she escaped from Loch Leven Castle, but she went south instead.

ORKNEY, WYRE

Car and passenger ferry from Tingwall and Rousay.

The small island of Wyre, south of **Rousay**, takes its name from its shape, Norse *vigr* meaning a spearhead, which it roughly resembles. It has eight farms, a population of about 40, a pier and its own school. Interesting remains include a ruined 12th-century chapel and Cubbie Roo's Castle, named after Kolbein Hruga, a Norwegian also of the 12th century who settled here. Wyre was the birthplace of the author Edwin Muir, who wrote movingly in his autobiography of his days on the island.

OYKEL BRIDGE
Highland

On A837 14m W of Lairg.

The road to Ledmore and the west from **Lairg** enters Strath Oykel at Invercassley, four miles east of the small settlement at Oykel Bridge. Oykel simply means 'high' from an old Brythonic word, the same root as the Ochil Hills near Stirling. Near Invercassley there was a bloody clan battle in 1397, a force of Mackays defeating their rival

MacLeods to such an extent that only one of the latter survived the affray, and he died later of his wounds. Today the road provides a drive through beautiful scenery, at first wooded then more open and wilder, with the western hills coming into view. There is fine **fishing** on the rivers and hill lochs. The people of Strath Oykel were noted for their opposition to the **Clearances** in the late 18th and early 19th centuries, and there were several skirmishes here. In the end, it was all to no avail: more powerful forces prevailed and they had to leave.

PENNAN
Grampian

On B9031 12m W of Fraserburgh.

Pennan is a cluster of white-washed sandstone cottages round a tiny harbour. It is familiar to many thousands of people who do not know its name, for this was the setting for the popular film *Local Hero*. The harbour is still used by fishing boats, but the cottages are mainly holiday homes. West of Pennan is Troup Head, with wild cliffs rearing over 350 feet above the sea. You can walk over it to the villages of Crovie and Gardenstown, the latter (called locally Gamrie) founded by Alexander Garden of Troup in 1720 and for long a stronghold of the Plymouth Brethren movement. The cliffs are split by deep clefts including Hell's Lum and the Tore of Troup, a ravine running inland for eight miles.

PETERCULTER
Grampian

On A93 6m W of Aberdeen.

The land either side of the River Dee just west of Aberdeen has long been known as Culter (pronounced 'kooter'). Knights Templar built two chapels here in the late 12th century; the one on the north bank was dedicated to St Peter, hence Peterculter, and the one on the south bank to St Mary – and Maryculter parish is still there today. Templars' Park is on the south bank of the river, with the ruined chapel; a mile or so east is Blairs College, a Roman Catholic foundation of 1827, which has a fine portrait of Mary Queen of Scots. Also here you will find the **Storybook Glen**, an attraction for children.

PETERHEAD
Grampian

On A952 32m N of Aberdeen.

The 'Blue Toon', as it is known, is one of the largest white fish landing ports in Europe, and is also a major service depot for North Sea oil installations, with two large bases around the harbour. The long southern breakwater was constructed by convicts from Peterhead Prison in the early 20th century; the prison is now a maximum security establishment. The coastline is marred here by barbed wire surrounding an RAF station and by the vast chimney of Peterhead power station; above the power station on a hill is a curious modern sculpture commissioned by the hydro board.

Peterhead was Scotland's main whaling port in the 19th century, and those days are recalled in the prosperous houses of the period, in the Arbuthnot Museum, at **Ugie Salmon House** and on the town's heritage trail, which takes in points with names like Blubber Jetty. The Dales Country Park opened in 1987, the 400th anniversary of the town's foundation by George Keith, Earl Marischal of Scotland. On the western outskirts, at Inverugie, is Faith Acres, a Christian centre involved in the training of missionaries. Five miles north of Peterhead is St Fergus, the UK's most important gas-gathering terminal, taking in many millions of cubic metres a day from the gas fields under the North Sea. To the south are the notable sea-bird cliffs of the **Bullers of Buchan**.

PITMEDDEN ESTATE
near Ellon, Grampian

Off A920 5m W of Ellon.
May–Sept, daily 1000–1800. D (P). NTS
(06513 2352).

The Pitmedden estate extends to about 100 acres, its centrepiece being a re-creation of Alexander Seton's Great Garden, originally laid out in 1675. It has four parterres, three based on designs thought to have been used in the gardens of Holyroodhouse, Edinburgh, and the fourth a heraldic design based on the Seton coat of arms. There are woodland walks, picnic areas, a herb garden, a museum of farming life with agricultural and domestic artefacts, visitor centre, tearoom and shop. To the north-west is **Tolquhon Castle and Gallery**, and a little way south is Udny Castle, a turreted tower which can be viewed from the road; the churchyard at Udny Green has a 'morthouse' once used by guards watching for body-snatchers.

PITSLIGO
near Fraserburgh, Grampian

Off B9031 5m W of Fraserburgh.

The small village of Pitsligo has two churches, one dating from 1634 (now disused) which has fine stonework by Dutch masons. The newer church, built in 1890, has a Forbes loft and interesting Jacobean carved panelling transferred from the older building. Pitsligo was known as 'the visible kirk' from its

use by fishermen as a landmark. At Pitsligo Castle, south-east of the village, Lord Forbes established a curious school of 'transcendental devotion' (a form of meditation) in 1700. The castle was bought by the American media millionaire, Malcolm Forbes, in 1989 but he died in February 1990 before restoration work could be completed. On the coast near Pitsligo is Rosehearty, established as a fishing port by Lord Forbes in the late 17th century.

PLOCKTON
Highland

On minor road 5m N of Kyle of Lochalsh.

The picturesque village of Plockton, which is part of the National Trust for Scotland's large **Balmacara** estate, is sited on an inlet of Loch Carron. Although it is on the west coast, the village faces east, and the mild climate means that sub-tropical plants flourish here. The village has an annual regatta in summer, and is a popular anchorage for pleasure-craft throughout the season. It was originally a fishing and crofting township but is now a holiday centre.

PLUSCARDEN ABBEY
near Elgin, Grampian

On minor road 5m SW of Elgin.
All year. Daily 0800–2000. D (P). Free
(034389 257 or 388).

Pluscarden was founded as a Valliscaulian house in 1230. Attacked by the Wolf of Badenoch in 1390, it survived as a priory until 1560. Thereafter it fell into ruin until Benedictine monks from Prinknash

Abbey in Gloucestershire came here in 1948 and began restoring the buildings, many of which are open to visitors.

POOLEWE
Highland

On A832 5m N of Gairloch.

The River Ewe rushes into the sea at Poolewe, a small village which is close to **Inverewe Gardens**. From Poolewe a minor road runs up the west side of Loch Ewe for ten miles to Cove, with fine views across the lochs to the mountains of Letterewe. The Tollie Path leads from Poolewe to Loch Maree, a walk of five miles.

PORTKNOCKIE
Grampian

On A942 20m E of Elgin.

The fishing village of Portknockie lies between **Findochty** and **Cullen**. It has a small, neat harbour and brightly painted houses. Portknockie was founded in 1677 by fishermen from Cullen, attracted by the natural harbour. Like so many other coastal villages, it thrived during the herring boom. Offshore is the curious arched Bow-Fiddle Rock. Below the headland of Scar Nose, where Norse invaders were defeated in 961, is Whale's Mouth Cave.

PORTLETHEN
Grampian

Off A92 7m S of Aberdeen.

A coastal path leads south from **Aberdeen** past Altens and Cove, with waves crashing into deep inlets, for nearly seven miles to Findon and Portlethen, which have grown as dormitory suburbs of Aberdeen. The original settlement of Portlethen, as the name would indicate, was on the coast above Cammachmore Bay.

PORTMAHOMACK
Highland

On B9166 10m E of Tain.

Portmahomack is on the south side of the Dornoch Firth, at the north end of the **Fearn** peninsula. West of the village – once a considerable fishery centre, with a harbour improved by **Thomas Telford** – are fine sands. Nearby is the ruin of Ballone Castle, a 15th-century, Z-plan tower. On Tarbat Ness is the second tallest mainland **lighthouse** in Britain, a white and red banded tower over 120 feet high, built by Robert Stevenson in 1830.

PORTSOY
Grampian

On A98 8m W of Banff.

The attractive village of Portsoy is noted for its marble, quarried locally; items made from it are on sale in a shop at the harbour. From the town centre, steep streets run down to the harbour, which was built by the Ogilvies of Boyne in 1692 and enlarged in the 1820s. The oldest building in the village is Soy House, dating from the 1690s; the Star Inn is 1727 and has a pend arch leading to a courtyard. It is, almost inevitably, connected with tales of smuggling. A walk along the cliffs west of Portsoy leads to the area known as the Breeks, the source of the serpentine green marble, some of which found its way to the Palace of Versailles, outside Paris. Four miles to the east is the ruin of Boyne Castle, dating from about 1580. Nearby, in a 17th-century mill, is Scotsmill Pottery, where haggis moneybanks are for sale.

THE PUMP ROOM
Strathpeffer, Highland

In the Square. Easter–Sept, Mon–Sat 1000–1700.

A reminder of Victorian times, this was where people came to 'take the waters'. They dipped in the sulphur-tainted spa supposedly to improve the health and the nerves.

RAASAY
Highland

Car and passenger ferry from Sconser, Skye, all year, Mon–Sat.

Raasay, an island about 15 miles long, lies between **Skye** and **Applecross**. It is generally fertile, rises to a height of 1450 feet on Dun Caan, and has a crofting population of about 150. The birdlife is excellent and the island offers good walking. Ironstone, found at the south of the island, was mined for a short period around 1915–20. The island was MacLeod territory and towards its northern end is the ruin of Brochel Castle, a MacLeod stronghold. The local chieftain later built Raasay House at Clachan, which is no longer occupied.

RANNOCH MOOR
Highland/Central/Tayside

Rannoch Moor covers a large area between Bridge of Orchy, **Glencoe** and Loch Rannoch. The A82 crosses its western end below the hills of the Blackmount, as does the West Highland Way footpath. Other paths cross from Bridge of Orchy and from Glencoe, meeting at Rannoch Station. The moor can be peaceful in summer, its lochs and lochans sparkling in sunlight, and extremely desolate in winter, when the A82 is sometimes closed by snow. Evidence that the moor was formerly forested is found in the many ancient pine stumps lying under the peat, and it is now host to experimental conifer plantations started by the Forestry Commission some years ago. A rare plant, the Rannoch rush, was discovered here.

RED DEER, see panel p194.

RHYNIE
Grampian

On A97/A941 12m S of Huntly.

The neat village of Rhynie with its attractive square sits in the shadow of the Tap o'Noth, a distinctive hill topped by a vitrified fort. In Rhynie churchyard are two Pictish symbol stones. South of Rhynie is Lumsden, home of the Scottish Sculpture Workshop, whose work can be seen displayed both here and at **Kildrummy**. Two old castles are also nearby. Craig, just south of Rhynie, was an L-plan tower built in 1570 and occupied by the Gordon family until 1892. It is still substantially complete. Druminnor, east of the village, was formerly known as Castle Forbes. The earliest parts date from about 1450. It later became neglected but has recently been restored as a house. Druminnor is on the road to Clatt, below the Correen Hills, a small village whose apt name means 'concealed'. In the 16th century it was a burgh of barony and had its own provost and bailies.

ROSEMARKIE
Highland

On A832 1m NE of Fortrose.

Rosemarkie means 'headland of the horse'. The village has fine cliffs to its north-east, with caves that can be seen at low tide; an attractive walk inland leads up the Fairy Glen to lovely waterfalls. **Groam House**

The Red Deer

The red deer is the largest mammal found in Scotland. Originally a creature of the forest, it has been forced by the virtual elimination of the native pine woods to adapt to a life on moorland and open hill. As a result, over the past two centuries the red deer has grown smaller and hardier. The romantic image portrayed by Sir Edwin Landseer in his famous painting *The Monarch of the Glen* is now some way detached from reality.

Shooting red deer has slowly evolved from a sport pursued by wealthy estate owners and their friends in Victorian times into something more akin to an industry. Large Highland estates offer shooting to guests – often from abroad – and the income thus derived is very important to the economy not just of the estate but of the whole area.

In Victorian times, guests were accommodated in large lodges built for the purpose, furnished in considerable style and with many servants. The quarry was pursued on foot, and long, hard days on the hill were the norm. Many of the lodges have gone, or have been converted into hotels; guests are more likely to stay in the principal house on the estate. Vehicles are commonly used to take guests far into the hills, but the final pursuit of the stag must be done on foot, and the expert guidance of a stalker is still needed to bring the hunter to the right position upwind of the stag and within range.

The stag shooting season is from July to late October, and hinds are culled from October to February. In general, the aim is to take the weaker beasts out, leaving the better animals to provide the basis of the herd in future years. Red deer mate in October, and the roaring of the stags at this time is one of the great hill sounds of the Highlands. Fertilization is delayed until the spring, and the calves are born in May or June.

Despite the organization of estates in some areas into deer management groups, in recent years the red deer population in Scotland has grown past the point where the level is sustainable through culling or natural wastage. Hard winters lead to the deaths of many thousands of deer, and overgrazing has become a problem in many places, causing erosion and seriously affecting the regeneration of tree cover.

(continued)

Red Deer *(continued)*

The Red Deer Commission (based in **Inverness**) was set up by government in 1959 to conserve and control the red deer population in Scotland (it also has responsibility for roe and sika deer). The commission carries out counts each year, using helicopters as well as men on the ground, and issues advice and information on the management of deer. It has no legal powers to require estates or deer management groups to carry out culls, however.

Unless there is a major increase in the natural tree cover across the Highlands, it seems unlikely that the red deer will revert to its former size and stature. Herds of deer are still a fine sight, though in summer you will most likely have to climb the hills to see them. In winter they come to lower ground in search of food and can be seen more easily.

Museum is notable for its Pictish relics. St Moluag is said to have founded a church in Rosemarkie in the sixth century. From nearby Chanonry Point you look across the narrows dividing the Moray and Beauly Firths at a strange conjunction of sites: the powerful stronghold of **Fort George** and the fabrication yard at Ardersier, the skeletal outlines of the cranes at the latter seeming somehow to underline the strength of the walls at the former. Chanonry Point is one of the best places in Britain for seeing dolphins, though they are becoming rarer.

(of 1781) had its clock tower added in 1870, the handsome timepiece being the former town clock from Nairn. Rothes is the home of the **Glen Grant Distillery**. At one time there were five distilleries in the town. Little remains of Rothes Castle, a 13th-century tower burned in about 1700: many of its stones were taken for local building use. Nearby is Boat of Brig. The explanation for the curious name is that there was a bridge (one of the earliest anywhere on the lower Spey) which collapsed and was replaced by a ferry – the 'boat of the bridge'.

ROTHES
Grampian

On A941 10m S of Elgin.

Rothes, above a bend in the River Spey, was founded in 1766 on the site of an older village. The church

ROTHIEMURCHUS
Highland

On B970 1m E of Aviemore.

The large estate of Rothiemurchus (the name means 'plain of the firs') stretches from the Spey to the high **Cairngorm** tops. It has been owned by the Grant family for over 400 years. Today the estate is still managed for farming and forestry. It contains a substantial area of remnant Caledonian pine wood, around the River Einich, which has an atmosphere of almost cathedral-like majesty. Birdlife here ranges from the small crossbill to the capercaillie. Higher up, the estate forms part of the Cairngorms National Nature Reserve, including the southern entrance to the Lairig Ghru pass and the summit of Braeriach at over 4000 feet. The **Rothiemurchus Visitor Centre** has literature on the estate and on the many paths and trails available, and there is a smaller seasonal centre at Loch an Eilean, which holds a castle on an islet, a former Comyn stronghold.

ROTHIEMURCHUS VISITOR CENTRE
near Rothiemurchus, Highland

On B970 2m E of Aviemore. All year. Mon–Sat 0900–1700 (0479 810858).

The visitor centre has displays on the estate and the ranger service is based there. Attractions include farm tours, a fish farm which can be visited, clay pigeon shooting, **fishing**, safari tours in a Land-Rover visiting the pine woods and a deer farm, guided walks, farm shop, whisky centre and pottery.

RUM, see SMALL ISLES.

RUTHVEN BARRACKS
near Kingussie, Highland

On B970 1m S of Kingussie. All reasonable times. Free. HS (031–244 3101).

The barracks occupy a large mound that formerly held a fortress associated with the Comyns, later the Gordons and also with the Wolf of Badenoch, son of King Robert II of Scotland, who is said to have lost his life here after playing chess with the devil. The castle was demolished in 1689. When communications in the Highlands were improved, Ruthven was a natural site for government barracks, being at the junction of several lines of communication. The barracks, built in 1716–18, had a short but stormy history. They were attacked by Jacobite forces in August 1745, but successfully resisted; attacked again in February 1746 and surrendered; and finally sacked by Highlanders retreating from **Culloden**, after they had received word that the campaign was over.

ST CYRUS
near Montrose, Grampian

On A92 3m N of Montrose.

The small village of St Cyrus is now atop its sandy cliff, but at one time the houses were down on the shore, nearer the salmon fisheries which are still there. The whole area of shore and marsh is owned by the Tay Salmon Fishery Co of Montrose but is managed by Scottish Natural Heritage as a national nature reserve, important for its plants, birds and butterflies., explained in the **St Cyrus Reserve Visitor Centre**.

ST CYRUS RESERVE VISITOR CENTRE
near Montrose, Grampian

On minor road off A92, 3m N of Montrose. Apr–Oct, Tue–Sun 0900–1700 (06748 3736).

The centre has displays on the wildlife and landscape of the reserve and the salmon fishing, an audio-visual show and an aquarium. The reserve holds up to 350 flowering plants and ferns and over 200 types of moths; 50 bird species have been recorded.

ST KILDA
Western Isles

No regular service; access only by arrangement with Scottish Natural Heritage or the National Trust for Scotland.

St Kilda lies 100 miles west of the Scottish mainland. This spectacular group of islands and rock stacks includes the cliffs of Conachair, at 1400 feet the highest sea-cliffs anywhere in Britain. Wildlife includes unique indigenous breeds of sheep, mouse and wren and the world's largest gannetry. The main island, Hirta, supported a small population until 1930, when the islanders asked to be evacuated. They were resettled, mostly in western Scotland. The islands are now owned by the National Trust for Scotland and leased to Scottish Natural Heritage as a national nature reserve. In 1987 St Kilda became Scotland's first World Heritage Site, under a designation promulgated by UNESCO. NTS workparties visit the islands every summer to restore the old village houses and to undertake historical and other studies. Incongruously, considering their very high natural and historical value, the islands hold a military base tracking missiles fired from **South Uist**, and there are radar installations on several of the hilltops.

SCOURIE
Highland

On A894 10m N of Kylesku Bridge.

Scourie, on a wide, sandy bay, is a crofting and holiday village. The most northerly palm trees in the world grow – survive might be a better word – in the gardens of Scourie House, bearing witness to the effects of the Gulf Stream in maintaining a mild climate here. North of Scourie is **Handa Island**; south is Badcall, on Eddrachillis Bay, dotted with islands and rich in birdlife.

SHETLAND

Shetland consists of five principal islands and innumerable smaller ones, most of the latter uninhabited. The culture is distinctly Norse, if anything more fiercely and deliberately so than in Orkney; perhaps not surprising as these most northerly of British islands are only 200 miles from Norway. Shetland has its own flag and there has been some campaigning for political separatism in recent years, and for closer links with Norway. The Norn dialect is still spoken.

The island economy has been based on agriculture, **fishing** and crafts, particularly knitting, for centuries, but has undergone a change with the advent of North Sea oil. There is a major onshore facility at Sullom Voe, where oil is piped in from several different fields. The islands have benefited through financial agreements struck between Shetland Islands Council and the oil companies. As a result, good leisure and recreational facilities are to be found even in quite remote places. The Shetland pony should not be forgotten when speaking of the economy. Sales are held each October, and buyers come from many parts of the world to acquire these hardy little animals.

Christianity came to Shetland early, and many remains are to be seen, as well as the striking stone records of people from more distant times, including **Jarlshof** and **Mousa**. Shetland today is steadily building a reputation as a holiday destination, with an appeal for anglers, walkers, ornithologists and those with a taste for the special atmosphere of island life. The light is a particular attraction: in midsummer it hardly gets dark at all for several weeks, and Shetland is one of those places fortunate to witness the Aurora Borealis, or 'Northern Lights', a spectacular display in the sky, quite frequently.

SHETLAND, FAIR ISLE

Passenger ferry from Grutness, near Sumburgh; flights from Lerwick and Kirkwall. NTS.

Situated halfway between **Orkney** and Shetland, Fair Isle has benefited from efforts encouraged and initiated by the National Trust for Scotland over the past 40 years to maintain the community and improve living conditions. A large wind generator provides power; a radio-telephone links the island with the outside world; a new pier has been built. There is a permanent population of about 70. The famous Fair Isle knitwear is exported by a co-operative, and is in great demand. The observatory, established in 1969, provides summer accommodation for visitors; the birdlife is superb, with over 300 species recorded here. Sheep are farmed (Sheep Rock is a noted landmark, and the name Fair Isle may mean 'sheep island'), and fishermen go out for lobsters.

SHETLAND, FETLAR

Car and passenger ferry from Unst or Yell; flights from Lerwick.

Fetlar (fat land) is a very fertile island, east of **Yell** and south of **Unst**, with a crofting and fishing community. There are many

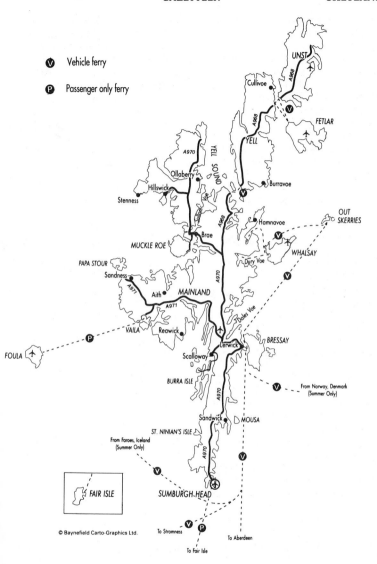

Shetland

standing stones, circles, cairns and tombs, including the mysterious Fiddler's Crus between Vord Hill and Skutes Water, three rings of stones with a triangular space between them. Their purpose is not known. Fetlar is renowned for its birdlife: not just the famous snowy owls (sadly, there has not been a breeding pair for over a decade), but also plover, dunlin, redshank and shearwater. Common and grey seals and otters may also be seen. Much of Fetlar is an RSPB reserve with restricted access.

SHETLAND, FOULA

Small passenger ferry, Tue and Fri in summer, Tue only in winter, from Walls, Mainland.

Foula lies almost 30 miles west of **Mainland**, from where on a clear day its silhouette can just be seen. The cliff of Kame on Foula, 1220 feet high, is one of the highest in Britain. There is one landing-place (not a harbour) on the east side at Ham Voe. Even here the boat has to be hauled out for safety. How long Foula's surviving population, now fewer than 50, can maintain their life here, with fishing no longer the sustaining industry it was, remains to be seen.

SHETLAND, MAINLAND

Shetland's largest island stretches for over 60 miles, north to south, with a westward bulge leading towards **Papa Stour**. It holds the islands' capital, **Lerwick**, the airport at Sumburgh (plus several smaller airfields), the oil terminal at Sullom

Voe, and a considerable number of small crofting, fishing and agricultural communities. The coast is deeply indented with bays or 'voes'. The hills are low, rising only to about 1000 feet, but wide views can be obtained from many places on the island. Important historical sites include **Jarlshof**, **Mousa**, St Ninian's Isle with its ancient church and Scalloway Castle, built in 1600 by Earl Patrick Stewart. There is a local history museum at Scalloway and an agricultural museum at Tingwall.

SHETLAND, MAINLAND, CLICKHIMIN BROCH

1m SW of Lerwick. Apr–Sept, Mon–Sat 1000–1900, Sun 1400–1900; Oct–Mar, Mon–Sat 1000–1600, Sun 1400–1600. Free.

The broch, which stands about 17 feet high, was built out into a small loch on the site of an even older fortification to form its own island.

SHETLAND, MAINLAND, JARLSHOF

Off A970 22m S of Lerwick. Apr–Sept, Mon–Sat 0930–1900, Sun 1400–1900; Oct–Mar, Mon–Sat 0930–1600 (but closed Tue and Wed pm), Sun 1400–1600.

This extraordinary archaeological treasure is near Sumburgh Head, the southernmost tip of Shetland. It is a place of frequent gales and a century ago, one such gale exposed some old stone walls. Curious, the landowner, John Bruce, began to excavate; he and others since have uncovered settlements from the Stone Age, the Bronze Age, the second and third centuries AD, from Norse times and medieval: a human story going back perhaps 3000 years. It is a site like no other in Britain. The name Jarlshof was coined by the author Sir Walter Scott, and has no basis in history. Nearby are the remains of a 16th-century house of the Stewart Earls.

SHETLAND, MAINLAND, LERWICK

Shetland's principal town (population about 7000) owed its 17th-century growth to the increasing use of the waters round about by Dutch fishermen; as a settlement it has a much longer history, as is seen at **Clickhimin Broch**. The name Lerwick is Norse, meaning 'clay creek'. Near the north end of Commercial Street, the main thoroughfare, is **Fort Charlotte**. The Shetland Museum in Lower Hillhead has displays on life in Shetland from earliest times to the coming of North Sea oil. The oil has brought prosperity, reflected in Lerwick's range of shops. The famous Shetland knitwear can of course be purchased.

Norse links are maintained with the staging each January of the Up Helly Aa fire festival, in which a galley is hauled through the streets and then burned as an offering to the gods to ensure the coming of spring. Offshore from Lerwick is the small island of Bressay with notable cliffs. The Bressay Stone, a Celtic relic found on the island, is now in the National Museum of Antiquities in Edinburgh. Off Bressay is Noss, a bird reserve noted for the 600-foot Noup of Noss, a cliff which is

an extraordinary metropolis of sea-birds.

SHETLAND, MAINLAND, LERWICK, FORT CHARLOTTE

Commercial Street, Lerwick. Apr–Sept, Mon–Sat 1000–1900, Sun 1400–1900; Oct–Mar, Mon–Sat 1000–1600, Sun 1400–1600. Free.

This pentagonal fortress was built by Cromwell's forces in 1653 with gunports pointing out to sea to guard the approaches to Lerwick. Sacked by invading Dutch troops in 1673, it was restored in the late 18th century and has survived more or less intact.

SHETLAND, MOUSA

Passenger ferry from Sandwick, Mainland.

The **broch** on the small island of Mousa is possibly the best preserved of all these remarkable Iron Age buildings. The outer walls still stand to a height of 40 feet and between outer and inner walls is a staircase which can be climbed to reach the parapet, from which the whole island can be scanned.

SHETLAND, PAPA STOUR

Daily passenger ferry from West Burrafirth, sea permitting.

The western bulge of Shetland **Mainland** ends at Sandness and Melby; across the treacherous Sound of Papa is the small island of

Papa Stour. The island is reasonably fertile, but the coastline is fretted and gouged into deep inlets, bays and high cliffs – geos and voes in Shetland landscape terms. They include Francie's Cave, Shepherd's Geo and the Hole of Bordie, a tunnel nearly half a mile long through a headland. The Maiden's Stack is said to have had a small house on it where a damsel was imprisoned by her father to protect her virtue.

SHETLAND, UNST

Car and passenger ferry from Yell, Mar–Sept daily; flights from Lerwick, Mon–Fri all year.

Unst, the most northerly of the Shetland islands, is known for superb cliff scenery, splendid birdlife, its tough little ponies, and its knitwear. Historical remains include Muness Castle (late 16th century) on the island's easternmost promontory. Offshore is the nature reserve of Haaf Gruney, where many sea-birds, including petrel, breed; the island holds a long-disused chromite mine. At Westing there is a large standing stone and a ruined 12th-century church, with the graves of two 16th-century traders from Bremen in Germany, showing how extensive were the trading links from these islands. Past Westing is a restored mill of Norse design.

Baltasound has the island airstrip, and the road continues over the moors to Haroldswick, Britain's most northerly village, where the post office will frank letters and cards with its special stamp. Further north is Saxa Vord, a hill just under 1000 feet high

topped by radio masts. In 1962 a windspeed of 177mph was recorded here. From the hill you look north over Burra Firth and Hermaness to the lighthouse on Muckle Flugga, the true northern extremity of the British Isles. Built in 1854 by David and Thomas Stevenson, it is still manned, and the relief of the crew by helicopter is often a hazardous operation. Hermaness is a sea-bird sanctuary, a national nature reserve holding many thousands of gannets, puffins, guillemots, kittiwakes and skuas. Its cliffs are 600 feet high.

SHETLAND, WHALSAY

Car and passenger ferry from Laxo, daily in summer, less often in winter; regular flights from Lerwick, all year.

Whalsay lies off the east coast of Shetland's **Mainland**. The island rises to 400 feet on Ward of Clett, with an economy based on fishing supporting its population of 500. Fish-processing goes on as it has at least since the 17th century; the Hanseatic store from that time can be seen by the pier at Symbister. Near the hamlet of Isbister are the Standing Stones of Yoxie and the Bunzie House, also Stone Age. Ten miles east of Whalsay are the Out Skerries; the two main islands are inhabited, and there is a modern fish-processing factory. The islands, among the most remote in Britain still supporting a community, are reached by ferry from Lerwick.

SHETLAND, YELL

Car and passenger ferry from Toft, all year.

ell is a large island, 17 miles
by seven. It has suffered some
depopulation and a decline in
both agriculture and fishing. The
population has stabilized at about
200 and efforts are being made
to improve facilities for visitors as
well as for the islanders themselves.
Much of the island is peat, which
tends to give it a dull appearance:
the name itself comes from a Norse
word meaning 'barren'. The ferry
from Toft, on **Mainland**, arrives
at Ulsta. Four miles north on the
west side of the island is the **Old
Haa of Burravoe**. At the north
end of the island is the medieval
Kirk of Ness. A minor road leads
to Gloup with its fishermen's
memorial. At one time there was
a sizeable community here, but
in July 1881, in a great storm, ten
vessels and over 50 men were lost.
From Gutcher, ferries go to Unst
and Fetlar.

SHETLAND, YELL, OLD HAA OF BURRAVOE

*On A968 4m N of Ulsta. Apr–Sept,
Tue–Thur, Sat–Sun 1000–1600. Free
(095 782 339).*

The Old Haa is a 17th-century
building converted to hold an island
museum with displays on local
history, landscape and wildlife,
video and tapes of local musicians
and storytellers. There is a craft
shop, art gallery and café.

SHIEL BRIDGE
Highland

On A87 20m E of Kyle of Lochalsh.

The A87 plunges down Glen
Shiel, with the superb mountains

of **Kintail** on either side, to reach
Shiel Bridge, where the minor
road over the Mam Ratagan
branches off towards **Glenelg**.
The settlement includes a hotel,
shop, filling station and camp
site. The bridge itself is a **Thomas
Telford** construction of 1820 with
a span of 65 feet. Near the site
of the 1719 Battle of Glen Shiel is
another Telford bridge over the Allt
Mhalagain, built in 1814.

SHIELDAIG
Highland

On A896 16m W of Kinlochewe.

With the considerable improvement
of the road from **Torridon** to
Shieldaig in recent years, the village
has become easier of access and
thus more popular as a holiday
destination. It has an inn and a
number of cottages for rental, on
the shore looking out to Shieldaig
Island, tree-clad and owned by the
National Trust for Scotland.

SKIING, see panel p204.

SKYE
Highland

*Car and passenger ferry from Kyle of
Lochalsh, daily all year. Car (summer
only) and passenger ferry from Mallaig to
Armadale, all year. Car and passenger ferry
(summer only) from Glenelg to Kylerhea.*

Everybody has an image of Skye,
for this is an island beset by cliché:
the Winged Isle, the Misty Isle,

Skiing in Scotland

For a long time, skiing was simply a means of getting around more easily in snow. Doctors and postmen on Deeside used skis in the very early years of this century. In the 1920s and 1930s it gradually developed as a sport, following the rapid rise in popularity of skiing holidays in the Alps and other European areas, but there was little attempt at developing proper facilities until after 1945, when a combination of growing enthusiasm and little foreign currency led to moves to provide proper uplift in Scotland.

The first areas to be developed were Beinn Ghlas near Killin (later abandoned in favour of Meall a'Bhuiridh, at the head of **Glencoe**) and Glenshee, soon followed by **Cairngorm** near **Aviemore**. The Scottish ski resorts were beginning to take embryonic shape.

By 1956 a proper tow was in operation at Meall a'Bhuiridh; by 1961 the ski road was open on Cairngorm and the first chairlift there was running. Development of tows was also under way at Glenshee and a new area, the **Lecht**, was provided with a portable tow. Enthusiasm, commitment and imagination overcame many difficulties as the ski areas developed.

Development continued, albeit slowly, through the 1970s and 80s. In some cases there was strong opposition from conservation interests; plans for further development on Cairngorm were twice rejected by the Secretary of State, in 1982 and again in 1990, but a new tow on Glas Maol, Glenshee, was approved despite part of it intruding into the Caenlochan national nature reserve.

Skiing is now established as a fully developed winter sport, bringing substantial economic benefits to Strathspey, Deeside and the Blairgowrie area in particular, while the Lecht and Glencoe tend to be patronized by day or weekend skiers. After a long struggle to obtain the necessary permissions and to raise funds, a fifth centre at Aonach Mor was opened in 1989, establishing **Fort William** as a four-season holiday centre. Aonach Mor has the first gondola in Scotland, taking skiers up to a high-level restaurant at the foot of the lifts and tows.

The one great imponderable is snow. Winters in the past decade have been erratic, sometimes starting early, sometimes late, with snow disappearing and returning in a frustrating manner.

Development has not only been in piste skiing: cross-country or Nordic skiing has also become much more popular, and several Nordic centres have been set up.

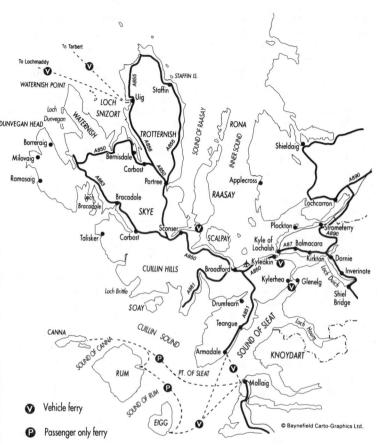

V Vehicle ferry

P Passenger only ferry

Skye

Over the Sea to Skye, and so on. In truth, it deserves superlatives. If you have an eye for landscape, Skye will captivate you, from the quiet charm of the Sleat peninsula through the power of the **Cuillin Hills** to the cliffs and rock spires of the long peninsula of **Trotternish**. The only large settlements are at **Portree** and **Broadford**; there are many smaller villages and crofting townships around the island. Skye has a long human history, ranging from the Neolithic people who left chambered cairns through to the Vikings to the Lords of the Isles and on to modern times. There is much **crofting**, fishing and forestry, and some light industry. Tourism is an essential part of the island economy. Access is at present by ferry, but this should change in the mid 1990s with the building of a bridge – long proposed and long fought over - between **Kyle of Lochalsh** and Kyleakin, a small village overlooked by the stark fang of the ruined Castle Maol, built to guard against raiders trying to get through the narrows (Kyle means 'a narrows').

Skye divides into several distinct parts. The peninsula of Sleat, to the south-west, is low-lying and fertile. It holds the Gaelic college at Sabhal Mor Ostaig and the **Clan Donald Centre** at Armadale. Strathaird, to its north, is indented by Loch Slapin and Loch Scavaig. From Elgol there is a superb view of the Cuillin. The area around Torrin has recently been acquired by a conservation body, the John Muir Trust. The Cuillin form the mountainous heart of Skye, a climbers' paradise with a multitude of rocky peaks. A minor road runs into Glen Brittle giving more fine views of the range. The north-west part of the island has lower but still notable hills including the two known as MacLeod's Tables (Healaval Mor and Healaval Beag), with their distinctive flat tops. Also in this area are **Dunvegan Castle** and the Talisker Distillery, producing a malt whisky with a very distinctive flavour. Finally, Trotternish thrusts a long stubby hand into the sea towards **Lewis**. From Uig the ferry departs for Harris and North Uist.

SKYE, BROADFORD

On A850 8m W of Kyleakin.

Broadford straggles round its eponymous bay, looking north-east to the hills of **Applecross**. It is the first place of any substance reached by most people visiting Skye, and offers accommodation, shops and other facilities – and the chance of visiting the unique **Skye Serpentarium**. From Broadford the A851 branches off south-west through the Strathaird estate to Elgol and its matchless view of the **Cuillin Hills**. South of Elgol is one of several Prince Charlie's Caves to be found in Scotland: it is known that the prince, by then a hunted renegade, was sheltered here before returning to the mainland in summer 1746. Skye's airstrip is two miles east of Broadford.

SKYE, CLAN DONALD CENTRE

At Armadale on A851 17m S of Broadford or by car ferry from Mallaig (restricted winter service). Apr–Oct, daily 0930–1730; gardens all year. D (P) (04714 305).

The award-winning centre, largely funded through donations from the considerable American membership of Clan Donald, has displays on the history of the clan and the Lordship of the Isles. Special events are frequently staged. There is a restaurant and gift shop. In the extensive grounds are the ruins of Armadale Castle. Woodland walks are laid out and there is a ranger service.

SKYE, COLBOST FOLK MUSEUM

On B884 3m W of Dunvegan. Apr–Sept, daily 1000–1800 (047022 296).

A traditional thatched 'blackhouse' shows typical living conditions of the 18th and 19th centuries, when people and livestock shared the same roof.

SKYE, CUILLIN HILLS

The Cuillin are unique: a range of gabbro hills crested with jagged spires, towers and pinnacles, offering the toughest test the hill-walker can be set in Britain: one of the summits, the Inaccessible Pinnacle of Sgurr Dearg, is a graded climb, with an abseil descent. The Cuillin were first properly explored, in mountaineering terms, in the late 19th century, by men such as Sheriff Nicolson, who had the unusual distinction of having a peak, Sgurr Alasdair, named after him following the first ascent in 1873. Similarly, Sgurr Mhic Coinnich commemorates the early guide John Mackenzie. Walkers of a nervous disposition will identify with Sgurr a'Ghreadaidh (peak of torment) as they wrestle with the complexities of the Cuillin Ridge: to add to the difficulty, the gabbro rock, though giving superb grip, makes compasses unreliable.

SKYE, DUNVEGAN CASTLE

On A850 25m W of Portree. Easter–Oct, Mon–Sat 1000–1730; gardens daily all year, 1000–sunset. D (P) (047 022 206).

Dramatically sited on a rugged coastline, Dunvegan has been the home of the chiefs of Clan MacLeod for 700 years. The castle has many clan relics including the famous Fairy Flag, said to have miraculous powers, Jacobite mementos including a lock of Prince Charlie's hair, and much else of interest. There is a craft shop and restaurant. The grounds are extensive, a beach walk is available, and in summer there are boat trips to a seal colony. life-size model portrays the giant.

SKYE, KILMUIR, MUSEUM OF ISLAND LIFE

Off A855 2m S of Duntulm. Apr–Oct, Mon–Sat 0900–1730 (047 052 279).

Seven thatched cottages hold displays on island life, furniture, farming and domestic implements, old photographs and papers.

SKYE, THE PIPING CENTRE

On minor road at Boreraig, NW of Dunvegan.

An old schoolhouse contains displays on the history of the Highland bagpipe and the *piobreachaid*, the great pipe music, and on the MacCrimmon family, pipers to Clan MacLeod for centuries.

SKYE, PORTREE

On A850 26m NW of Broadford.

Portree is the principal town on Skye, and the island's 'capital'. It was originally Kiltaragleann (church at the foot of the glen) but got its present name (meaning 'king's haven') after a visit by James V. The town is attractive with a fine setting, rising up from a lovely natural harbour. It was in Portree that Bonnie Prince Charlie said farewell to Flora Macdonald with the words 'For all that has happened, Madam, I hope we might meet in St James's yet.' It was a forlorn hope. From Portree roads lead west to **Dunvegan** and north round the long **Trotternish** peninsula.

SKYE, SERPENTARIUM

The Old Mill, Harrapool, Broadford (on A850). Easter–Oct, daily 1000–1800 (0471 822533).

A unique private collection of snakes, lizards, tortoises and amphibians housed in large glass tanks in a former water mill. Snakes can sometimes be handled, under supervision.

SKYE, TROTTERNISH

By A855/A856 N of Portree.

Skye's northern peninsula thrusts out for 25 miles to its tip at Rubha Hunish. The interior has a chain of hills giving one of the finest ridge walks in Britain. North of Portree on the east coast road, a path leads up to the Old Man of Storr, a rock spire giving a severe test for climbers. Past Culkaknock is the Kilt Rock, resembling that garment in its basaltic columns and colours. The road continues to Staffin, a small holiday resort on a sandy bay. Inland from here, reached from the minor road running west to Uig, is the fantastic assembly of rock spires, towers and other shapes known as Quiraing. A path leads into the heart of this extraordinary place, reaching a grassy area known as the Prison, once used for hiding cattle.

The main road cuts across the northern tip of the peninsula to the ruin of Duntulm Castle, a Macdonald stronghold. Flora Macdonald is buried at **Kilmuir**, where the **Museum of Island Life** is also found. She brought Prince Charlie ashore near here, at Kilbride Point. She had intended to take him to Monkstadt, home of Sir Alexander Macdonald, but government forces got there first and the couple had to go south instead. From Uig the car ferry leaves for **Harris** and **North Uist**. Near here on an impressive headland is an Iron Age fort, Dun Skudiburgh. The road continues along Loch Snizort past Kingsburgh, where Flora and the prince found shelter. There is a prehistoric burial cairn and above Tote is Clach Ard, 'the high stone', with Pictish symbols. The road meets the A850 from

Dunvegan before returning to **Portree**.

SMALL ISLES (RUM, CANNA, EIGG AND MUCK)
Highland

Passenger ferry from Mallaig, all year, Mon, Wed, Sat plus Fri May–Sept; and from Arisaig, May–Sept, Mon, Wed, Fri, Sat.

The Small Isles are a cohesive group, but with very different characters. They make up one scattered parish, and their total population is only about 200.

Rum is the largest and most mountainous of the islands. Until 1826 it had a considerable crofting population, but in that year the island was cleared and most people went to America. The island was turned over to sheep farming. In 1845 it became a sporting estate and for the next century was almost a 'forbidden island', especially during the ownership of the Bullough family, Lancashire cotton magnates who built the extraordinary Kinloch Castle, a fantasy in Arran sandstone full of objects collected from all round the world. It now offers accommodation to visitors.

In 1957 the island was bought by the Nature Conservancy Council (now Scottish Natural Heritage) and since then has been run as a large outdoor laboratory, notably for the study of red deer and as the base for the successful reintroduction of the sea-eagle to Scotland. Much work on woodland regeneration also goes on. Rum has a fine central chain of hills, all with ringing Norse names, the highest being Askival (2650 feet). They are the haunt of thousands of shearwater, who breed here every year. There are two nature trails around Loch Scresort. Permission to stay on the island must be obtained from SNH. The name is often spelt 'Rhum' but this is a Victorian aberration, perhaps induced by the alcoholic connotation of the correct spelling.

Canna is low-lying and fertile. The island has been owned and managed by the National Trust for Scotland since 1981, when it was transferred to them by the previous owner, Dr John Lorne Campbell, a noted Gaelic scholar who still lives on Canna.

Eigg is dominated by its Sgurr, a sharp prow of rock visible from the mainland and rising to 1300 feet. Its dark pitchstone has columns and pillars. At the north-west of the island are the Singing Sands of Camus Sgiolaig, which make a semi-musical sound when walked upon. The churchyard has a fine Celtic cross-slab. Eigg today supports a crofting and fishing population of about 100 people.

Muck (island of pigs) is the smallest of the Small Isles group and has a population of about 25. It is low and reasonably fertile, and is the least visited of the four.

SMOKEHOUSE
Achiltibuie, Highland

In Achiltibuie. All year. Mon–Fri 0900–1730; Easter–Oct, Sat 0900–1730. (085482 353).

Here, right by the sea, you can learn about the curing and smoking of fish, including salmon, meat and other products, sample the results, and perhaps take some away with you.

SOUTH UIST
Western Isles

Car and passenger ferry from Oban, regular service, all year.

South Uist, like its neighbouring islands, is of two distinct parts: the east coast is hilly, with finely shaped mountains rising to Beinn Mhor at 2033 feet, and below them a flat landscape of lochan and bog, while the west coast has sandy beaches backed by machair, with a glorious summer display of flowers. The ferry arrives at Lochboisdale, one of two sizeable communities on the island (the other is at Daliburgh). Those apart, the population of around 2200 is scattered amongst crofting townships.

A south–north look at the island starts at Garrynamonie, which has a new church, Our Lady of the Sorrows (built 1964). From Ludag, a ferry runs to **Eriskay**. At Kilpheder are remains of an Iron Age wheel house, and at Kildonan a cairn marks Flora Macdonald's birthplace. West of the main road is the ruin of Ormiclate Castle. Howmore church has an unusual central communion pew; on Loch an Eilean is a small island with a ruined tower, Caisteall Bheagram. The B990 runs east to Loch Skipport, passing the national nature reserve on Loch Druidibeg, the principal British wintering ground of the greylag goose. Two artificial islands have recently been created here in an attempt to encourage black-throated divers to breed.

The main road continues past Rueval, a hill holding the 30-foot statue of Our Lady of the Isles (Hew Lorimer, 1957), which contrasts oddly with the radio masts (known locally as Space City) on the summit of the hill. The installation is connected with the missile firing base on the machair to the west here; the missiles are tracked from **St Kilda**. Passing West Gerinish, the road crosses Loch Bee, one of many angling lochs on the island, on a causeway. Shortly afterwards, the causeway to **Benbecula** is reached. South Uist has associations with Bonnie Prince Charlie: he landed at Corodale Bay, on the east coast, in May 1746, and was hidden in the inevitable Prince's Cave nearby for some while before escaping to **Skye**, dressed as a maid, in the company of Flora Macdonald.

SPEAN BRIDGE
Highland

On A82/A87 10m N of Fort William.

Thomas Telford's 1819 bridge, which still crosses the River Spean here, was preceded by one built by troops under General Wade in 1736. Here the road through Glen Spean and by Loch Laggan to Strathspey branches off from the one that goes up the Great Glen. The latter continues to reach the Commando Memorial, an impressive sculpture by Scott Sutherland erected in 1952 as a memorial to the men who trained in the country around here, many of them being based at **Achnacarry**. It stands on a knoll with superb views to **Ben Nevis**, Aonach Mor and the hills known as the Grey

rries. **Blarour Nursery** is at Spean
idge.

TONEHAVEN
rampian

A92/A94 15m S of Aberdeen.

onehaven has developed
nsiderably in recent years, the
d part of the town around the
rbour from which it takes its
me contrasting with the new
tates up the hill. The oldest
rviving building is the Tolbooth
1600) on the old pier, built as
storehouse for **Dunnottar Castle**
d now a museum. The harbour
elters both fishing vessels
d yachts. Stonehaven was the
rthplace of R.W. Thomson,
ventor of the pneumatic tyre in
45 – and of much else including
e hydraulic dry dock and
e self-filling fountain pen. A
omson Memorial Rally of vintage
hicles is held each summer.
onehaven's year starts and ends
ith the unique Fireball ceremony.
t midnight on Hogmanay, wire
ntainers containing combustible
aterial are attached to ropes, set
fire and swung round the heads
the carriers as they process along
gh Street.

TORYBOOK GLEN
aryculter, Grampian

f South Deeside Road, Maryculter, 6m W
Aberdeen. Mar–Oct, daily 1000–1800;
v–Feb, Sat–Sun 1100–1600. D (P)
224 732941).

e glen has walks passing
aterfalls and other features based
on nursery rhymes and children's
stories. Special attractions for
children include the Three Bears'
House and the Old Woman's Shoe.
They can also visit Troll-land, try
a rescue helicopter, and meet the
teenage mutant turtles. There is a
restaurant and picnic areas.

STRATHDON
Grampian

On A944 16m SE of Tomintoul, 18m W
of Alford.

Strathdon is the name both of the
valley of the River Don and of a
small village. It has an impressive
church, built in 1851, large and
imposing even in this splendid
setting. Strathdon is the setting
for the Lonach Games each year, a
rival to **Braemar**. In 1991 the Lonach
Highlanders revived an old habit
and marched all the way to Braemar
to meet their sovereign, a stiff
hike of 20 miles. The Strathdon
fiddlers were renowned in **Queen
Victoria**'s day, and a local piper,
Jamie McHardy, became servant
and companion to the queen in her
later years. **Candacraig Gardens** are
nearby.

STRATHISLA DISTILLERY
Keith, Grampian

In Keith. May–Sept, Mon–Fri 0900–1630.
D (P) (05422 7471).

Strathisla claims to be the oldest
working distillery in the Highlands,
having celebrated its 200th
anniversary in 1986. The whisky
it produces is used for the Chivas
Regal blend. The distillery has a
reception centre with audio-visual

presentation, tours with a tasting, and a gift shop.

STRATHNAVER
Highland

On B873/B871 between Altnaharra and Bettyhill.

In the early years of the 19th century, the long valley of Strathnaver saw some of the most infamous scenes of the **Clearances**. People were evicted from their houses, which were then burned, and they were herded to the coast to scratch a living as best they could or take their chance on an emigration ship. The story is told in the museum at **Bettyhill**. Today the strath, which runs in a broad sweep from the hotel at Altnaharra under Ben Klibreck past Loch Naver and Syre to the sea, is quiet, its farmsteads interspersed with forestry plantations.

STRATHNAVER MUSEUM
Bettyhill, Highland

At east end of Bettyhill village on A838. May–Sept, Mon–Sat 1000–1300, 1400–1700. Times may vary from year to year; check locally on 04612 330. D (P).

The former Farr Church (1774) has been converted into a museum with displays on wildlife and local history, telling particularly the story of the **Clearances** of Strath Naver, when the people were removed from the land and forced either to live a harsh life on the coastal strip or emigrate. There are also mementos of Clan Mackay; in the churchyard is the ninth-century Farr Stone.

STRATHPEFFER
Highland

On A834 3m W of Dingwall.

Strathpeffer, known locally as 'the Strath', became a popular spa in Victorian times. The large, grand hotels date from that period, and the former **Pump Room** can be visited, as can the **Dolls Museum**. This was all prophesied by the Brahan Seer, a local visionary, 200 years earlier. He said that 'the day will come when crowds of pleasure and health seekers shall be seen thronging its portals'. Strathpeffer still a popular holiday destination, but for coach tours rather than health-seekers. To the north is Castle Leod, seat of the Earls of Cromartie, chiefs of the Clan Mackenzie (not open to the public) There are many fine walks in the area.

STRATHSPEY RAILWAY
Aviemore, Highland

Jun–Sept, daily 0930–1800; Easter–May, Oct, Sat–Sun 0930–1800 (0479 810725).

The Strathspey Railway Company operates steam trains from Aviemore to **Boat of Garten** several times a day. There is a small railway museum at Boat of Garten, and it is hoped that in time the line may be extended to **Grantown-on-Spey**.

STRICHEN
Grampian

On A981 8m S of Fraserburgh.

riginally called Mormond,
richen is a planned village,
tablished by Lord Strichen in
'64. It is designated a conservation
ea. Among a number of fine
uildings is the turreted Tower
ouse of 1816. On Mormond Hill,
oove the village, are a large white
orse and stag cut into the hill by
aptain Fraser of Strichen (founder
 New Leeds village) 200 years
go. The summit of the hill holds
a RAF radio station.

TROMA
ighland

*rry from John o'Groats by arrangement
95 581 252).*

ae island of Stroma seems to
 neither of the mainland nor of
rkney. Sitting in the Pentland
rth a couple of miles off **John
Groats**, it once held a considerable
opulation but is now inhabited
aly by cattle and sheep. The
ghthouse, built in 1896 to a David
evenson design, now operates
atomatically. The last family left
roma in 1962: as recently as the
'30s there were 40 pupils in the
land school, but times change,
ad work on the mainland, in
onstruction or farming, took them
l away. The island has fine cliff
enery and a notable whirlpool,
e Swelkie. Beside it is little
voma, also with whirlpools called
e Wells of Swoma.

STRONTIAN
Highland

On A861 15m W of Corran Ferry.

Strontian (accent on the 'ti') is a
neatly laid out village on an inlet
of Loch Sunart. Lead was worked
here in the 18th century, some of it
used for bullets in the Napoleonic
Wars. In 1790, Strontianite, of
which Strontium-90 is an isotope,
was discovered here. Some of the
mines have recently been reopened
for the extraction of barytes, an
essential component in North Sea
oil exploration drilling. Below the
mines is the Ariundle National
Nature Reserve, a remnant of the
oak woods which once liberally
graced the western seaboard. It also
has fine mosses and lichens. A walk
leads through the reserve.

SUMMER ISLES
Highland

*Ferry from Ullapool, all year: enquire locally
for times.*

The Summer Isles are a scattered
group of a dozen islands in outer
Loch Broom. Tanera Mhor, the
largest, has a hotel. The islands
are noted for their wildlife, and as
well as the ferry, there are regular
cruises in summer to Isle Martin, a
bird sanctuary, and to other smaller
islands to see the seals.

TAIN
Highland

On A9 22m N of Dingwall.

Tain's name may derive from Norse *thing*, a meeting place, the same root as Dingwall. Tain received its charter as a royal burgh from Malcolm Canmore in 1066. Even before that, St Duthus founded a chapel here. The lovely old mid 14th-century collegiate church bearing his name was a place of penitence and pilgrimage, and has superb stained-glass windows. Another notable building is the Tolbooth (16th century, rebuilt 1707), with its spire and turrets. This was the place from which many of the possession orders were issued during the dark times of the **Clearances**; it was also used for imprisoning those who resisted. Next to it is the Clan Ross Museum. Tain today is an attractive town of about 2000 people, its industries including cheese production and the **Glenmorangie Distillery**. A water-driven mill at Aldie still produces oatmeal.

TAMDHU DISTILLERY
Knockando, Highland

On B9102 6m W of Aberlour. Jun–Sept, Mon–Sat 1000–1600; Easter–end May, Mon–Fri 1000–1600 (03406 486).

The Tamdhu distillery, founded in 1896, was closed from 1927 to 1947 and then restarted production. The visitor centre is in the former railway station and is on the Speyside Way footpath. Tours are available and there is an exhibition

with a collection of over 130 whiskies, a gift shop and picnic area.

TARLAND
Grampian

On B9119 7m N of Aboyne.

This attractive village with its fine square sits in the district of Cromar, lands belonging to the Gordons of Haddo. Tarland is a quiet place, which has its own show in the summer. To the north-east is Culsh Earth-House, dating from the Iron Age, and a mile south-east is Tomnaverrie Stone Circle.

TARTAN, see panel p215.

THOMAS TELFORD, see panel p219.

THURSO
Highland

On A836/A882 20m NW of Wick.

Thurso (Thor's river) has doubled in size in the past 40 years, since the opening of the nuclear research station at **Dounreay**, and now has a population of 9000. The influx of people has led to improved facilities including a leisure centre at Meadow Lane. The old part of the town around the harbour includes St Peter's Church, possibly 13th century, and attractive old cottages

Tartan

The check-patterned cloth known as tartan, woven in a design identifiable with a particular clan or family, is often thought of as the traditional dress of the Highlander. There is some truth in this, but the real emergence of 'clan tartans' came only in the late 18th and early 19th centuries.

The word tartan possibly comes from a French word, *tiretaine*, used to describe a cloth half of wool, half of linen, woven in a check or stripe pattern. This cloth was certainly used in Scotland as early as the 16th century, but the colours and pattern depended as much on the preference of the wearer and the dyes available as on the area or clan. Clan identity was expressed through emblems such as plants or trees rather than the cloth worn.

By the late 17th century weaving had become more sophisticated and Martin Martin of **Skye** could write that the plaid, the common garment of the time, 'consists of divers colours, and there is a great deal of ingenuity required so as to be agreeable to the nicest fancy . . . Every isle differs from the others as to the stripes in breadth and colour.' There is still no mention of a clan affinity.

Soon after this the short kilt became more common. Called *fhileadh beag* in Gaelic, it was anglicized to 'phillibeg'. When General Wade formed his 'independent companies of Highlanders' in 1739 they were supplied with kilts in a 'government tartan' of green, blue and black. The regiment was called the Black Watch, a name which survives today.

After the Battle of **Culloden** in 1746, the Disarming Act was passed, outlawing the wearing of Highland dress. It laid down that 'no tartan or party-coloured plaid or stuff shall be used for great coats or upper coats'. The penalty for offenders was transportation to the colonies.

The Act was repealed in 1782, and after that, identification with things Scottish grew steadily, and tartan became a fashionable cloth to wear. Clans now adopted their own tartans, often using a cloth from a particular locality. In 1815 the Highland Society (established not in Scotland but in London) wrote to clan chiefs asking for samples of tartans so that they could be fixed. About 40 samples were submitted, certified by the clan chiefs, and these remain in the society's archives today.

(continued)

Tartan *(continued)*

Fanned by the writings of Sir Walter Scott and others and by the visit to Edinburgh of King George IV in 1822, interest in tartan continued to grow. The firm of Wilsons of Bannockburn, near Stirling, became recognized as tartan specialists, and developed many new tartans, with fanciful names such as Robin Hood, Large Gipsy and Caledonia.

Two books of the period also 'authenticated' tartans which in fact had dubious origins. John and Charles Hay Allan, who claimed (falsely) to be grandsons of Bonnie Prince Charlie, published *Vestiarium Scoticum* in 1842 and *The Costume of the Clans* in 1845, in which year James Logan and the artist R.R. Maclan produced *The Clans of the Scottish Highlands*, turning fiction into fact with great conviction and facility. Queen Victoria also adopted tartan, ensuring its popularity.

Tartan is now as fashionable as it has ever been. New tartans are still being produced – not for clans, but for organizations such as British Gas and the Royal Air Force and even for football clubs, who have developed them largely for commercial marketing purposes. Clans all have their separate tartans for normal wear and dress occasions, and there are tartans laid down for Highland Dancing competitions.

Thurso has been an important port for centuries. In medieval times it exported meat, fish and hides and more recently Caithness flagstone. Rotterdam Street provides a link with Holland: Scandinavia is recalled by Harald's Tower, burial place of Earl Harold, 12th-century ruler of Caithness, **Orkney** and **Shetland**.

Thurso and the surrounding area are associated with Sir John Sinclair (1754–1835), a noted agricultural improver. His daughter Catherine made her name from writing novels. Sinclair's life and times are featured in the museum in the Town Hall. Another notable Thurso man was Sir William Smith, founder of the Boys Brigade, who was born at Pennyland House in 1854.

TIMESPAN CENTRE
Helmsdale, Highland

Off A9 in Helmsdale village centre. Easter–mid Oct, Mon–Sat 1000–1700, Sun 1400–1700 (to 1800 in Jul–Aug). D (P) (04312 327).

Imaginative displays with lifesize figures and artefacts recreate the past including Picts and Vikings, murder at Helmsdale Castle, the burning of a witch, the **Clearances**, and the gold rush. The gardens beside the Helmsdale River have medicinal plants and herbs used for healing, cooking and dyeing cloth.

TOLQUHON CASTLE
near Pitmedden, Grampian

Off B999 1m W of Pitmedden. Apr–Sept, Mon–Sat 1000–1900, Sun 1400–1900; Nov–Mar, Mon–Sat 1000–1600, Sun 1400–1600.

The castle is approached by a large forecourt with old yew trees. The building is early 15th century and has survived much as it was built, a mansion being added later. The castle was occupied until the mid 19th century.

TOMATIN
Highland

On A9 15m SE of Inverness.

The village is notable for **Tomatin Distillery**, which has one of the largest bonded warehouses in Scotland. This is all Clan Mackintosh country: the chief still has his seat at Moy Hall, to the east. In the 1745 Rising, the then chief was on the government side while his wife supported the Jacobites. Hearing that Prince Charlie was at Moy, a force of 1500 government troops was despatched under cover of darkness, but five men of Moy ran around them firing guns and shouting, and panicking them to such an extent that they retreated.

TOMATIN DISTILLERY
Tomatin, Highland

Easter–Sept, Mon–Thu 0900–1600, Fri 0900–1500. D (P) (08082 234).

The distillery, one of the largest in Scotland, produces over five million gallons of whisky every year; the process has been sophisticated to such an extent that its 23 stills are controlled by only half a dozen operators. Tours and a tasting are offered, and there is a reception area and gift shop.

TOMINTOUL
Highland

On A939 14m SE of Grantown-on-Spey.

Is this the highest village in the Highlands? At over 1100 feet it disputes the title with **Braemar** and **Dalwhinnie**, though none is the highest village in Scotland, for Wanlockhead claims that honour. Tomintoul village was established by the Duke of Gordon in 1776, showing the common pattern of a central square and gridiron streets. **Queen Victoria**, passing this way in 1860, called it a 'tumbledown, poor-looking place' but today it is neat and trim. The name means 'barn hillock'. It is an excellent centre for **walking**, riding and **fishing**, and in winter for **skiing**, for the **Lecht** ski centre is only a few miles away. Tomintoul is the southern end of the Speyside Way footpath. There is a small museum in the square, and the large **Glenlivet Estate** nearby offers tours and walks.

TONGUE
Highland

On A836 50m N of Lairg, 44m W of Thurso.

The Kyle of Tongue, shallow and with extensive sandbars, extends inland for ten miles from Tongue Bay, and the village of Tongue (meaning a spit of land) is on its east side. The Kyle is crossed by a causeway, saving nearly ten miles of road. Tongue House was once the home of the chiefs of Clan MacKay, one of whom (Donald MacKay, first Lord Reay) was said to be a familiar of the devil. South of Tongue is the multi-peaked Ben Loyal, while westward the road runs on round Loch Eriboll to **Durness**. Tongue Church, dating from 1724, has a MacKay loft usually hung with the clan tartan. The Kyle is a notable place for waders and sea-birds.

TORPHINS
Grampian

On A980 7m NW of Banchory.

Torphins grew with the coming of the Deeside railway, which has long since gone. It is said locally that the village got its name from Thorfinn, Earl of Orkney and an ally of Macbeth; or it might be *torr fionn*, the white hill. East of Torphins is the Hill of Fare on which the Battle of Corrichie was fought in 1562.

TORRIDON
Highland

On A896 10m W of Kinlochewe.

The National Trust for Scotland's 16 000-acre Torridon estate is a mountain treasure-house of the highest quality, with hills of individual character which still form a cohesive group. Liathach (the grey one) and **Beinn Eighe** rise too steeply above the road from **Kinlochewe** to be well seen, though their presence is powerful. At the west end of Liathach (named from the quartzite on its upper slopes) is the small village of Torridon, and nearby is the Trust's **Torridon Countryside Centre**. A minor road continues west to **Diabaig**, passing the car park from where Beinn Alligin – clearly seen after a short walk up the Abhainn Coire Mhic Nobuil – is usually climbed.

TORRIDON COUNTRYSIDE CENTRE
Highland

At junction of A896 and the Diabaig road. Late May–end Sept, Mon–Sat 1000–1800, Sun 1400–1800.

The centre has displays and an audio-visual presentation on the landscapes and wildlife of the area.

TOWIE BARCLAY CASTLE
near Turriff, Grampian

Off A947 3m S of Turriff. Open by arrangement: enquire locally or telephone (08884 347).

A Barclay stronghold since the 12th century, the castle was the site of the Trot of **Turriff** in 1639. Extensively restored in recent years, it has won several architectural awards. The hall has a fine ribbed vault and there is a walled garden.

Thomas Telford

In the summer of 1801 the British government asked the eminent civil engineer Thomas Telford to survey the Highlands to select suitable sites for new fishing stations and to consider the possibility of a canal linking the lochs of the Great Glen. He reported with his usual speed and thoroughness; impressed, the government asked him to go back the following year and look at the state of roads and bridges in the area.

Telford was forthright in his second report: 'It is incalculable the loss which the public has sustained and are about to suffer from want of roads in this country', he said. Somewhat optimistically, he asked for £1 million. There was never any likelihood of that sum being granted, but in June 1803 the House of Commons agreed a sum of £20 000 – a very large amount for the time – for 'the making of roads and bridges in the Highlands'. It was the start of a mammoth enterprise that was to engage Telford for the next 30 years.

He had risen from humble beginnings. Born in Langholm in the Borders in 1757, the son of a shepherd, he worked as a mason, first in Edinburgh and then in London. His appetite for learning was insatiable. 'Knowledge is my most ardent pursuit', he wrote. 'I am not contented unless I can reason in every particular.'

Telford was appointed engineer of the Ellesmere Canal in 1793 and of the Shrewsbury Canal a year later. His first connection with Scotland was in 1796, as engineer to the British Fisheries Society, whom he advised on plans for the new harbour at **Wick**.

In all, Telford supervised the building of over 1000 miles of roads in the Highlands and 1200 bridges. He also designed harbours, churches, manses and other buildings – and of course oversaw the construction of the **Caledonian Canal**, the largest civil engineering project of its day, lasting 18 years from its start in 1804 to final completion in the autumn of 1822.

Telford was an engineer of genius, with a mind capable of making the boldest leap of imagination. Many of his bridges still grace the Highland scene. The masterpiece among them is perhaps the iron bridge over the River Spey at **Craigellachie**, but the stone bridges all show not only fine engineering but a true sensitivity towards their location.

The poet Robert Southey, a close friend of the great engineer, summed up his life perfectly. 'Telford's is a happy life,' he wrote, 'everywhere making roads, building bridges, forming canals and erecting harbours – works of sure, solid, permanent utility.' Thomas Telford died in 1834.

TUGNET ICE-HOUSE
near Fochabers, Highland

On B9104 at Spey Bay, 5m N of Fochabers.
Jun–Sept, daily 1000–1600. D (P). Free
(0309 73701).

A large ice-house of 1830, formerly
used for storing fish caught in the
Spey estuary, has been converted
into a museum with displays on the
River Spey, its fishing and wildlife.
The Speyside Way path starts here.

TURRIFF
Grampian

On A947 11m S of Banff.

Turriff is an important agricultural
market town of some 3000 people,
on the River Deveron. Its church
has a carved belfry and interesting
carvings, and the town's mercat
cross is 16th century. Three castles –
Craigston, Delgatie and Towie Barclay
– are within five miles of the town.
Turriff is chiefly remembered for
the skirmish known as the Trot
of Turriff in 1639, when a party
of Royalist Gordons routed the
Covenanters, led by the Master of
Forbes: the first action of the Civil
War. The town is also remembered
for the Turra Coo, an incident
which shows the independent turn
of mind of the people of Buchan. In
1911 Lloyd George's government
brought in legislation requiring
employers to pay insurance stamps
for their workers. Many farmers
objected, and one, Robert Paterson
of Lendrum, refused to pay and
had a cow impounded in lieu.
The beast was to be auctioned in
the square at Turriff to raise the
necessary cash, but folk rallied
round Paterson and no bids were
made. The cow was taken to
Aberdeen and auctioned, and farmer
Paterson's friends then clubbed
together to buy her back, parading
her through the streets of Turriff
in celebration. There is a cairn at
Lendrum Farm, outside Turriff, and
the Turra Coo has inspired songs,
poems, chinaware and at least
one book.

TWEED, see HARRIS TWEED
panel p135.

UGIE SALMON HOUSE
near Peterhead, Grampian

Off A952 1m N of Peterhead. All year.
Mon–Sat 0900–1200, 1400–1700. Free
(0779 76209).

This is the oldest salmon fish house
in Scotland, and dates back to
1585, when it was built for George
Keith, the founder of the town
of **Peterhead**. Visitors can see how
salmon is smoked and purchase the
results.

ULBSTER
Highland

On A9 6m S of Wick.

This small village is almost
surrounded by cairns, standing
stones and **brochs**. To the
north-west near Loch Watenan are
the Cairn of Get, a passage-grave,
and the stone rows of Garrywhin,
which radiate from a central cairn.
Around Loch of Yarrows are more
cairns, and there are brochs at
Bruan, Borrowston, and Thrumster,
a larger village to the north which
also has a standing stone alongside
the road. The coast around Ulbster
is superb, and nearby is the
extraordinary harbour of Whaligoe,
with its long flight of steps
(reputedly 365) leading down from
the clifftop. Sarclet Haven, below
Thrumster, is a charming natural
anchorage.

ULLAPOOL
Highland

On A835 32m NW of Garve.

Ullapool was one of a number of
villages established in the late 18th
century by the British Fisheries
Society to provide bases for the
expanding fisheries industry,
taking advantage of a naturally
sheltered position on Loch Broom.
Since then, the village has grown
up the hill from the waterside.
Fishing is still important and it
is common to see large factory
ships or 'klondykers', often from
Eastern Europe or Russia, in the
harbour. In recent years Ullapool
has become very much a tourist
centre. The pier has been enlarged
to take the Stornoway ferry, and
many boat excursions are offered
in summer. Angling, both sea and
loch, is excellent, as is the walking,
with fine coastline and hills in the
surrounding area. It is all a long
way from the original settlement,
almost certainly Norse, for the
name Ullapool means 'Olaf's farm'.

URQUHART CASTLE
near Drumnadrochit, Highland

On A82 2m S of Drumnadrochit.
Apr–Sept, Mon–Sat 0930–1900, Sun
1400–1900; Oct–Mar, Mon–Sat 0930–1600,
Sun 1400–1600.

The castle, on a promontory
commanding Loch Ness, dates from
the 13th century. John Grant, then
Lord of Urquhart, undertook major
restoration in the 16th century, but
the castle later fell into disrepair.
Extensive ruins remain. It is a
much-favoured, atmospheric spot
for sightings of the Loch Ness
Monster.

Queen Victoria in the Highlands

Queen Victoria first visited Scotland in 1842, five years after she came to the throne and two years after her marriage to Prince Albert. Apart from a brief visit by George IV in 1822, she was the first British monarch to travel this far north since Charles I. Both she and her consort were captivated by Scotland and its people, and came again in 1844 and 1847.

They determined to find a Highland home, and on the advice of Lord Aberdeen went to look at **Balmoral**, a castle by the River Dee, not far from the village of **Braemar**. It was felt that the climate, relatively dry and with pure air, would benefit the prince's health. Balmoral was an inspired choice. The queen wrote in her diary: 'All seemed to breathe freedom and peace.' The estate was purchased in 1852 and work started on the new castle, completed in 1855. It is still the royal family's Scottish country home today.

Victoria and Albert explored the Highlands extensively, and the queen has left us delightful descriptions, recorded in the diary she kept faithfully for most of her life. They climbed hills, on ponyback as far as possible, then walked; they travelled through the glens; Albert stalked deer; the queen sketched. The wilder the scene, the more she seemed to like it. Returning to England after her 1847 visit, she comments, 'the English coast appeared terribly flat.'

They went to the **Small Isles** and to Staffa, visiting Fingal's Cave. They visited the Trossachs, and the western Highlands where the queen noted that 'the country is very fine, but the weather was dreadful.' But it was Deeside that they held most dear. They climbed **Lochnagar**, above Balmoral, in thick mist, and then on the way down the sun came out – 'most provoking' said the queen at having missed the view from the summit.

Prince Albert died in 1861 but Queen Victoria continued to visit her beloved Scotland until her own death 40 years later. It was truly a love affair between a sensitive woman with a genuine feel for wild landscape and a country with everything to offer to inspire and satisfy that feeling: a love affair continued by members of the royal family today.

Walking in the Highlands

The area covered by this guide offers, without doubt, the finest walking to be found in the British Isles. The variety of landscape and scenery is exceptional. All eight of our 4000-foot mountains are here as are over 200 peaks of 3000 feet plus many, still fine, of lesser height. The coastal walking is without parallel, and the long inland glens offer through treks of sublime beauty and wildness.

There is little in the way of 'formalized' walking. The West Highland Way enters Highland Region at the high point of **Rannoch Moor**, continuing through **Glencoe** to **Fort William**; the Speyside Way runs for nearly 50 miles from Spey Bay to **Tomintoul**. These are fully waymarked walks set up under the auspices of the Countryside Commission for Scotland (now part of Scottish Natural Heritage). These walks apart, most of the area is an open book of discovery for the visitor to explore.

But less experienced walkers need not feel too constrained. There are many excellent local walks guides available which describe walks of up to six miles in length – microcosms of the wider scene giving an introduction to the beauties of the area. In some places (**Braemar** is an example) community councils and other voluntary bodies have waymarked short local walks for visitors.

With the appetite thus whetted, the possibilities are endless. A lifetime could be spent exploring the historic passes and through walks such as the Lairig Ghru and Lairig an Laoigh in the **Cairngorms**, the walk through Glen Tilt and Deeside from Blair Atholl to **Braemar**, the magnificent walk through **Glen Affric** from Cannich to **Kintail**, or the old military roads such as the **Corrieyairack Pass** from **Fort Augustus** to Strathspey.

The legal aspect of walking in Scotland is rather different from that elsewhere in Britain. There is a law of trespass, but the simple act of walking on private land is not of itself an offence: damage must be proven. In general terms, there are few restrictions to countryside access, though during the main stalking and grouse-shooting season from mid August to late October, local advice should always be taken in case of disturbing the shoot, which is a most important economic factor in the Highlands and Islands.

(continued)

Walking *(continued)*

Good equipment, especially waterproofs and boots, is essential if venturing into wilder country, and the ability to use map and compass is also a prerequisite for anyone walking the hills and glens. For those with the necessary equipment and confidence, the mountains offer experiences of great variety and satisfaction. Each season has its own delights, and once some knowledge of the country has been gained, it is not difficult to enjoy the priceless gift of solitude.

The islands too have a very special atmosphere which walkers can capture to the full. Be it cliffs, canals, dramatic mountains or lovely glens, the Highlands and Islands can provide scenery to satisfy all tastes, time and again.

VATERSAY
Western Isles

This small island is now joined by causeway to **Barra**, giving its 80 inhabitants a much firmer link to the outside world. The causeway was provided partly because the population had been declining. The houses are mainly at the south of the island, which rises to 625 feet on Heishival Mor, and there is a crofting and **fishing** economy. At one time cattle were swum to Barra. For 54 years Vatersay was owned by Lady Cathcart, who only visited the island once, but after an uprising in the early part of this century, it was purchased by the Congested Districts Board and divided into 58 separate crofts. Off Vatersay is the islet of Uinessan, once the site of a church, Cille Bhrianain.

QUEEN VICTORIA, see
panel p222.

WALKING, see panel p223.

WALTZING WATERS
Newtonmore, Highland

In Newtonmore. Easter–Nov, daily 1000–1900 plus late show at 2030. Limited winter opening: enquire locally. D (P) (05403 752).

Opened in 1990, this 'aqua theatre' presents a spectacular water, light and music show in a specially built auditorium. There are craftwork displays, a coffee shop and a children's play area.

WEST HIGHLAND MUSEUM
Fort William, Highland

Cameron Square, Fort William. Jul–Aug, Mon–Sat 0930–2100; Jun and Sept, Mon–Sat 0930–1730; Oct–May, Mon–Sat 1000–1300, 1400–1700 (0397 2169).

The Whisky Trail

There are over 100 distilleries in Scotland; more than half of them are in a relatively small area around the lower reaches of the River Spey. The whisky producers in the area have collaborated with tourist boards to set up what they proudly proclaim as 'the only malt whisky trail in the world'.

Malt whisky is produced by a process involving barley, yeast, and water; the water makes a significant difference to the final taste, along with the number of years the whisky is allowed to mature, and the type of cask used during that long process. The 'island malts' from Islay, Jura and **Skye** have a significantly different taste from those of Strathspey, due in large part to the influence exercised by the peaty water on the islands. The water used by the Strathspey whisky-makers is purer, giving a lighter taste. All this is explained at the distilleries on the Malt Whisky Trail, where visitors can see each part of the process – malting, mashing, fermentation, distillation, maturation and bottling – for themselves, and then sample the finished product.

Whisky takes its name from the Gaelic *uisge a beath* – literally 'the water of life'. It has been produced in Scotland for many centuries, but it was only in 1823 that an Act of Parliament put the industry on a proper footing and ended illicit distilling and smuggling, which had been rife. One of the distilleries on the trail, the **Glenlivet**, was the first in the Highlands to be licensed, in 1824; another, **Strathisla**, is the oldest, dating from 1786.

The distilleries on the Malt Whisky Trail are **Cardhu, Glenfarclas, Glenfiddich** (Dufftown), **Glen Grant** (Rothes), Glenlivet, Strathisla (Keith), **Tamdhu** and Tamnavoulin. All are different, and all have their own story to tell. A trail leaflet giving more details is available from tourist information centres in the area.

There are of course many other fine distilleries which welcome visitors, from **Orkney** to **Skye** and from **Fort William** to **Aberdeen**shire. They too are listed in the gazetteer. But there is only one Malt Whisky Trail.

The museum holds varied and interesting exhibits on the history and wildlife of the area with Jacobite relics including the 'secret portrait' of Bonnie Prince Charlie.

WHISKY TRAIL, see panel p225.

WICK
Highland

On A9 37m N of Helmsdale,

Wick – from Norse *vik*, meaning a bay – has been an important fishing port for many centuries. The photographs in Wick's museum show the harbour packed with vessels in the days of the herring boom: there are fewer boats today, but it is still a busy place. The town's modern expansion started

in 1808 when the British Fisheries Society commissioned **Thomas Telford** to plan a new village, Pulteneytown, on the south side of the bay. The harbour was completed in 1810 and improved in 1868. Soon after that the railway reached Wick, making communication with the south easier.

Most historical interest is in the older, northern part of the town. The parish church of 1830 is adjoined by Sinclair's Aisle, burial place of the Earls of Caithness. A major industry established more recently can be visited at Harrowhill, the premises of **Caithness Glass**. On Noss Head are the twin ruins of Castles Sinclair and Girnigoe, both residences of the Earls of Caithness. The ruins are somewhat precarious and care should be taken if visiting them. Wick has become a shopping and tourist centre as well as a fishing port.